MANAGEMENT OF INFORMATION IN LIS

THEORY AND PRACTICE

Ansaar Hussain
Tabasum Zehra

ATLANTIC
PUBLISHERS & DISTRIBUTORS (P) LTD

ATLANTIC
PUBLISHERS & DISTRIBUTORS (P) LTD
7/22, Ansari Road, Darya Ganj, New Delhi
Tel.: +91-11-4077 5252, 2327 3880
E-mail: orders@atlanticbooks.com
Web: www.atlanticbooks.com

Published by Atlantic Publishers & Distributors (P) Ltd 2024

Printed & bound in India by Atlantic Print Services

Contents

PART 2
DOCUMENT PROCESSING (PRACTICE)

Preface

This book has been prepared keeping in mind the syllabus of BLIS/ MLIS students of University of Kashmir, University of Jammu, IGNOU and other higher education institutes of India. It can be used by JKSSB/JKPSC and other state recruitment aspirants to prepare for different recruitment examinations/interviews, like that of College Librarian, School Librarian, Public Library Librarian, Library Assistant and for other related posts. The book has two main parts with following headings, viz:

1. ORGANISING AND MANAGING INFORMATION
2. DOCUMENT PROCESSING: PRACTICE

The first part of the book deals with topics like classification and classification schemes, uses/importance of classification in a library, postulational approach in classification, cataloguing concept along with types and forms, standards and formats associated with cataloguing, concepts related to subject indexing like indexing principles/languages/techniques, impact of technology on cataloguing, metadata along with some other important concepts.

The second part overlays topics that enclose Dewey Decimal Classification (DDC), transcription of a class number, structure and organisation of DDC, different types of notes and instructions in DDC, three summaries of DDC, relative index in DDC, tables and schedules in DDC, use of auxiliary tables in DDC, structure of AACR-2R, headings in cataloguing, cataloguing of multivolume publication, MARC standards, history of the Sears List, principles of vocabulary control, indexing process, chain indexing along with some other important topics.

While preparing the book different open e-resource platforms have been consulted and used which include DOAJ, DOAB, e-gyankosh, etc.

Ansaar Hussain
Tabasum Zehra

PART 1

ORGANISING AND MANAGING INFORMATION

Unit 1

Basic Concepts in Classification

Meaning of Classification

Classification is the process of grouping similar or like entities. It may be noted that there can be no grouping without division, as there can be no shadow without light or no parting without meeting. Thus, grouping implies division. Grouping and division are two sides of the same coin. It may be understood that grouping and division are the basic processes of classification. In other words, classification is related to categorisation, a process in which ideas and objects are recognized, differentiated and understood. Classification is the grouping of related facts into classes.

Classification and Organisation

Since grouping and inter-group ranking are acts of organisation, classification is the organisation of ideas, items, entities, etc. In fact, classification and organisation are inseparable. Today, classification is considered a tool for organising in every sense of the word. So, classification is structuring and mapping. The difference between a heap of bricks and a mansion is classification. In a mansion, every brick is positioned in an organised way. Similarly, the difference between a disciplined army and a chaotic mob is classification.

Uses of Classification

Classification is a mental act and logical process of association and relation. It goes on in every moment of life knowingly or unknowingly, deliberately or unconsciously. As far as uses of classification are concerned:

- Any system, be it biological (man), social (government, libraries and institutions) or mechanical (computers and machines), needs to be classified for successful functioning.
- All human beings, whatever they do, need to be classified in every sense of the word. The more sophisticated and intelligent a person, the better their sense of classification.
- A postman classifies postal items for efficient and timely delivery. For quick, efficient and easy delivery, a postal item is sorted (classified) many times between the posting and delivery stages.
- A fruit seller sorts his fruits into categories, like oranges, apples, grapes and so on.
- Record files in an office are arranged in some order, and within each file, letters and memos are arranged in some known order. Without such an arrangement, the previous record cannot be located and used.
- Books and other reading materials in libraries are arranged to increase their usability.

Scope of Classification

There is no act of life where classification is not used. It is applied everywhere. It is a basic process of learning. The opposite of classification is disorder and chaos. All objects, entities, actions, thoughts and concepts can be classified. We can classify people, countries, natural phenomena, plants, flowers, animals, libraries, philosophies, literature, artifacts, automobiles and what not. It is a universal phenomenon. It is the only method to simplify, understand and comprehend a complex universe to discover its structure and impose some order over the otherwise chaotic world.

Process of Classification

Classification is a process of co-relation. It is a way of thinking systematically and purposefully. It is an aid to memory and reasoning power. Nothing can be identified without it. It means to define an entity is to classify it first. For example, a gun is a firearm, a chair is a piece of furniture, a car belongs to the class of vehicles and so on. A group is divided or a member is included into a group on the basis of some characteristic. A characteristic is an attribute, quality or property of an entity that relates it with, or separates it from, a group. For example, a group of people may be divided into males and females. Here, 'gender' is the characteristic of division. All the students of a university may be divided into undergraduate, postgraduate and research degree students. Here, the level of education is the characteristic. Books in a library may be arranged on the basis of their subject content. Thus, a characteristic is the basis of division. Successive application of right and relevant characteristics produces deeper and finer classification.

Genus-Species Relationship

'Genus' may be defined as a class, kind, or group marked by Some common characteristics or by one common characteristic. A genus can have multiple sub-groups having certain common characteristics or framed on the basis of a few collective features. Each sub-group is referred to as a species. A table is a genus, while multiple articles of a table, like glass tables, wooden tables, etc., are species of tables. Ancient philosophers applied the dichotomous method to divide the universe into two groups at every step. Greek philosopher Porphyry (232–304 AD) used this method, and the resulting groups and subgroups are known as the Tree of Porphyry. This method, however, is artificial, as every phenomenon is not dichotomous in the universe: there are many shades between white and black. The modern approach is to divide by genus-species or by whole-part methods.

Nature of Classification

Logically speaking, classificatory groups are not absolute; classifications are relative as something is classified with reference to others. An entity cannot be classified or ranked in itself. It takes two aspects to create a classification. It means a unique entity cannot be classified. It is a class of its own. No classification is absolute, that is, classifications are not permanent. Classifications are not even real. No classification exists in nature. All classifications are man-made and made for a purpose. No classification is good or bad; these are helpful or unhelpful to a varying degrees. It all depends upon the purpose of classification. A classification that serves its purpose well is the best, whether logical or not. The logic of classification depends upon the chosen characteristics and the order in which these are applied. A large group of persons could be divided by age; gender; religion; race; nationality; mother tongue; the colour of skin, hair or eyes; and many more characteristics. Each time, it will result in a different grouping.

Classification as a Tool

According to Aristotle (384–322 BC), classification is a theoretical, practical and productive science. As the saying goes, theory is the most applied knowledge. We can arguably say that classifications are always practical and designed for some purpose. As already stated, classification is a tool for simplification, understanding and organisation. Without organisation, nothing works. All the uses of classification may be summed up as 'management, aesthetics and knowledge creation.'

Organisation helps in better management. Classification helps in organise anything and everything—life to a shoe store, knowledge to libraries. A library, archive, postman and grocery shop—all use classification to save time. It ultimately leads to an economy of time, money and manpower.

Aesthetics is the science of beauty. An arranged store appeals visually to the visitors. Classification is also described as pairing and matching. So, a housewife matching the colour of her room curtains with other items in the room is essentially doing an act of classification.

Philosophers, scientists and researchers classify to study and understand the growth and structure of knowledge.

Knowledge Classification

Classification can be of any object, phenomenon, concept or act. Classification and categorisation of knowledge per se is called knowledge classification. From time to time, philosophers, scientists, educationists and the like have formally categorised the entire known knowledge to outline its boundaries and show the structure of knowledge. For example, Hindu Vedas (1500 BC) divided knowledge into four categories in the order of *Dharam*, *Arth*, *Kam* and *Moksh*. Aristotle (third century BC) divided knowledge into three parts: Theoretical, practical and productive, further dividing them into ten categories. A propedia is the classification of knowledge and vice-versa. Knowledge is defined as the sum total of ideas, theories, experiences, history, feelings, values, sciences, symbols, arts, facts, fiction and myths conserved by a society. Classification of knowledge is essential for its simplification, understanding and progress. Without its in organisation, no further growth and progress can be made.

Library Classification

A library classification is a system of organisation of knowledge by which library resources are arranged and ordered systematically. Library classifications are a notational system that represents the order of topics in the classification and allows items to be stored in that order. Library classification systems group-related materials together, typically arranged as a hierarchical tree structure. A different kind of classification system, called a faceted classification system, is also widely used, which allows the assignment of multiple classifications to an object, enabling the classifications to be ordered in many ways.

Libraries are established to house and preserve books and other documentary heritage of mankind. Books and other information sources are knowledge objects and can also be classified like other physical objects. Since antiquity, librarians have classified books to produce convenient groupings and to facilitate their location at the time of need. An unarranged collection is a heap of books, not a library by definition. Finding a book from such a library will be like locating a needle from a huge heap of hay. In earlier times, books were grouped and arranged on the basis of their language, size and colour of binding, authorship or broad subject categories. Those methods were perfectly useful in those times as the main aim of libraries was to store and preserve documents rather than serve them to scholars. Access to knowledge was the preserve of the privileged few.

Modern Library Classification

In the then-emerging industrial society of the late nineteenth century, there was an attitudinal shift in the values of education and libraries. The importance of literacy was recognised for aware and responsible citizens. In a democracy, access to education was democratised and opened to all. 'Education for all' became the objective of the welfare state. To meet the needs of society, not only many new libraries were established by law, but the doors of libraries were open to all and sundry—scholars, students, neo-literatures, poor, children, housewives, old and challenged, and other marginalised sections of the society, without any discrimination. Further, to maximise their use, books were placed in free stacks, and users were allowed open and direct access to the books. That open access policy required a new and better arrangement of books for the browsers. Then, Melvil Dewey (1851–1931) designed his Decimal Classification, which divided knowledge by academic disciplines of study and used decimal notation to denote subjects. The latter aspect provided almost infinite capacity for expanding and inserting new subjects at proper places. Since then, books have been classified predominantly on the basis of their subject content, that is, knowledge. Thus, library classification is knowledge classification as applied in libraries. In other words, library classification is applied knowledge classification. However, library classification is much more than knowledge classification as it also has to consider the physical aspects of the documents, the way knowledge has been formatted and presented in them and the viewpoint of the author. It includes aspects such as language, media, form, format, viewpoint and many more. The designer of a classification scheme is known as a classificationist. Operating a classification system to assign class numbers to documents in a library is also classification; in this context, the operator is called a classifier.

Uses of Classification in a Library

Classification is vital to library services. In fact, classification is implied in the definition of a service library. It supports all library services. Classification is to a library as a skeleton is to a human body on which all the body organs rest. The classification of a library collection is like the map of a city. In a library, classification serves all the functions stated above—it is a tool for management, aesthetics and knowledge creation. All the Five Laws of Library Science formulated by Ranganathan's library classification (1931 and 1957) have specific implications in designing quality classification systems. Without classification, a library is an unorganised dump of books. Therefore, without it, the full value of a library collection cannot be obtained. However, its specific uses can be broadly listed as follows:

- Classification brings together books on the same subject. Thus, a user gets all the books in one place, which is much more convenient for the users.
- It facilitates the browsing function of a library. Browsing refers to looking at library collections without any specific purpose—a sort of window shopping.
- It is a location tool; without it, the library catalogue will not be able to function properly. It is also used for preparing shelf lists.
- It is the basis of all information retrieval systems and methods, both in manual and electronic systems.
- It helps replace the books at their correct places when the books are returned to the stacks after home use or use within the library.
- Library classification has been claimed to serve three functions: Cognitive, information retrieval and shelf arrangement. The cognitive function is to represent the structure of knowledge and the intra-relation of subjects.
- Many bibliographies, catalogues, etc., are classified for better use. Universal Decimal Classification (UDC) was created to arrange entries in a universal bibliography.
- Classification has been found useful in reference services for the facet analysis of users' questions in

reference interviews. It is useful for the arrangement of circulation records.

- It helps build a balanced collection of documents in a library.

Limitations of Classification

- Classification has been described as the mathematics of librarianship, yet like the value of π (pi), it is never exact.
- Classifications are social, not natural.
- These do not satisfy the needs of all the library users. Only the majority are served, while some users with specialised needs require a different arrangement.
- It is a costly process and subjective too.
- Two classifiers may differ widely on the correct classification of a given book. Not only this, a classifier may classify a given book differently at different times. No classification can comprehensively represent all the subjects dealt within a book.
- Side topics cannot be represented by the class number and hence remain hidden from needy users.
- Classification by discipline also scatters subjects. For example, a book on 'Family Life' may be placed in different main classes, such as Ethics, Sociology, Anthropology, Social Welfare and Medicine. Hence, it results in scattering.
- A particular classification may not satisfy all the users as they have individual needs. Classifications are not based on the survey of the needs of library users.

Unit 2
Types of Classification

Introduction

Classification of documents and other reading materials is indispensable for any library. Various standard and local methods for arranging library materials, including clay tablets, papyrus rolls, monographs and other print documents; audio-video material; CDs; multimedia and now web sources, have been employed from time to time by librarians to organise their collections. Their classification has varied from homemade or ad hoc systems to somewhat adapted from some universal knowledge classification systems. Since the late nineteenth century, librarians have developed many standard classification systems pioneered by the Dewey Decimal Classification (DDC) in 1876.

Fixed and Relative Location Systems of Classification

Fixed Location Systems: These systems are from the pre-Dewey era. They assigned a fixed place to a book on the shelves. The call number indicated the shelf ground on which the book was stacked. For example, a call number of, say, 2.4.6.25 meant that it was the 25th book on the 6th shelf of the 4th almirah in the 2nd room of the library. Thus, a book could be located even by a blind person. Its advantage was saving shelf space, as such systems require a vacant place only at the end of the shelf or almirah. In a fixed location, maintenance of subject grouping was difficult. New books could be accommodated at the end of the shelf. When the books needed to be shifted to another place, their call number also needed to be changed frequently. It involved a lot of labour and wastage of time and money. Melvil Dewey (1876–1931), while working in the library of Amherst College (Massachusetts), could not tolerate this wasteful task of frequent reclassification. He invented a relative classification system to solve this problem, giving permanent call numbers to books in a library.

Relative Location Systems: In relative systems, the class number refers to the intrinsic subject of the book rather than the shelf place. The decimal notation used by Melvil Dewey provided a neat technique for dividing knowledge by denoting each division and subdivision by decimal fraction numbers. The call number indicated the subject rather than any fixed places on the shelves. It was a masterstroke that brought a paradigm shift in library classification. The new books could be accommodated at their proper places without disturbing the relative location of the existing books. In the new method, the shelf location of books changes with the addition of more books. Books on the shelves keep shifting to the right side, but their relative location remains the same; on the right and left of a book, it will always have the same subject as its neighbours. The great advantage of this system is the maintenance of strict and finely divided subject collocations.

Classification by Design Methodology

Enumerative Systems: A classification is a map of knowledge that lists every subject and its subdivisions in a top-down approach. Each subdivision is given a notational mark to denote it. Known as the class number, this notation, or a cluster of digits, is assigned to a document having that topic as its specific subject. These are also known as 'mark and park' systems. Enumerative classifications comprise the pre-defined and frozen lists of subjects of the past, present and near future. These only provide readymade pigeonholes for documents rather than finally individualising them according to their subjects and their various documentary aspects. Most of the time, these prove square holes for round pegs. Now, these are considered rather old-fashioned classification systems.

Faceted Systems: An enumerative system produces systematic but linear lists of subjects. Knowledge is multidimensional and growing dynamically. An enumerative classification can represent only one aspect of the specific subject at a time. Many aspects have to be left out. For example, in the earlier editions of the DDC, a simple subject like 'Anatomy of Dogs' could either be classified as 'Zoology of Dogs' or 'Anatomy of Animals'. Both aspects could not be taken together. Thus, such systems fail to co-extensively classify the present-day knowledge, not to speak of the subjects to emerge later.

By the beginning of the twentieth century, these enumerative models were not very effective, yet no other model was available, though the UDC (1895+) had made some improvements in the DDC to denote some more auxiliary aspects of a document. S.R. Ranganathan (1892–1972), after a long study and experimentation in the late 1920s, developed a different method to classify multidimensional knowledge thrown by the twentieth-century industrial society. These are now known as faceted systems. A facet is any of the many sides of a cut diamond. Ranganathan used this term in classification to designate different aspects of a specific subject. Instead of making a long list of subjects in some systematic order, he divided each subject horizontally into different categories and then vertically into different subdivisions known as facets and isolates, respectively. For example, the subject of library science could be divided into 'Kind of Library' facet, 'Kind of Document' facet, 'Kind of Operation' facet and 'Kind of Service' facet. Later, Ranganathan developed a theory of 'Five and only Five Fundamental Categories.' These categories comprised of Personality, Matter, Energy, Space and Time. He postulated that every subject comprises some or all of these categories. This faceted system was later refined and developed into a dynamic and effective model based on postulates and principles for which Ranganathan developed a theory in his famous book *Prolegomena to Library Classification* (Madras Library Association, 1937). All the new library classification systems are faceted, while old systems like the DDC, or the

Bibliography Classification (BC), and UDC are getting faceted through revision.

Synthesis Grafted on an Enumerative Base: It is a mix of the above two systems. The enumerative systems later developed some special tables of documentary aspects to combine with the base number. The first such example is of the UDC, which started simply as an enhancement of the DDC in 1895. A multiplicity of auxiliary subdivisions were added to the DDC base to make a class number multifaceted. As a survival approach, some additional internal tables have been devised, and many more provisions of number synthesis have been invented to make them more hospitable and faceted to combat the dynamically growing knowledge. The DDC, in its eighteenth edition (1971), introduced five more tables and made many more provisions for number synthesis through instructions and special tables here and there. Being added quite late, such a structure is not regular or uniform. It is an add-on provision that has its own problems.

Knowledge Classification and Library Classification

Classification is a process, a logical visual method of simplification and understanding. No phenomenon or object can be understood without classifying it. It organises all sorts of entities and depicts their due place in the universe. Classification can be both of abstract and concrete entities, of ideas and things. It is essentially a life process of learning, doing and living successfully. It was another (more sophisticated) act of classification when man related clouds with rain, rain with the growth of vegetation and life and certain herbs with certain diseases. All that became knowledge by and by. It has rightly been said that all knowledge is classification. Knowledge is defined as the sum total of facts, beliefs, experiences, memories, expressed feelings, arts, sciences, fiction and myths conserved by society. Thinkers of all ages have tried to categorise knowledge to understand its nature, categories, boundaries and growth. That became knowledge classification. Knowledge classification is outlining and mapping to depict its structure and boundaries. It leads to a better understanding of its history, nature, kinds, properties and growth and the gaps in it. It becomes a guide for educationists, scientists and librarians. Knowledge classification is both speculative and empirical and a province of philosophers and scholars. One example of knowledge classification is Vedic categories (1500 BC) of knowledge in *Dharam*, *Arth*, *Kam* and *Moksh*.

Library classification is a book or a document classification. Documents are nothing but carriers of knowledge and information. In modern libraries, documents are classified on the basis of their knowledge content. Therefore, knowledge classifications have become the basis of library classifications. But knowledge is abstract and fluid and takes the shape of its container and carrier. Books, on the other hand, are physical and solid entities to be arranged on shelves. Documented knowledge has some non-subject aspects, such as language, the viewpoint of the author, format, media, etc. All these have to be accounted for in a library classification. Library classifications are, in fact, more detailed and have notations/symbols to be assigned to documents, separate common tables for physical aspects and a detailed index of subjects. Therefore, library classifications are more formal and complex than the knowledge classification on which these are based.

Web Classifications: Ontologies

Ontology is a powerful classification tool for the Semantic Web, describing and representing an area of knowledge. It specifies a description for classes, relationships that exists among entities and properties that entities have. Ontology characterises well-defined concepts, their taxonomy and many-sided relationships. It is a hierarchical collection of concepts arranged in categories combined with multidimensional relations in order to reflect the vocabulary of that area of knowledge. It is a web of connections. An ontology used for knowledge organisation and retrieval in an electronic environment has the power of traditional hierarchical classifications, subject heading lists and thesauri. It combines elements of the three. Ontologies are sources of controlled and standardised terms that help organise information in more precise and multidimensional ways. They yield better search results by using new search techniques and natural language processing.

Some examples: Biogen Idec: Using semantics in drug discovery research.

MINDSWAP: Using ontologies to aid terrorism intelligence gathering.

Classification by Areas of Applications

Another division of library classifications can be by the subject area covered. There are general classification systems that cover the entire universe of knowledge. The other categories are special classifications covering a specified subject or limited area of knowledge. These, by default, are broader and depth classifications, respectively. These can broadly be of three types: Special classifications, users' interest classifications and general classifications.

1. Special Classifications

A special classification is a classification for a specific area of knowledge, such as economics, banking, occupational safety, diamond technology, women studies, indology, etc. Some examples of special classification schemes are Uniclass: Unified Classification for the Construction Industry (London: RIBA, 1997); London Education Classification, University of London, 1974; etc.

Special classifications inevitably are depth classifications used for classifying and indexing micro literature in the form of journal articles, research reports, theses, etc. These are eminently useful for information retrieval in special libraries and information centres. Ranganathan also called them depth classifications.

Special classifications usually do not exist alone. Every special library has documents on its special area and also on related subjects. For instance, a nuclear science library might also have books on fiction, sociology, management, etc. A special classification, such as the classification of business studies, might require another general classification for classifying documents in other areas, such as political science, sociology, psychology and mathematics. Usually, for classifying in related and other areas, a standard system is adopted. On the other hand, a special classification might be a mere extension of a certain class of the general classification system. For example, in India, many local-made detailed extensions of the Dewey Decimal Classification class numbers exist, such as 954 Indian History, 294 Indic Religions and 181.4 Indian Philosophy, to adequately classify such subjects in Indian libraries.

2. Users' Interest Classification

The ultimate function of a lending library is to serve its users to their satisfaction. Classification is a tool to manage a library. By definition, it is an arrangement of information material in a way useful to the majority of the users. In other words, it is a rational sequence of maximum utility. The convenience of library users is a weighty consideration, if not the overriding one in a classification. It is always advised to put a book in the most useful place. Many librarians and classifiers feel that practical utility must govern all arrangements.

In fact, different user communicates and organisations need different arrangements transcending the traditional division by orthodox disciplines. A user-oriented library classification need not be overly logical. The essence of reader interest arrangement is to classify material in a bold and utilitarian way that cuts across traditional groupings. The aim is to group library materials in ways that coincide with the user's thinking, interest, activity and needs.

3. General Classification

A classification of the entire universe of knowledge is known as a general classification. These are also known as universal classifications. Dewey Decimal Classification (DDC), Universal Decimal Classification (UDC), Colon Classification (CC) and Library of Congress Classification (LCC) are some outstanding examples of this category.

Classification by Levels of Detail

Universal classifications are further divided into three kinds, known as full, medium and abridged editions, depending upon their level of detail and use in a kind of library.

***Full Edition*:** These are the standard editions with full details and generally aim at large general libraries, say, a university library or large public library.

***Abridged Edition*:** These are meant for small libraries where medium coverage is adequate. Abridged versions, being comparatively inexpensive, are also popular in developing countries. Abridged Dewey Decimal Classification (DDC) is also very useful for teaching. It may also be used in conjunction with some special classification to cover remaining general areas of knowledge.

***Medium Edition*:** These carry details between a full edition and an abridged edition. These are the least costly and very easy to use. Historically speaking, till the 1980s, the Universal Decimal Classification (UDC) was available in three versions of details, namely full, medium and abridged editions, having about 2,30,000 (100%), 70,000 (70% of the full), and 20,000 (10%) entries, respectively.

Classification by Forms of Literature

Apart from subject specialisation, special forms of documents, such as official reports, patents, standards, maps, CDs and videos are arranged by different methods. Some official documents, such as reports, patents and standards, bear some special code number. These are arranged by that official number. Pamphlets are usually arranged by title. Popular fiction is mostly arranged alphabetically by author. There is also what is called a user-oriented system. These are local even ad hoc arrangements to place together all books in one place likely to be required by a single group of users. J. Mills has listed the following sections or forms of documents that might require a different type of arrangement in a library:

1. Age and grade of the reader
2. Books for a short loan or those for reference
3. Current and reserve stock
4. Size of documents
5. Other physical considerations, such as films, cassettes, CDs, etc.

6. Factual and imaginative literature
7. Language of the documents
8. Documents of temporary significance
9. Values of documents like manuscripts, rare materials, special editions, etc.
10. Form of presentation, like bound periodicals, etc.
11. Date of printing, incunabula
12. Documents for abnormal readers, such as the blind.

Print and Electronic Versions

Not only are traditional classifications being used for classifying electronic and web documents, but information technology (IT) has also been used as a tool and medium for designing and publishing classification systems. As a result, many classification systems are now available in electronic form. The twenty-first edition (1996) of the DDC available on a CD was known as Dewey for Windows (DfW), which has many more useful features over and above the print version. The electronic and much-enhanced version of the DDC-23 (2011), known as Web Dewey 2.0, is now available only through 'OCLC Connexion' to licensed users on the Internet. Abridged Web Dewey is also available in the same way. Electronic versions are updated monthly. All the electronic versions are easy-to-use, easy-to-update and versatile, with many more features, including expert systems for number building. Unlike the print or CD versions, web versions cannot be pirated or duplicated.

Unit 3
Postulational Approach

Introduction: Historical Perspectives

Modern library classification began in the late nineteenth century. Initially, classification systems, such as DDC, UDC and LCC, were developed without much theory to guide the technical work. Classification design was the field of a few geniuses who were guided mostly by their intuition and flair. W.C.B. Sayers (1881–1960), a respected teacher at the University College, London, derived the theory of classification in the form of canons in his famous books. The other two pioneering names are E.W. Hulme (1859–1951) of the UK and E.C. Richardson (1860–1939) of the USA. Their work on the theory of classification was mostly descriptive of the existing schemes. It was a descriptive phase of the theory of library classification. Then came H.E. Bliss (1870–1955), a par excellence philosopher and designer of classification. He spent his life designing his classification entitled Bibliographic Classification (1940–1953). But prior to that, he delved deep and long into the theoretical foundations of library classification based on the empirical foundations of knowledge and its organisation in his two famous books: *Organizing of Knowledge and System of Sciences* (1929) and *Organization of Knowledge and Subject Approach to Books in Libraries* (1933, second edition in 1939).

Bliss formulated many canons and principles of classification to guide the designing of classifications. But that was a phase of descriptive theory.

Postulational Approach

The postulational approach means going about the task of classifying by a premediated theory in the form of laws, canons, principles and postulates. When Ranganathan designed his CC in (1924, 1928-33), ironically, he did it without any formulated theory. Indeed, he had learnt some canons of classification in the classification classes of his most revered teacher W.C.B. Sayers. After the publication of his CC in 1933, Ranganathan started thinking about the theory behind it that lay in his unconscious mind while designing the CC. That theory was so comprehensive and objective that it became the theory of classification in general. He formulated objective, even mechanical, methods to design a classification system. Apart from the five (normative) laws, he formulated 55 canons, 22 principles, 13 postulates and 10 devices for the synthesis of class numbers and the evaluation of classification systems. To this end, he divided the whole work into three planes, namely idea plane, verbal plane and notational plane. He neatly divided the work to be carried out in each plane. Ranganathan, thus, liberated classification design from the elusive flair and intuition and raised it to the status of a science.

Idea Plane

An idea plane is a plane of foremost importance where core intellectual work is done. Mostly, the work here pertains to the choice of the model, defining the subject, its scope and sources of terms and concepts. Core classificatory work is the choice of characteristics and order of their application to produce categories of concepts called facets and isolates. Further, it is to arrange the isolates into arrays and chains. Ranganathan has given the following five sets of canons for the work in the idea plane:

1. Canons of Characteristics
2. Canons for Succession of Characteristics
3. Canons for Formation of Arrays of Classes
4. Canons for Formulation of Chains of Classes
5. Canons for Filiatory Sequence

Canons of Characteristics

The terms are collected on small slips from the identified standard sources of the subject. This mass of terms is broken into smaller groups, called facets of the subject, by choosing suitable characteristics. A characteristic is an attribute to divide a group into smaller groups. It is a sort of hammer. It is a basis of division. The choice of characteristics, amongst many attributes, of an entity is vital and momentous. The ultimate quality of the final classification will crucially depend on the chosen characteristics. The three canons of characteristics are:

- Canon of Differentiation
- Canon of Ascertainability
- Canon of Permanence

The canon of differentiation means that the characteristics that we chose should be able to divide the group into at least two sub-groups. A group of entities cannot be further subdivided or differentiated on the basis of characteristics common to all (canon of differentiation). For example, bicycles cannot be divided on the basis of the number of wheels, as all of them have two wheels. But they can be differentiated into subgroups on the basis of the kind of rider, such as gent's bicycles, ladies' bicycles and children's bicycles. Further, the chosen differentiated characteristics should not be unverifiable or uncertain (canon of ascertainability). For example, a group of living people cannot be divided on the basis of their previous birth or the date of their death. The date of death of living persons is uncertain, and so is the previous birth. But living people may be divided on the basis of gender, nationality or skin colour; all these are ascertainable characteristics. Further, the chosen characteristics should be of permanent nature, not transitory or changing (canon of permanence). Chameleons cannot be grouped on the basis of their colour as it is changeable. The political party hopper Ganga Charan Rajput cannot be classified on the basis of his party. People should not be classified on the basis of the colour of their clothes, as they can easily change.

Canons for Succession of Characteristics

There may be many relevant and permanent characteristics for dividing a group. All may be needed to divide and subdivide a group. But the order in which these are applied one after the other is very important for the kind, quality and ultimate value of classification. Therefore, this set of canons is related to the sequence in which the various characteristics are applied. These are:

- Canon of Concomitance
- Canon of Relevant Succession
- Canon of Consistent Succession

Concomitant means happening at the same time. Therefore, this canon means that two characteristics applied to a class should not produce the same sub-classes. For example (in 2009) a class can be divided into two groups by applying the characteristics of below and above 20 years of age. Then, applying the characteristics 'born in or before 1989' and 'born after 1989' will result in the same grouping. In this case, the 20 years of age or 1989 born are concomitant characteristics. Relevant succession means that the sequence in which these characteristics are applied should be relevant to the purpose. To cite an example, literature has four relevant characteristics: Language, form, period/author and name of the literary work. Lastly, the canon of consistent succession only advises that the order of application of characteristics once chosen should be followed consistently unless the purpose of classification itself changes. As a result of successive applications of characteristics, we obtain numerous individual concepts. These concepts have to be arranged in what are called arrays and chains.

Canons for Formation of Arrays of Classes

An array is a long line of entities of equal rank arranged in some systematic order. For example, all the children of a father make an array. In the same way, all the continents of Earth make an array. States of India make an array, and further, all the district towns of a state make another array. Ranganathan has prescribed the following canons for their formation:

- Canon of Exhaustiveness
- Canon of Exclusiveness
- Canon of Helpful Sequence
- Canon of Consistent Sequence

Exhaustiveness means an array should be all-inclusive of its eligible members. On the other hand, exclusiveness means that an entity should belong to one and only one array. In other words, a member should not be included in two groups at the same time. Helpful sequence demands that entities be arranged in a logical, predictable and helpful order. For example, all the children of a father can be arranged by age. Lastly, consistent sequence means that if a set of entities occurs at different places, their arrangement should be the same everywhere. For example, the terms 'male', 'female' and 'child' occur in the main classes of psychology, education, and even law.

Canons for Formation of Chains of Classes

As a result of successive application of characteristics to a group, not all members will be of equal rank. This could be wholes, their parts, kinds and various species and subspecies of an entity. Such whole and their parts should be kept together to form a chain of classes. A chain is a sequence of entities in successive subordination. For example, 'grandfather, father, sons, grandchildren' make a chain. There are two canons for arranging entities in a chain:

- Canon of Decreasing Extension
- Canon of Modulation

The first canon means that the entities should be arranged in a broader to narrower, general to specific or whole to parts order. For example, 'Asia, South Asia, India, North India, Punjab, Amritsar' makes a chain of classes in decreasing extension. Modulation means no intervening link should be missed in the classes arranged in decreasing extensions.

Canons of Filiatory Sequence: According to this canon, all the subordinate classes of a class, in whatever chain they may occur, should immediately follow it, without being separated from it or among themselves by any other class.

Principles of Helpful Sequence

As already stated, an array is essentially a systematically ranked and arranged group of equal entities. The members of a group may be arranged in many ways. Librarians need to choose a sequence that is helpful to the majority of the users and also logical. Entities in an array may be arranged in a chronological or historical sequence. A group of boys and girls may be arranged by age. Kings of a country may be arranged according to their period of rule. Indian prime ministers may be arranged in order: Nehru, Shastri, Indira Gandhi, Morarji Desai... Vajpayee, Manmohan Singh. Extending this analogy a bit, a queue waiting for a bus or before a booking window is also according to this order. It is an order that may be called 'First come-first-served'. A related principle is of 'Later in Evolution.' Some entities can be arranged as they have evolved. Animals can be arranged from amoeba to mammals. Plants can be arranged from Thallophyta to Dicotyledons. Society can be arranged as follows: Hunting society, agriculture society, industrial society and information society. Another principle involves geographical proximity or spatial contiguity, etc. If no other principle applies, then the entities may be arranged alphabetically. All the UN member states are arranged in alphabetical order. In a nutshell, for the arrangement of members in an array, use any systematic, predictable method that you think will be helpful to the majority of library users.

Verbal Plane

In this phase of classification work, we give standardised names to the concepts arranged in arrays and chains in the idea plane. Ideas are something airy in the mind. They cannot be well expressed and communicated without having a proper name. In this phase, we dress the airy ideas in proper and visible garments of language to make them standard terms to handle. It is important as ideas need some medium for expression and communication. It is rightly said—an idea in words is worth thousands in the mind. No idea can be communicated without apt words. In the field of science and all other technical subjects, like accountancy or literary criticism, these names for concepts are known as 'terms'. And the science of assigning terms to ideas is called terminology. Verbal plane deals with terminology.

Nature of Language

No doubt language is a vehicle of thought; without it, there could be no civilisation, no progress and perhaps no art or science. Without a developed language, we will not be able to think even. Without language, there will be only animals living. But any language spoken by any community is both rich and poor. It is rich in the sense that, usually, it has many words for a single concept. For instance, wages, pay and salary mean the same thing. Similarly, in Indian languages, Suraj, Surya, Dinkar, Prabhakar and Aditya all mean the sun. Different words having the same meaning are called synonyms. Thus, these are synonymous words.

It is poor in the sense that one word might denote more than one meaning. 'Cricket' is both a popular game and an insect. 'Bridge' is a construction over a river and also the name of a game. A word having more than one meaning is called a homonym. In English, there is hardly a word having only one meaning. It is said that the word 'order' has 250 meanings in the English language. Ranganathan found five meanings of the word 'classification'. Homonyms and synonyms are vitally useful for literary writers. They make the writings delicious, imaginative and rich with aesthetic pleasure.

Homonyms and Synonyms

Synonyms and homonyms are a great barrier in communication and even harmful for legal and business transactions and science and research communication. In scientific communication, we should be precise to the extent that one word should have one and only one meaning and vice versa. It means an ideal situation of one-to-one correspondence between concepts and terms. It means that the language of any science and academic field of study and research should be strictly free of homonyms and synonyms. It has already been achieved to a great extent in natural sciences. Social sciences, including library and information science (LIS), are struggling with the standardisation of terminologies in their subjects. The maturity of a discipline of knowledge can easily be measured by its standardised terminology. Ranganathan always urged librarians to learn and use technical terminology of library science for research and communication in their field. He also advised librarians to learn the technical terminology of other subjects for better information retrieval and to provide satisfactory reference service to scholars of various subjects.

Canons for Terminology

Ranganathan not only himself coined many new terms, but he also formulated many principles for the coining and display of new terms. As stated earlier, the first and foremost quality of any terminology is to be free of homonyms and synonyms. For this purpose, he formulated following canons:

- Canon of Context
- Canon of Enumeration
- Canon of Currency
- Canon of Reticence

Canon of Context: It lays down that the terms in the classification schedules be written and read in the context of the upper class. For example, instead of writing simple salts, double salts or complex salts, we should write 'salts'.

Canon of Enumeration: The scope of terms or disciplines is not universally settled. For example, the subject 'Dynamics' is considered a part of Mathematics by some and of Physics by others. In such circumstances, it is safe to delineate the scope by listing, that is, enumerating its subdivisions.

Canon of Currency: As already stated, terminology in any discipline is not static or frozen. It is always dynamic and moving. Even the old concepts get new meanings, and an old concept might get a new term. Old terms may denote new concepts. A classification system must always update its terminology using current terms. According to this canon, "Terms used to denote a class in a scheme for classification should be one that is current among those specializing in the subject field covered by the scheme".

Canon of Reticence: It means that the terms that are used in the classification schedules should be neither judgemental nor critical. The DDC (fourteenth edition) used the term 'humbugs' for parapsychologists. For example, one should not use the terms 'major authors' or 'minor authors' while dividing literary writers.

Notational Plane: Definition

Notation is a system of short-hand symbols to denote subjects and their subdivisions by ordinal digits. A digit is an element of notational systems. These digits have only ordinal value, that is, they only show order. These digits are not cardinal or quantitative. To explain, in a notational system comprising 1, 2, 3,...9, etc., the value of 2 is not greater than 1, but will only come after it. Similarly, if it comprises symbols A, B,....Z, it means that C is not greater than A or B but will fall between B and D. Thus, notation conveys only the order, not value or weight.

Notational Plane: Need and Purpose

In the idea and verbal planes, every concept is given a due place in a classification system; however, these terms cannot be assigned as index terms to the documents in a library. The notational plane overcomes this limitation. The need and purpose of this plane can be understood from the following points:

- Names/terms for subjects in the verbal plane are too long to be written as labels. Hence, we require short symbols to denote subjects through the notational plane.
- Names of subjects are different in different languages, while a library contains books in many languages. Mathematics is called '*Ganit*' in Hindi. Then, where should a book of mathematics in Hindi be placed? Under 'G' or 'M'? Names keep changing. For example, Economics was once called Political Economy. The Education Ministry is now called The Ministry of Human Resources Development. Sri Lanka was once

called Ceylon. There is no such provision in the verbal or idea plane.

- It is an indispensable component of library classification that is usually not required in knowledge classifications.
- Apart from arranging documents on shelves, this plane arranges entries in classified catalogues and shelf lists.
- It shows the relationships among subjects in the overall scheme of mapping knowledge.
- In a faceted classification, the plane makes the structure of the subject transparent.
- It is essential for chain indexing.
- It may be essential for the arrangement of (books) circulation records in a library.

Canons of Notation

To design a qualitative and effective notation, Ranganathan formulated and prescribed some canons for the choice and design of a notational system.

These are:

1. Canon of Homonym and Synonym
2. Canon of Relativity and Uniformity
3. Canon of Hierarchy
4. Canon of Mixed Notation
5. Canon of Faceted Notation
6. Canon of Co-Extensiveness

Canon of Homonym and Synonym: Ranganathan described notation as a servant of the idea plane, yet it is more than a mere series of symbols. He expected much from notation. He always treated it as a device to translate the subject of a document into an artificial language of ordinal numbers. And he wanted to endow it with the qualities of a language. In the same way, his canon of homonyms and synonyms prescribes that a class number should denote one and only one subject, and conversely, a subject should be denoted by one and only one class number.

Canon of Relativity and Uniformity: It means that the length of a class number (that is, the total number of digits in it) is usually an indication of the breadth and depth of the subject it denotes. Breadth and depth are technically known as the extension and intension of the subject, respectively. For example, 02 – Library Science, 025 – Library Operations and 025.3 – Bibliographic Analysis and Control. In this example, the subject becomes more and more specialised as the number (quantity) of digits goes on increasing.

Canon of Hierarchy: It is implied in the canon of relativity. It means that every characteristic used in the division of a universe of entities must be represented by a digit. In other words, the class number must faithfully depict the deepening hierarchy of subjects. For example, 5 – Sciences, 51 – Mathematics and 516 – Geometry.

Canon of Mixed Notation: Usually, there are two types of notation: Pure and mixed. A pure notation comprises single species of digits, say, only A/Z as in RIC or 0/9 Arabic numerals as in the DDC. There was a time when purity was considered a virtue due to ease of use. Mixed notation comprises a mix of two or more species, as in LCC, which uses a mix of alphabets and numerals to denote subjects. UDC, which mainly uses 0/9 notation with a host of punctuation marks and mathematical signs, also has a mixed notation.

Canon of Faceted Notation: Faceted notation must be structurally transparent to show various facets or elements of a class number. For example, in UDC, 82 Shak-2 denotes the plays of Shakespeare. Here, '8' refers to Literature, '2' refers to English Literature, 'Shak' stands for Shakespeare, and '-2' refers to Drama. In the DDC, 822.33 means the same thing. It is structured internally, that is, '8' refers to Literature, '22' refers to English Drama, '822.3' refers to Elizabethan Plays and '822.33' refers to Shakespeare.

Canon of Co-Extensiveness: It means that every aspect of the subject should be indicated by a digit. That is, a class number should be totally comprehensive of the characteristics used in dividing a subject. It again brings us to the question of hierarchy and relativity. For example, Indian History: 954, Mughal History: 954.02, Akbar: 954.02 and Court of Akbar: 954.02.

Qualities of Notation

Notation should have the following qualities:

- Notation should be user-friendly.
- Among the desirable qualities, a notation should be brief and not highly mixed so that digits convey a self-evident order. Proportionate or equitable allocation of digits to subjects will result in brief numbers.
- Digits should be easy to write; in fact, they should be available on the computer keyboard.
- Another desirable quality of notation is being mnemonic. A mnemonical notation denotes the same or similar recurring concept by the same digits. The DDC and the CC are highly mnemonic systems.
- Class numbers should be easy to pronounce and remember for a short while.
- The brevity of class numbers in the print environment is a necessity as a class number had to be written on the book spine, which has a limited breadth. Lengthy class numbers also pose difficulties in arrangement on the shelves.
- Hierarchical and faceted notation with high recall and relevant ratios are the best for information retrieval.
- The mixedness and length of a notation do not matter in an automated library, whereas in a print or manual library, these are weighty and influential considerations.

Hospitality in Array

Hospitality is the most essential, rather vital, quality of any notational system. Notation can accommodate new subjects at their proper places without disturbing the existing sequence. Non-technically, it is also known as flexibility or resilience of classification. It is essential as knowledge is simultaneously growing exponentially in multiple directions. Therefore, any living and practical classification must have the capacity to give place to the new subjects at their proper places. Thus, library classifications are revised from time to time to include new subjects in their natural places. For example, the DDC (1876) of 44 pages has grown gradually to more than 3000 pages (DDC-22 (2003)). Hospitality can be at two levels.

1. Hospitality by classifiers
2. Hospitality by classificationists in new editions

Hospitality by Classifiers

Almost all standard library classification systems recommend that classifiers not tinker with the schedules. They should not make local numbers in case a number for a new subject is not available in the classification. Usually, in such situations, it is advised that a classifier should wait for the new edition and temporarily may place the new subject with its broader class. But Ranganathan made provision for the classifiers to synthesise a class number for a topic not explicitly listed in the schedules. These are devices for hospitality and number building by the classifiers. These devices include subject, chronological, geographical, super-imposition and alphabetical devices.

Hospitality by Classificationists in New Editions

Every system designer is aware of making provisions to properly accommodate new subjects at later stages. Therefore, in every system, some conceptual, structural and mechanical provisions are made to accommodate new subjects at proper places (sometimes at not-so-proper places). The sophistication of a notational system can be measured by its instant hospitality to new subjects.

Gaps in Arrays

An array is a sequence of coordinate classes. A gap device, a method to accommodate future subjects, is used at every level of arrays in almost all classifications. A gap device leaves some vacant numbers here and there to be filled in with future and unborn subjects. In the CC, for example, arrays U2 and U7 are vacant positions that can be filled with new topics in Geography.

Limitations in Gaps

Though used by almost every classification, a gap device is not the real solution. This method does not ensure a rightful place for the new subjects. There may not be any vacant place available at a needed place; on the other hand, many vacant places remain unfilled for as long as no new subjects emerge. In the DDC, many new subjects are misplaced, as due to a lack of space at the right place, they are allotted a vacant place nearby. It distorts the structure or mapping of knowledge. No gaps are left in classes like technologies, where new subjects are popping up every day. Therefore, gaps are not the solution but alibis to postpone the crisis.

Sectorising Digits

These devices accommodate a subject at a proper place in an array, even if no vacant place exists. Ranganathan invented this ingenious method of empty digits, now also called sectorising digits. He set aside 0, 9, z and Z as empty digits. These digits are never used alone but are used as repeater digits to extend an array. For example, 1, 2, 3,...8, 91, 92...99, 991, 992,...999 are all coordinate classes. Similarly, we can extend an array like A, B, C,...Y, ZA, ZB, ...ZY, ZZA, ZZB,...ZZX and so on.

Emptying Digits

Digits T, V and X are set aside as emptying digits as these empty a preceding digit of its meaning but allow it to retain its ordinal value. For example, in the CC, K represents Zoology and L represents Medicine. No space is left between the two to insert a new subject Animal Husbandry. Using X as an emptying digit, KX is given to Animal Husbandry.

Empty-Emptying Digits

To make further rather almost unlimited interpolation in the CC, U, W and Y have been postulated as Empty-Emptying digits. It means not only are these digits empty of any meaning, but they also make other digits empty to which these are attached. For example, in the CC-7, Y represents Sociology, YYT represents Sociometry, YT represents Demography and YYU represents Socio-Cybernetics.

Hospitality in Chain

A chain is a sequence of classes of successively decreasing extension. The DDC provides infinite hospitality in a chain using decimal fractions. New subjects can be added by a decimal fraction at the end of a chain. This method is now used almost by all classifications. Using decimal numerals is almost a norm while designing classification systems. For example, 328 represents Legislative Process, 328.3 represents Parliaments, 328.33 represents Members of Parliament and 328.334 represents Basis of Membership. Hierarchy showing relationships of subordination and coordination, and relativity are scientific and logical qualities of any notational system.

Problems of Notation

There cannot be any library classification without notation. For many library users, notation is the library classification. In fact, it is one of the three forms to designate and denote concepts, the other two being terms and definitions. But notation is only skin deep and should not be overburdened with tasks. Apart from subject designation, it preserves and mechanises the chosen order of subjects and documents. Though indispensable, it has many problems. In many systems, the notation has become too complex. Lengthy class numbers are inevitable in depth classification, posing many problems. They are not user-friendly. The order of digits in a mixed notation may not be comprehensible to ordinary library users. In addition, in the UDC, punctuation marks pose a problem in the automatic arrangement as their value is incompatible with the ASCII. Late French classification thinker Eric de Grolier (1911–98) regretted that we have not applied to library classification the progress that notation has made in other fields, such as mathematics, logic and chemistry. One hindrance is the library users, who are laypersons and may not understand very advanced or sophisticated notation. The emergence of digital libraries might provide a virgin field to realise the full potential of notation in library classification.

Unit 4

Comparative Study of Schemes of Classification

Comparative Librarianship

Comparative librarianship is a branch of international librarianship to study and compare the library systems of different countries and organisations. This methodology can equally be applied to various systems and services offered by different libraries. Quite often, a comparative study of classification systems and their elements is made by comparing the features of various systems. A model library classification can be designed by borrowing the best features of each. S.R. Ranganathan's *Prolegomena* (1937, 1957, 1967) uses this comparative method to evolve a theory of library classification.

Introduction to the Major Schemes of Classification

The modern history of library classification began in 1876 with the publication of Dewey's system. Its use spread very quickly as it neatly and instantly solved many of the problems being faced by the librarians in the shelf arrangement and display of books. In its wake, many new general classification systems emerged, mostly to improve upon Dewey's system or explore some alternative approaches. Noticeable among these systems are:

- Dewey Decimal Classification (DDC) (1876+)
- C.A. Cutter's Expansive Classification (1893)
- Universal Decimal Classification (UDC) (1895+)

- Library of Congress Classification (LCC) (1903+)
- J.D. Brown's Subject Classification (SC) (1906)
- Ranganathan's Colon Classification (CC) (1933+)
- Bliss' Bibliographic Classification (BC) (1940–53)
- Rider's International Classification (IC) (1961)
- Broad System of Ordering (BSO) (1978)
- Bibliographic Classification, Second Edition (BC) (1977+)

Systems by Cutter, Brown, Bliss (first edition) and Rider are no more in use. Bibliographic Classification (second edition), being revised by J. Mills, is still not complete, though it is considered one of the best classifications of the present times. DDC, UDC and LCC are considered the three major living classification systems, are highly popular and, at times, are in competition with one another. S.R. Ranganathan's CC is the most scientifically designed system. It rather brought a paradigm shift due to its revolutionary method of facet analysis and postulational approach. It is sort of a mother to subsequent classification systems. All other systems, like DDC, UDC, BC-2 and BSO, have borrowed its methods to the extent possible for their revision and modernisation.

Discipline and Main Class

All the library classifications are first divided by discipline. A discipline is a fundamental field of teaching and learning. A discipline is a major chunk of knowledge characterised by the similarity of objects of study or the use of a common research methodology. Disciplines are academic in nature and are ways of looking at the world by academicians. Three classic and traditional disciplines in order are Sciences, Humanities and Social Sciences. Now many more disciplines have emerged, such as Physical Sciences, Biosciences and Behavioural Sciences, though some call them sub-disciplines. The number of such disciplines keeps growing as the knowledge grows. The obverse of a discipline is an isolated object or phenomenon, such as copper, child, tree and school, which could be studied in the context of any discipline.

A discipline or sub-discipline is further divided on the same basis into smaller chunks called main classes. All current classifications are based on main classes, which make the primary or basic facet. The main classes in any system form the first and mutually exclusive array of the division of the universe of knowledge. A main class may be defined as a homogenous, coherent and interrelated area of knowledge within the comprehension of an ordinary intellectual being. The scope and number of main classes vary from system to system and from time to time. For example, Astronomy is a part of Mathematics in CC (1963), but in DDC, it is an independent class. Many smaller topics in the sixth edition of CC (1963) got the status of a main class in its seventh edition (1987). Nevertheless, the number, scope and order of main classes form the core of any library classification system.

Notation

Every classification scheme arranges different subjects in order of their likeness and then assigns an artificial number or letter to represent that subject. The different artificial numbers or letters used to represent subjects in a classification scheme are collectively known as notation. Different classification schemes use different notation. DDC uses only Indo-Arabic numerals (0 to 9) for representing different subjects, while CC (seventh edition) uses 74 different symbols (26 capital Roman letters; 23 small Roman letters, excluding i, l and o; 1 Greek letter Ä; 10 Indo-Arabic numerals; and 14 other signs used for connecting these symbols) as notation. The total number of symbols used as notation by a classification scheme is called its notational base.

Some Important Definitions

Call Number: The call number is the number that distinctly identifies a book in a library. There are thousands or even more books in a library. A call number is used to identify one particular book in that collection. It also helps in finding the relative location of that book in the whole collection. Thus, if you know the general sequence of arrangement of books in a library, the call number of a book will guide you to the area and the exact place where the book is kept. The call number has three parts: Class number, book number and collection number.

Class Number: The class number of a book represents its subject. A classification scheme organizes all the subjects in a systematic order and uses an artificial scheme of numbers, alphabets and symbols called notation for each subject. The notation used for a particular subject in a classification scheme is called its class number. For example, the class numbers of Library Science and Mathematics are 2 and B, respectively. All the classification schemes use notation to represent different subjects; however, they use different class numbers for different subjects. Thus, the class number of Library Science in CC is 2, whereas, in DDC, it is 020.

Book Number: Books of different subjects will have different class numbers. But in a library, there might be many books on one subject, and all these books will have the same class number. For instance, in a school or college library, if two textbooks of a subject are acquired in a large number, say, 20 each, then all these 40 books will have the same class number. We need some method to distinguish all the books with the same class number so that they can be arranged in some order and find their unique place on the shelf. Books of the same class can be arranged according to book number. According to Dr. S.R. Ranganathan, "the book number of a book is a symbol used to fix its position relative to the other books having the same ultimate class". So, different books of the same subject will have the same class number but different book numbers.

Collection Number: Libraries generally do not have a single sequence of books. Reference books are separated from other books in most libraries. In school and college libraries, textbooks are kept separately. In university libraries, there might be separate departmental libraries besides separate reference collections. Some books are too small to be kept on the shelves; others are too large to be kept with other books. The above-mentioned situations lead to more than one sequence of books (called a collection) in the library. Thus, a book may be in any of the collections in the library, and it is necessary to mention the collection where that book is. The collections are indicated by symbols called collection numbers. A library may devise its own collection number scheme, which might help indicate the collection.

Some Important Classification Schemes

Dewey Decimal Classification (DDC)

DDC is the first general library classification scheme. It was designed by Melvil Dewey in 1876. The first edition of DDC had only 44 pages, including a 12-page schedule or scheme of subjects. Dewey used Indo-Arabic numerals (that is, numbers from 0 to 9) as notation for the scheme. It is the most popular scheme in the world. Since its first edition, published in 1876, DDC has been regularly revised to keep it up to date. The twenty-third edition of DDC was published in May 2011. Its electronic version, Web Dewey 2.0, was also released simultaneously. Every class number in DDC comprises three digits (numbers). As an aid to the eye, after the third digit, a dot is inserted, and then the fourth, fifth and subsequent digits are written. At the beginning of the schedule, three summaries of class numbers are given. The first summary gives ten main classes, the second summary gives 100 divisions where each main class is divided into ten branches and the third summary gives 1000 sections where each division is further divided into ten branches. The first summary of DDC (twenty-second edition) is reproduced below:

000 Computer Science, Information & General Works
100 Philosophy & Psychology
200 Religion
300 Social Sciences
400 Language
500 Science
600 Technology
700 Arts & Recreation
800 Literature
900 History & Geography

In the second summary, each main class is further divided into ten branches called divisions. The ten divisions of main class 000 are listed below:

000 Computer Science, Knowledge & Systems

010 Bibliographies

020 Library & Information Sciences

030 Encyclopedias & Books of Facts

040 [Unassigned]

050 Magazines, Journals & Serials

060 Associations, Organizations & Museums

070 News Media, Journalism & Publishing

080 Quotations

090 Manuscripts & Rare Books

In the third summary, each division is further divided into ten sections. The sections of 020 – Library & Information Sciences are given below:

020 Library & Information Sciences

021 Library Relationships

022 Administration of Physical Plant

023 Personnel Management

024 [Unassigned]

025 Library Operations

026 Libraries for Specific Subjects

027 General Libraries

028 Reading and Use of Other Information Media

029 [Unassigned]

Further branches of each section are given in the schedules. In addition to the numbers given in the schedules, six tables can be used for number building. These tables are as follows:

Table-1: Standard Subdivisions

Table-2: Geographic Areas, Historical Periods, Persons

Table-3:	Subdivisions for the Arts, for Individual Literatures, for Specific Literary Forms
Table-3 A:	Subdivisions for Works by or About Individual Authors
Table-3 B:	Subdivisions for Works by or About More than One Author
Table-3 C:	Notation to be Added Where Instructed in Table 3B, 700.4,791.4, 808–809
Table-4:	Subdivisions of Individual Languages and Language Families
Table-5:	Ethnic and National Groups
Table-6:	Languages

DDC (twenty-first edition) also had a Table-7 – Group of Persons, which was removed in DDC (twenty-second edition).

Universal Decimal Classification (UDC)

UDC is the only classification scheme that was not designed for the classification of books. It was designed for arranging the entries of the universal bibliography at the International Institute of Bibliography (Brussels). Two Belgians, Paul Otlet and Henri La Fontaine, revised the DDC (fifth edition) to such an extent that UDC was born in 1905. So, UDC has a base of DDC, or we can say that, broadly, the main classes and their divisions are similar in both schemes. But UDC has many more features for building a class number than DDC. Due to these features, it is quite popular among special libraries all over the world. It will vacate 61 of its current class, Medicine, to expand 620 – Engineering. Its auxiliaries and special tables are a sort of cosmetic surgery over the DDC to improve its structure and efficiency in classifying micro literature.

Library of Congress Classification (LCC)

LCC scheme, as its name suggests, was designed for the Library of Congress of the USA in 1901. The scheme serves the requirements of the world's largest library, the Library of Congress (LC), and is updated regularly. Though it is only a practical scheme without much theoretical base, it is quite popular, particularly in the libraries of the USA, because of the easy availability of class numbers for most of the books. There is some influence of Cutter's Expansive Classification on the main outline of classes of LCC. LCC consists of 21 main classes denoted by A/Z and based somewhat on the Expansive Classification (1893) of C.A. Cutter (1837–1903).

Colon Classification (CC)

CC was designed by the father of library science in India, Dr. S.R. Ranganathan, in 1933. Dr. Ranganathan was a teacher of Mathematics before shifting to Library Science. After joining Library Science, he became so interested in it that he started thinking towards a new classification scheme. He was very disappointed with the classification schemes available at that time, and soon, he designed a different type of classification scheme known as CC. CC is a faceted scheme, that is, it does not have schedules of classes or subjects as in other schemes, but each main class has one or more schedules of facets that can be added to the main class number. The universe of knowledge is divided into some subjects known as main classes. During the lifetime of Dr. Ranganathan, six editions of CC were published, but after his death, his work could not get the attention it deserved. The seventh edition of CC was published in 1987 without an index, so it could not be used by libraries. The libraries still using CC are either using its sixth edition or incorporating the revisions brought out in 1963.

The scheme of main classes given in CC (sixth edition) is as follows:

z	Generalia	LX	Pharmacognosy
1	Universe of Knowledge	M	Useful Arts
2	Library Science	Ä	Spiritual Experience and Mysticism
3	Book Science	MZ	Humanities and Social Sciences
4	Journalism	A	Natural Sciences
N	Fine Arts	AZ	Mathematical Sciences

NX	Literature and Language	B	Mathematics
O	Literature	BZ	Physical Sciences
P	Linguistics	C	Physics
Q	Religion	D	Engineering
R	Philosophy	E	Chemistry
S	Psychology	F	Technology
Ó	Social Sciences	G	Biology
T	Education	H	Geology
U	Geography	HX	Mining
V	History	I	Botany
W	Political Science	J	Agriculture
X	Economics	K	Zoology
Y	Sociology	KX	Animal Husbandry
YX	Social Work	L	Medicine
Z	Law	MZA	Humanities

Between M and N, a unique main class, Mysticism, has been interposed. Generalia or form classes, such as Bibliography, Encyclopaedias, etc., have been denoted by a/z, while the newly emerging main classes, such as Library Science, Mass Communication, etc., have been denoted by 1/9. A/M – Sciences and Technology have been arranged in order of their increasing concreteness, with M representing Useful Arts, which is an assortment of applied arts and crafts and the most concrete in the group. Mysticism is at the confluence of sciences and humanities and is considered the highest knowledge in Hindu tradition. Coupled with the form of documents, the arrangement of books on shelves is in what Ranganathan calls the APUPA pattern. This order is pedagogical. No other classification comes near to such a fine and systematic order of subjects as the CC.

Notation in Different Classification Schemes

Notation, an adjunct of classification, is the most visible feature of a library classification system. Its efficiency and user-friendliness primarily determine the quality and popularity of any system. A notation should consist of familiar digits that convey their obvious order, showing synthesis and hierarchy of subjects. Further, it should be brief, mnemonic and hospitable to new subjects.

DDC

DDC invented the use of Indo-Arabic decimal notation to denote subjects and their further subdivisions. A dot is put after the third digit only as a partitioning device that has no mathematical or semantic value. Its notation is pure, hierarchical and mnemonical. Its hospitality is poor as only gaps and decimal fractions are devised for this purpose. For example, 787.87 denotes Guitar.

UDC

UDC based on DDC denotes its main classes decimally 0/9, which can be further divided hierarchically as in the DDC. But more powerful is its kit of synthesis and auxiliaries for number building. In addition, there are special auxiliaries applicable only to a given small area. Thus, the notation of UDC is mixed and quite hospitable to new subjects with the use of hierarchy, gaps, letters and auxiliaries.

LCC

LCC uses two Roman capitals for its main classes. Each of these two-digit letters is further divided by arithmetical notation. The notation being moderately mixed, the large base from A/Z and further divisions, like AA to VZ and Z, give it enormous capacity for future expansions. For example, QD 149.5 denotes General Works.

CC

Notation of CC is a high watermark of library notation. It is a comprehensive system in itself and is bred on systematic canons and devices. The only problem is its complexity and frightening class numbers. But Ranganathan was not daunted by its or his own criticism on this account. CC notation comprises 74 digits belonging to six species of digits, including Greek letters and special characters.

Extent of Use and Popularity

Library classifications are designed for practical use; some were even designed for use in a specific library. But soon, their use extended outside their specific institutions. The extent of their use determines their survival and consequent their teaching, research and published literature on them. The popularity of a system depends on many factors, such as the time of its origin, inherent technical qualities, ease of use, use in centralised cataloguing such as MARC, constant revision, support services, institutional backing and its marketing.

DDC

It is the pioneer system and also the most popular one. Used in about two lakh libraries in 140 countries across the globe, it is said the sun never sets on it. Apart from this, it has been translated into about 34 languages of the world, including Hindi, Arabic and Vietnamese. Some sixty national bibliographies use this system to arrange their contents. Its Internet-accessible version, known as Web Dewey, is available through 'OCLC connexion.' It is also used in organising and searching some search engines. For example, Webrary.

UDC

By birth, UDC was not designed for the shelf arrangement of books. It aimed at documentation and information centres. Today, in terms of its applications, it is the most diversely used tool, from organising libraries, websites and bibliographies to artifacts and realia. It is used in 125 countries. In 34 countries, it is the main classification system used across national information centres. In 45 countries, it is used in certain kinds of libraries. It has been translated into 39 languages. National Information Services and Systems (NISS), UK, now called Intuit, provides information for education. It uses UDC to organise its directory of Networked Resources. For example, selecting a specific class number, say, 34, will list all the resources on Law, while 343 will only list resources on Criminal Law.

LCC

Though the LCC was designed only for the LC, it is being used in about 60% of the large public, academic and research libraries in the US. LCC numbers appear on MARC records, which are used by many libraries for copy cataloguing throughout the world. Even some national bibliographies of Asia and Europe are using this system. Due to the depth of details, constant revision and institutional backing, it has a very bright future. Its online version, known as Classification Plus, also includes Library of Congress Subject Headings (LCSH) and is much more versatile. In the web environment, the potential of using LCC as a tool for organising Internet resources has proved quite successful.

CC

CC is an influential system, though not a highly used one. It is claimed that in the 1960s, about 20 university libraries, along with many public and college libraries in India, used this system. The CC numbers are given as an element in the Indian National Bibliography (INB) entries though its main arrangement is in accordance with the DDC. No new library is opting for this system due to its dated schedules and lack of support or backup service. But it is still being taught in library schools of India.

Historical Contribution of Classification Schemes

DDC

Contributions of DDC are many and everlasting. The use of decimal notation was an ingenious stroke of discovery. Though simple and efficient to represent subjects and place new subjects, it has many inherent limitations in portraying a true structure of knowledge. Subsequent classifications have used decimal notation in one way or the other. Even the LCC is now resorting to this method for the hospitality of new subjects. Its other contributions include division by discipline, depiction of hierarchy and invention of the relative index. It is 135 years old and going strong and getting popular day by day. The lesson is: Well-governed schemes remain rejuvenated and are trusted by librarians.

UDC

UDC, credited to be the first bibliographic classification, was introduced for the first time in any classification of powerful synthetic equipment in the form of auxiliaries. It performs the jobs of shelf arrangement and information retrieval with equal ease. Some also credit it as the first faceted scheme that heralded the Ranganathan methods. It was also the first classification to be tested for its usefulness of classification in computerised databases. Also known as European Dewey, it was the first classification sponsored by a professional organisation, which ultimately became International Federation for Information and Documentation (FID). Further, it was the first classification available in three official languages: French, German and English. Its translations are available in 24 languages. It again is the first classification to be owned and managed by a consortium of publishers (UDC consortium; UDCC) spread across the globe. Its contributions to classification are both technical and organisational.

LCC

It has the distinction of being the producer and the consumer at the same time—Alvin Toffler would say. It is a general classification with a series of depth schedules and can be used in general and research libraries. Its great support base from the LC and use in centralised and cooperative cataloguing services cover many of its technical drawbacks. Support of the world's largest and greatest library and its use in its excellent bibliographic services impose greatness on this system despite its many technical faults and weaknesses.

CC

It is a pioneer-faceted scheme that revolutionised classification thinking and practice. Its methods of facet and phase analysis have become the general theory of classification. It has devised an objective mechanism for designing and evaluating library classification systems by dividing the entire work into the idea, verbal and notational planes. By finely formulating canons, principles and postulates for the process of classification, S.R. Ranganathan raised classification work to the status of science. Now many schemes, both general and special, have sprung up using facet analyses. BSO is one such example. Many old systems, like DDC and BC-2, have used CC's methods for their revision. It started a new paradigm that is the basis of all indexing languages useful for print and electronic environments.

EXERCISE UNIT 1 – UNIT 4

1. What do you mean by the term classification?
2. Highlight some uses of classification in general.
3. Define genus-species relationship.
4. Define library classification.
5. What are the uses of classification in a library?
6. State the limitations of library classification.
7. Describe fixed and relative location systems of classification.
8. What do you understand by 'classification by design methodology'? Explain in detail.
9. What do you mean by ontology?
10. Describe the postulational approach in classification.
11. Discuss, in detail, Ranganathan's five sets of canons for the work in the idea plane.
12. Discuss canons for arrays of classes in detail.
13. What do you understand by principles of helpful sequence? Discuss in detail.
14. Describe the notational plane. Explain its need and purpose.
15. Explain six canons of notation given by Ranganathan.
16. What do you understand by comparative librarianship?
17. Name some prominent classification schemes.
18. What do you understand by the class number of a book?
19. Define call number.
20. How is the collection number different from the accession number?
21. Discuss DDC in detail. Throw some light on its three summaries.
22. Describe CC as a scheme of classification.

Unit 5
Basic Concepts in Library Cataloguing

Library Catalogue: Definition

The term 'Library Catalogue' has been formed from the Greek phrase 'Katalogos', with 'Kata' meaning 'according to' and 'Logos' meaning 'order' or 'reason'. Logos also refers to a logical concept that is based on reasoning. A library catalogue is a list of books and other graphic material in a library arranged according to a recognized order and containing specific items of bibliographical information to identify and locate the catalogued material. Thus, a library catalogue is a listing of all the items within a library. In pre-computer times, library books were indexed in card catalogues, which were cabinets of drawers of index cards: Author cards, title cards and subject cards.

A library catalogue, said to be the mirror reflecting the holdings of a library, helps the user locate and access the material required by them. It identifies to the user the bibliographical details of books for the purpose of selection and study. The catalogue groups the books in the library according to author, subject, collaborator, etc. By consulting the catalogue, a user can know the availability of all types of reading materials, both print and non-print, in the library. It is a time-saving device both for the user and the library staff.

Need for a Library Catalogue

Libraries generally acquire reading and reference materials both in print and non-print forms for the benefit of readers to study, reference and research. All the time, the desired documents might not be available physically on the bookshelves as these are issued, and if the users go to the shelves directly without consulting the catalogue, they will think that these documents are not acquired by the library, though these are actually possessed by the library. Besides, the non-book materials (NBMs), which are likely to miss the notice of readers, cannot be browsed. Here, a catalogue can be helpful for the user. The need for the catalogue can be summed up in the following points:

- It enables a person to find a book of which either the author, the title or the subject is known.
- It assists in the choice of a book as to its edition (bibliographical) and its character (literary or topical).
- It shows what the library has from a given author, on a given subject or in a given kind of literature.
- It locates a resource within a library.
- It saves the time of users as well as the staff in searching and finding a particular book.

Objectives of a Library Catalogue

Library catalogues are prepared to accomplish certain objectives, as mentioned by the legends and geniuses in the field of cataloguing, including Cutter, Ranganathan and Lubetzky. In the opinion of Cutter, a catalogue should:

1. Enable a person to find a book of which (a) the author, (b) the title or (c) the subject is known;
2. Show what the library has (a) by a given author, (b) by a given subject or (c) in a given kind of literature; and
3. Assist in the choice of a book (a) as to its edition by describing the work adequately for easy identification or (b) as to its character.

According to Ranganathan, "if a reader is interested in a subject which takes him to the library, his wants will be better served if the catalogue can spread before him a full, connected, panorama of all the materials on his desired subject, all its sub-divisions and all broader subjects of which it is itself a sub-division". He further devises the objectives of a library catalogue as follows:

1. To disclose, every reader their documents
2. To secure every document for its reader
3. To save the time of the reader
4. To save the time of the staff

However, Lubetzky is of the view that a library catalogue should serve: "First, to help for quick location of a particular publication, i.e. of a particular edition of a work which is available with library. Second, to display the relevant and related documents of a given author".

Functions of a Library Catalogue

The basic function of a library catalogue is to inform an enquirer whether or not a particular publication is in the collection of the library and, if so, where it can be found. It also reveals what material the library has on a given subject, author, etc. Thus, the functions of a library catalogue can be summarized as follows:

- It is the most important finding tool for staff reference, but its primary task is to enable the readers to ascertain what books a library possesses.
- It provides records in an order that helps the reader know what those materials are, where they are and to determine their character and suitability for that purpose.
- It serves as an exhaustive bibliography on a subject.
- It helps the library staff order new books and avoid the duplication of the materials by checking the catalogue.
- It displays the record of the library's resources to make them easily accessible for study and reference.
- It serves as a dependable tool for the communication of ideas and subjects dealt within the books to readers who use the library.

- It bridges the wide gap between the resources of rich collections of a library on one side and the users on the other side who are looking anxiously to satisfy their thirst for information by getting their desired documents without any loss of time.

Qualities of a Library Catalogue

A functional library catalogue must have the following qualities:

(i) ***Accuracy***: Errors of spelling and style or format may be avoided. Inaccuracy of any type might lead to misunderstanding, loss of time and even dislocation of a card leading to disappointment of a reader. Cards should be carefully checked before filing.

(ii) ***Consistency***: The rules of cataloguing should be strictly adhered to so that consistency can be maintained. If an amendment in rules is required due to some practical exigencies, it may be made only after careful consideration of all the pros and cons. But once an amendment has been adopted, it should be followed consistently, and there should not be afterthoughts and frequent changes. All changes should be recorded in a file or on the cataloguing code for future reference and guidance.

(iii) ***Needs of Users***: A librarian should always keep the needs of the users in mind while deciding about the various entries in the catalogue. The librarian should keep in mind the type of queries frequently made by the users. The catalogue should be so designed that it is able to satisfy the needs of the majority of the users.

(iv) ***Arrangement***: The arrangement of content in an entry should be simple, uniform and easy to understand. It should not confuse the reader but give clear-cut guidelines about the nature of the book and its location.

(v) *Up-to-Date*: There should be no time gap between the acquisition and processing of books and between the preparation of catalogue cards and their filing in the catalogue cabinet.

(vi) *Multi-Pronged Approach*: The cataloguer should try to provide at least a few added entries in order to enable the users to locate a document from various angles, that is, author, title, editor, subject and joint author. The chances of retrieval of documents on demand increase with this multi-pronged approach.

(vii) *Standard*: A good library catalogue must comply with international metadata standards.

Laws of Library Science and Library Catalogue

All the activities of the library revolve around the Five Laws of Library Science because these are the guiding principles for effective scientific planning of a library. For preparing an effective catalogue, several guidelines are implied in these Five Laws enunciated by Ranganathan.

First Law and Library Catalogue: 'Books are for Use'—the first law implies the need for organising the collections of a library for optimum utilisation by providing a number of physical facilities and reader services. The physical form of a catalogue should be such that it is flexible, can be kept up-to-date, is easy to consult and allows a speedy search. It allows for the addition of entries for new documents as and when added to the library. The users should know the scope, contents and coverage of documents by means of annotation and useful notes in a catalogue so as to make an appropriate choice among various documents. The catalogue is the only medium that brings together the users and the collections leading to maximum use and satisfying the thirst for knowledge.

Second Law and Library Catalogue: The second law states that 'Every Reader Her/His Book', which implies that various approaches of the users, that is, search by author, subject, title, etc., should be satisfied. Many books are of composite nature. Neither the title nor the main entry may disclose the contents.

This law requires that hidden contents should be brought to the notice of the readers by preparing subject analytical entries.

Third Law and Library Catalogue: Third law, that is, 'Every Book its Readers', requires the preparation of analytical entries and cross-reference entries as and when necessitated, especially in the case of books published under the editorial direction (where a number of contributors contribute papers). Seminar/conference proceedings and journals in which some of the articles/papers are highly needed by the readers are likely to miss the notice of the readers if only added entries are prepared. Instead, readers they will be helped if analytical entries are prepared.

Fourth Law and Library Catalogue: The fourth law, 'Save the Time of the Reader', ensures the saving of the precious time of the users. A catalogue should be not only simple in its design and construction but also up-to-date and communicable with elaborate guides. For effective use of the catalogue, user education/orientation programmes should be organised for the users.

Fifth Law and Library Catalogue: 'Library is a Growing Organism' is the fifth law, which implies that the catalogue also grows because of the addition of books to the library. Keeping in view the changes and growth in nature and variety of publications, other forms of documents, needs of users and the advent of ICT has an enormous impact on changes both in the physical form and internal structure of the catalogue. Change is must, and the library should prepare to face such challenges. Hence, while selecting a physical form, decision should be taken on the basis of features like longevity, durability, space, simplification, portability, selectivity, flexibility and cost.

Library Catalogue vis-à-vis Other Library Records

Difference between a Catalogue and an Index

Index means 'to indicate' or 'to point out' and is usually present at the end of a book. There is an exhaustive index showing the list of terms along with the relevant page numbers for instant reference for easy retrieval of the information. The main differences between a library catalogue and an index are mentioned below:

Characteristic	Library Catalogue	Index
Arrangement	A catalogue can be arranged alphabetically or in a classified sequence	An index is always arranged alphabetically
Entry	Includes some descriptive specifications of a document containing a subject	Index entry only specifies the subject
Flexibility	New entries can be inserted in a systematic order at any time	New subjects can be inserted at any time
Purpose	It is a record describing the documents acquired by a library	Provides access to any bibliographical entries of the catalogue by author, title or subject
Entries	Analytical entries may be prepared depending on the nature of the document	No such entries are required in the case of an index

Difference between a Catalogue and a Shelf List

A 'Shelf List' is an inventory that records bibliographical data of items arranged exactly the same way as arranged on the shelves. The main differences between a shelf list and a library catalogue are mentioned below:

Characteristic	Library Catalogue	Shelf List
Users	It is an indispensable tool for readers as well as library staff	It is consulted only by the staff of the library
Degree of Use	Used frequently	Used usually at the time of book selection and stock verification
Arrangement	Arranged either alphabetically or in a classified sequence depending on the choice of the inner form of the catalogue	Always arranged in a classified order
Form	Might be in various forms, like card, register or computerised	Generally in card form
Added Entries	Needs added entries to satisfy various approaches of the readers	No such entries are found in a shelf list

Difference between a Catalogue and an Accession Register

It is a very important administrative record in which books either purchased or received through gift and exchange are listed in chronological order date-wise and assigned a number sequentially. The main differences between an accession register and a library catalogue are mentioned below:

Characteristic	Library Catalogue	Accession Register
Purpose	Helps identify and locate a book in a library	Indicates the total collection of a library
Use	Extensively used and brings all like documents together	Used by staff only
Items of Information	Detailed information about a document is given	Contains bibliographic details
Degree of Use	Used intensively by users and staff	Used comparatively less and by staff only
Arrangement	Systematic: Either alphabetically or by call number	Systematic in the sequence of their serial number
Form	Might be card, register, book-type or computerized	Mostly on register

Library Catalogue, Bibliography and Publishers' Catalogue: A Comparison

Characteristic	Library Catalogue	Bibliography	Publishers' Catalogue
Purpose	To serve the users and satisfy the laws of library science	Depends upon the kind of bibliography	Promotion for the sale of books
Function	Serves as a retrieval tool	To bring the notice of the readers, a selected list of documents relevant to the study; inventory functions	Inventory functions restricted to book purchase
Scope	Collection confined to a particular library or a group of libraries	Normally, it is restricted to a particular subject region, person or language	Restricted to a particular publisher or group of publishers

Characteristic	Library Catalogue	Bibliography	Publishers' Catalogue
Arrangement	Either alphabetically or acceding to a call number	Usually, it is arranged alphabetically	Subject-wise and alphabetically
Users	A large number of users, including research scholars and library staff	Mostly the scholars and library staff	Librarians, faculties and scholars
Physical Form	Found generally in card, register and computerized form	Usually found in the form of a book	Occurs in the form of a book (both printed or mimeographed)
Bibliographical Information	Maximum information about the document, along with availability and location mark, is provided	Likely to have useful information with an annotation for selecting the best document	Information is inadequate; highlights the special feature and revision, if any, about the document
Preparation of Entries	With the help of catalogue codes containing the rules for the preparation of entries made based on the needs of users	Prepared acceding to some citation standards, such as BIS: 2378 or 2381	Prepared from documents themselves; does not follow any cataloguing codes

Cataloguing and the Role of Technology

The needs and requirements of users differ from one another. Consequently, a number of entries are prepared for the document to satisfy the various approaches of readers. The main entry and added entries usually serve this purpose. The main entry provides maximum relevant and useful information about the documents. Further, the added entries are prepared under several access points, such as joint authors, editors, translators, titles and series of the document consisting of brief information for easy location. Cataloguing is the process of preparing entries for a catalogue. The steps involved in making entries are enumerated as follows:

1. Choice of access point/determination of heading and rendering for the above entries.
2. Recording of the information under various sections/ areas of the description of the entries.
3. Determination of the style of writing, punctuation marks, etc., as per the International Standard Bibliographic Description (ISBD).
4. Writing call number in all the entries.
5. Filing of catalogue cards.
6. Preparation of guide/reference card, proper maintenance and updating of entries in the catalogue.

All these processes and procedures are involved in the act of cataloguing. The provision of detailed information facilitates a reader in selecting the needed documents. To help the cataloguer catalogue properly, keeping in mind the expected approaches of the readers, catalogue codes have been developed, designed and revised. The Classified Catalogue Code (CCC) was formulated by S.R. Ranganathan in 1934 is a user-oriented code that provides rules for subject entries and exhaustive rules for choice and rendering of bibliographic items for descriptive cataloguing. Similarly, Anglo-American Cataloguing Rules (AACR) editions 1 and 2 and 1988 revised edition, amendments and regular incorporation of new rules for new items, like 'electronics resources', prove to be the most popular catalogue code. It follows the ISBD format for the purpose of cataloguing to achieve uniformity, consistency and standardisation for preparing catalogue entries. Besides, it is amenable to the computerisation of library activities and leads to international library cooperation, resource sharing and global networking.

Due to the unprecedented growth of publications, it is difficult to know the location and availability of publications with the help of traditional/manual methods. But with the advent of IT and Information Communication Technology (ICT), it is possible to ascertain what information exists and where. Many libraries are computerized and networked so that they can have access to the resources of other libraries through online access, that is, the catalogue entries are stored and searched for display as desired by the user. In the context of the cataloguing process, there is no scope for a computer to create the basic entry as it involves technical skill and expertise in the subject field. But once the data is entered and a suitable software package is in use, the computer is capable enough to prepare highly complicated types of catalogues for control of information. We need to grab this opportunity offered by IT so that maximum benefit can be given to the users for the best exploitation of the resources of other libraries.

Symbiosis

Classification helps arrange documents on the shelf in a logical order, bringing together documents on like subjects and separating those on different subjects. Library catalogue interprets the collection of the library and helps the user select and locate the desired document. These two interrelated processes help the readers lay hands on their requisite information. Classification and cataloguing satisfy the laws of library science and work for their mutual help. Where classification fails to satisfy the need of the users, catalogues come to the rescue by preparing suitable entries and vice-versa. This mutual relation between classification and cataloguing is termed symbiosis.

Unit 6

Types and Forms of Catalogues

Inner Forms of a Catalogue

The inner form of a library catalogue refers to the arrangement of a catalogue entry in a logical and systematic order to fall into a helpful sequence for storage and retrieval. There are three types of inner forms of a catalogue:

1. Alphabetical: Entries are arranged on the basis of alphabets
2. Classified: Entries are arranged by the class number or notation
3. Alphabetico-classed: Combines qualities of both 1 and 2

Author name, title, subject and dictionary catalogues fall in the category of an alphabetical catalogue. A classified catalogue is so named because it is arranged in a classified order. Classified order is an artificial order that may be difficult to use. Hence, a classified catalogue has two parts, the other part being alphabetical, which is easy to use and leads the user to the classified part. An alphabetico-classed catalogue is a variation of the classified catalogue. It overcomes the shortcoming of the artificiality of a classified arrangement by making it classified alphabetically. All of these catalogues have been discussed below.

Author Catalogue

Author is the person who is chiefly responsible for the intellectual thought content of a work. In simple words, the author is the creator of a work. In an author catalogue, the entries of documents are under the author's name and arranged alphabetically. It provides access to documents by the names of their authors. In other words, the leading section of an author catalogue would comprise the name of an author. An author is generally a person or a corporate body who is responsible for the thought content of the document brought out under the name. The listing of personal names of authors varies greatly because of the cultural traditions in the naming of persons in different regions of the world. Which part of the names should be taken as the lead in a catalogue has been set by cataloguing codes, and there are established practices. Thus, a catalogue whose entries are listed by author, editor, compiler, translator or other party is considered to have responsibility for the creation or assembly of the work specified.

Advantages

- It brings together the titles of books of the same author in one place in the catalogue.
- It helps a user determine which books are available in the library by a given author. This function can, however, be fulfilled by author entries in other inner forms of a library catalogue. In a classified catalogue, this function is performed by the alphabetical index of the dictionary part.
- It ensures that there is no scattering of works of the same author through the catalogue.

Disadvantages

- Approaches of readers under the subject, collaborators, distinctive titles, etc., cannot be satisfied.
- It requires that the reader knows the exact name of the author and the title.
- In case the author is known by different forms of name or pseudonym, the reader may find it difficult to locate a resource.

Name Catalogue

A name catalogue is a variation and extension of an author catalogue. It contains entries for works of one author and books written by him, that is, it brings in one place the entries for all the books written by one author. All entries are arranged alphabetically by the name of the author. In other words, a name catalogue is a compound or mixed type of catalogue which combines the author and subject entries (the subject entries representing the author as a subject) into one alphabetical sequence. In this type of catalogue, autobiography, biography and other critical studies, such as memoirs and diary of an author, are arranged along with his original work. Author entries include:

- Corporate authors, both as an author as well as subject;
- Name series; and
- Place name forming part of an author heading.

A name catalogue serves as an author catalogue and also as a subject catalogue. Any reader interested in the works by or on an author might find this type of catalogue very useful for finding specific material of his interest.

Advantage

- It is useful and valuable for the collection of books of an author and books on her/him.

Disadvantages

- Subject entries are limited to personal and corporate names only.
- There is no title entry in this type of catalogue.

Title Catalogue

In a title catalogue, the titles of documents occupy the leading section of entries, which are arranged in alphabetical order. Queries of readers who remember only the exact title can be answered with the help of a title catalogue. However, it is noticed that many of the readers do not spell out a title exactly the way it appears on the title page, particularly non-fiction titles. To fulfil the title approach of readers, entries can be selectively provided in catalogues of public libraries for fiction and for those that are well-known by their titles. It is a part of the dictionary catalogue or the author-title index of the classified catalogue. For books in classical language, particularly Sanskrit and Pali, this catalogue is somewhat preferred. Thus, a library catalogue in which books and other works are listed only under their titles, usually arranged alphabetically, is referred to as a title catalogue.

Advantage

- This type of catalogue satisfies the approaches of readers, especially in cases of fiction, drama, poetry and class literature and classical languages.

Disadvantage

- It cannot alone satisfy all approaches of the readers, except the title approach.

Alphabetical Subject Catalogue

It is a list of books in a collection, each entered under the name of the specific subject as a heading, the entries being arranged alphabetically. Several books on the same subject will be brought together in the catalogue. When there is more than one book on one subject, the author of the book is selected to determine the alphabetical order. If the author's name is common for several books, then the title of the book is taken into account for the arrangement of entries. Thus, in an alphabetical subject catalogue, entries are made under the name of the specific subjects of documents. Irrespective of their affiliations, specific subject entries are strictly arranged in alphabetical order.

If a reader approaches the catalogue intending to find a book or books on a specific subject, this catalogue provides excellent service as they can refer to it like a dictionary. However, if at all, a reader wants to see all the materials on a field of knowledge systematically, the catalogue fails to respond to their query, that is, a book on BOTANY will be separated from books on ZOOLOGY. Similarly, books on CHEMISTRY will be separated from books on PHYSICS. Hence, a reader has to look under separate headings at different places in the alphabet if all the materials available in a given field of knowledge are to be gathered.

Advantages

- With the help of this catalogue, a specific subject approach of the readers can be satisfied.
- This catalogue is prepared with the help of a standard list of subject headings, like the Sears list of subject headings (SLSH) or the LCSH, giving it consistency, uniformity and standardisation.

Disadvantages

- The related subjects are scattered throughout the catalogue owing to their alphabetical arrangement. For example, Money and Banking, Electricity and Magnetism, Astronomy and Planet, etc.
- The standard list of subject headings fails to cope with the ever emergence of new subjects, and newer editions need to be brought out regularly; otherwise, the cataloguer is unable to assign exact subject headings for newly published books.

Dictionary Catalogue

It is a catalogue in which all the entries (authors, title, subject, series, etc.) and their related references are arranged together in one alphabetical reference. It resembles the arrangement of entries in a dictionary where the words are strictly arranged alphabetically. The various entries of this catalogue are arranged just like a dictionary, that is why it is called a dictionary catalogue. It is a mixed type of catalogue, where we find two distinct approaches merged together. It is a combination of two distinct and different approaches, the author and title approach for the reader who knows the book they want by the author and the subject approach of the reader who does not know either the name of the author or the title of the book but wants material on some specific subject. As a result of this type of arrangement, quite unrelated headings will come together, and related headings will be dispersed (for example, classification and cataloguing, flowers and rose will be dispersed).

Advantages

- It is the most popular form of catalogue used in public, school and college libraries, and even in university libraries. Its popularity is due to its arrangement like a dictionary, that is, in alphabetical order.
- It can satisfy the different specific needs of the readers.
- The users need not be aware of class numbers to refer to this catalogue.
- With the help of cross-references and general references, readers are guided from one heading to another.
- A direct approach to any specific subject can be satisfied easily. For example, if a reader wants books on 'CRICKET', he will refer to the catalogue directly under this term and immediately know all the books available on 'CRICKET' in the library.

Disadvantages

- For readers who need information on a subject with all its ramifications, the dictionary catalogue is the most difficult to use. It is slower in yielding information and less satisfactory in its result than the classified form.
- The extensive use of cross-references to bring together the related subjects makes the catalogue bulky. Its maintenance is more difficult. Moreover, the cross-references often prove to be tiresome.
- It is a tedious and time-consuming affair on the part of the readers to find out information on the various aspects of a particular subject and its related subjects from this catalogue.
- Dictionary catalogue suffers from all the consequences of excessive dependence on verbalisation.
- Replacing the old subject terms with new subject terms is a tedious and time-consuming process.

Classified Catalogue

The classified catalogue provides access to information by subject. It differs from an alphabetical catalogue in that the arrangement is by class numbers. It brings in an artificiality as the user is expected to be aware of the scheme of classification. To help the user, a classified catalogue is in two parts: The first part (as defined earlier) is the notational representation of its subject, while the other part is alphabetical in nature that guides the user in navigating through the classified part and reaching the desired information. Thus, a catalogue of subject entries arranged in systematic order according to a scheme of classification is referred to as the classified catalogue.

Classified Part of Classified Catalogue

It is the arrangement of entries of documents by class numbers, giving a systematic and structured display of subjects in a classified catalogue. It maps out the subordinate and coordinate subject divisions and puts them in a logical sequence. This systematic arrangement, to a certain degree, reflects the logical thinking of specialists in different subjects and gets their appreciation. It is absolutely necessary to give verbal equivalents of the divisions of class numbers, as common users do not understand such numbers.

Alphabetical Part of Classified Catalogue

The alphabetical index to a classified catalogue, consisting of the author, title (wherever necessary), subject entries and other entries for collaborators, series, editors of series and a host of cross-references, is meant to support the classified part of the catalogue. It can fulfil all the functions of a dictionary catalogue, that is, collect the works of an author together, bring all the different editions of a title, cross reference for subjects, etc. With the classified part bringing all the related subjects together and the alphabetical order bringing together all the distributed relatives, the classified catalogue can fulfil all the functions of a library catalogue.

Advantages

- In a classified catalogue, the main entry not only falls under the subject a book deals with but also falls in close proximity to related subjects.
- The logical or systematic arrangement of subjects is assumed because the catalogue is based on a recognised system of classification.
- The close identity of arrangement between catalogue entries and books on shelves tends to increase the readers' familiarity with a large number of books.
- It discloses the strengths and weaknesses of a library by subjects, broad and specific.
- It is easy to bring out printed parts of a classified catalogue, class by class, with a consolidated index at the end of the volume when the parts are printed.
- Specific sections of classes of the classified catalogue in a large library with a fairly balanced and representative active collection can be used as relative subject bibliographies.
- More readers can consult the catalogue at a time because of the facility of separate catalogue cabinets both in classified and alphabetical parts.
- Changes in subject terminology do not seriously affect the classified catalogue. Only the subject index cards in the alphabetical portion need to be re-filed according to the changed terminology.
- The index entries of a classified catalogue are easier to use and consult.

Disadvantages

- In a classified catalogue, the reader needs to consult the alphabetical part first, then taking the call number, they need to again go to the classified part for detailed information about the document.
- The success of this catalogue depends on the chosen classification scheme. Because if there is any drawback

in the classification scheme, it will be reflected in the catalogue.

- Revision of the classification scheme necessitates revision of the relevant part of the subject catalogue.

Dictionary Catalogue and Classified Catalogue: A Comparison

Characteristics	*Dictionary Catalogue*	*Classified Catalogue*
Arrangement	One single alphabetical sequence of author, title, subject, etc.	Two parts: (i) Classified part and (ii) Alphabetical part
Author and Title Filiations	Works of the same author, different editions of the same work and different translations of a work kept together	The alphabetical index gets these filiations of authors and works
Subject Filiations	Related subjects get scattered because of the alphabetical arrangement	Presents a structured and organized arrangement of subjects
Distributed Relatives	All distributed relatives are collected and brought together	The alphabetical index can perform this function
New Subjects	It can be inserted into the catalogue without any difficulty	To be fitted properly in the subject filiation
Classification as a Basis	It does not depend on any scheme of classification	Successfulness depends solely on the qualities of the scheme of classification
Use of Cross-References	Extensively used	Less used
Ease of Use	Simple, easy and straight-forward	Two-step search is necessary
Printing	Cannot be done in parts	Printing of subject is possible
International Cooperation	Difficult to achieve	Possible, if UDC is used

Alphabetico-Classed Catalogue

The alphabetico-classed catalogue may be considered a combination or mixture of the best points associated with the dictionary and the classified catalogues. In other words, it represents an attempt to combine some of the advantages of a classified catalogue with the directness and ease of consultation of the alphabetical catalogue. A catalogue with entries under broad subjects alphabetically arranged and subdivided by topics in alphabetical order. It is out and out a subject catalogue. It does not stand independently by itself as in the case of a dictionary catalogue. An alphabetico-classed catalogue provides alphabetically arranged broad subjects. Topics subordinate to the main subjects are listed as sub-divisions. Thus, a catalogue of this kind consists of an alphabetical sequence of mutually exclusive broad subject headings, under each of which appears the further alphabetical sequence of sub-headings. The process of alphabetical divisions can be carried down to the degree of minuteness required by the catalogue material.

Advantage

- In this type of catalogue, there is an attempt to incorporate the advantages of the dictionary and the classified catalogues with the simplicity of an alphabetical arrangement of broad subject headings where, again, sub-divisions are arranged alphabetically.

Disadvantages

- It is a complex type of catalogue. The references are made from the specific heading to the complex heading.
- Subject headings are complex, creating confusion for the reader.

Choice of Inner Forms of a Catalogue

The essential requirements in the choice of an inner form of a catalogue are as follows:

1. A good library catalogue should satisfy the different approaches of the readers.
2. Works of the same author or collaborator or on the same subject should come together.

3. The catalogue should be logically constructed so that closely related classes can be brought together.
4. It should be prepared in such a way that a reader can easily understand without much trouble.
5. The catalogue should be selected keeping in mind the type of user community, their information needs and the nature of documents.
6. The library must provide a user-oriented catalogue.

Outer/Physical Forms of a Catalogue

Catalogues have different outer or physical forms. The type of physical form selected for a catalogue depends on its relative requirements, that is, the criteria for selecting the best possible outer form of the catalogue is to ensure that it can be used efficiently by the maximum number of users. It is prepared at the least cost and occupies less space.

Criteria for Selection of the Best Physical Form of a Catalogue

In the recent past, due to the advent of IT, most of the libraries are in the process of computerisation and developing computerised catalogues. However, card catalogue still exists and is in operation, especially in colleges and university libraries. Whatever physical form a catalogue might have, it should possess all the features of the most suitable catalogue, if not all. The selected physical form should ideally fulfil most of the following criteria:

- It should be possible to keep it up to date, which implies that one should be able to insert or withdraw entries easily as and when required. It means the catalogue should be flexible in nature.
- It should bring like entries together, that is, on the same author and same subject.
- It must be easy to use and should be possible to consult it inside or outside a library. This is related to portability.
- It should be economical to produce and maintain and should have a facility for making several copies.

- It must be compact in size so that it does not occupy much space.
- It should provide multiple access points and save the time of the readers so that, at a time, more readers can use the catalogue.

Different Outer Forms of a Catalogue

Bound Register Form

In this form, the entries of documents of a library are written in hand in a bound register or ledger. The information about each document, like the author, edition, accession number, number of copies and class number, is provided, and separate registers for author, title and subject can also be prepared.

Advantages

- The ease with which readers can use this catalogue is unquestionable.
- Xerox copies of the catalogue can be placed at different locations in libraries, facilitating the readers to consult the catalogue in any corner of the library so that, at a time, more readers can use it because it has the quality of portability.
- Several entries that a reader can see on a page at a time without the necessity of turning one card after another is definitely an added advantage, saving precious time of the readers. Sometimes a card may be skipped while consulting hurriedly.
- It needs neither much space nor special equipment for its display due to its compactness.
- Since readers are in the habit of reading and consulting books from childhood, they feel it is much more convenient to consult being like a book.

Disadvantages

- It does not possess the quality of flexibility; hence, when new books are added, entries cannot be filed in their appropriate places as the left-out space is filled soon. Hence, such books will be entered at the end of the register, or a supplementary catalogue will be prepared, which is a delaying process. The addition of books is an inherent feature of a library. This catalogue is unable to keep good company as one is fast, while the other is slow.

- It cannot be kept up to date.
- The quality of the paper is not thick as the card catalogue; hence, its durability is less and cannot withstand constant use by the readers.
- In case books are stolen, damaged, torn out, mutilated and outdated, then immediately, the relevant entries are to be deleted from the catalogue, which looks confusing and indecent.

Printed Book Form

It is a catalogue of books and other reading materials available in a library bound in a volume or volumes where entries are printed on pages. It is also known as a printed page catalogue or a bound book catalogue. These are prepared in conformity with standard principles and rules of cataloguing. Some of the big libraries like the British Library, the LC, the National Library, Kolkata, Glasgow and Liverpool Catalogues printed their catalogues in book form. To keep the catalogue updated, they regularly issued supplements to these catalogues.

Advantages

- Since this catalogue resembles the printed reading materials, it creates a less psychological barrier to the readers for use as they are familiar with the conventional printed books.
- The speed of search is fast as compared to other forms of catalogues.
- Multiple copies of this catalogue can be made on demand and sold so that readers can comfortably consult the catalogue at home and in hostels.
- No thoughtless and careless reader can make any alteration in the pagination or in the order of arrangement of entries. The volumes of it can be kept

on a table without any special equipment and are easy to handle. Experience shows that the printed book catalogue is psychologically attractive to the public and that it is easy, simple and conventional to use. There are no long trays for pullouts and pullbacks.

- In small libraries, it is considered economical to use this catalogue as in such libraries, books are added in small numbers. Subsequently, supplementary catalogues can be prepared.
- It is easy to consult as a reader can glance at many entries on one page.
- It does not occupy much space.
- It can be segmented into various sections and issued subject-wise to satisfy the needs of different subject groups of users.

Disadvantages

- Insertion and withdrawal of entries or their deletion is not possible as it is not flexible.
- It is highly expensive for its production, and the issue of supplements takes much time; hence, it cannot be kept up to date.
- Printing of the catalogue consumes a lot of time, and in the meantime, new books are acquired by the library whose entries cannot be included. As a result, the information about such books cannot be brought to the notice of the readers. As such, the catalogue cannot indicate the complete collection.

Sheaf Form

The sheaf form of the library catalogue is also known as the loose-leaf form. A sheaf form of the catalogue is one in which slips of paper are put into a loose-leaf binder and bound by some mechanical device into a volume. This is a loose-leaf binder format, which provides the convenience of handling a book. In the sheaf form, each entry is made on a separate slip. But there may also be more than one entry on each slip or page. The entries are either handwritten or typed. New slips can be inserted in appropriate places without disturbing the existing order of arrangement of entries. It is also possible to remove entries for specific documents in case such documents are withdrawn from the library stock. Roughly, each volume of a sheaf catalogue might contain about 500 to 600 leaves. The volumes so constituted may be displayed on special shelves with appropriate labels on their spines, indicating the order (either alphabetical or classified) of arrangement. At one time, this form of catalogue became somewhat popular in countries like England and other European countries.

Advantages

- "Generally one slip is used to record the particulars of one document only. This leads to wastage of space on slips, which are larger in size".
- It is possible to bring like entries together, that is, books by the same author and on a specific subject.
- It is easy to consult and can be referred to inside and outside the library.
- It is the most economical to produce and can be kept in a small wooden/steel rack, resulting in occupying less space due to its compact nature.
- A mobile library collection may be entered in a sheaf catalogue, and it can be carried in a van.
- Duplicate entries can be made easily.

Disadvantages

- There is a wastage of space as the size of each clip is too large.
- Since the size of a clip is 7-¾ by/4 inches/the particulars of one document may be recorded, resulting in a waste of space.
- The entries be struck off as and when the relevant document is lost, damaged or withdrawn. Otherwise, the whole slip will be again rewritten or retyped on the entire page.

- The filing and fixing of sheaves into a loose leaf binder is a time-consuming and tedious process as it involves unlocking and locking time and again. Hence, it creates problems in the proper maintenance of the catalogue.
- Those libraries that follow this catalogue cannot conveniently participate in any cooperative venture where unit cards are used for entries.

Card Form

Library catalogue in the card form is by far the most popular physical form. It is widely prevalent in libraries throughout the world, including India. In this form, the bibliographical elements of every document are recorded on a single card. This method of representing every document on a single card is known as the unit card principle. These cards stand in card trays or cabinets with a punched hole of about half a centimetre from the bottom for inserting a locking rod. This locking system keeps the cards from falling out and also prevents unauthorised persons from removing any card from the tray. Because of its wide usage all over the world, many aspects pertaining to the card catalogue are standardised. For example, 12.5 × 7.5 centimetres or 5 × 3 inches is the universally adopted size for a catalogue card.

Advantages

- It is flexible in keeping it constantly updated with the quality of expansion and withdrawal of entries.
- The users and the library staff can handle it with ease.
- It is possible to bring together entries with the same handling.
- The cards are single, self-contained units. This feature permits additional approach points and cross-reference in the catalogue.
- The entries for lost books can be withdrawn, and like entries can be filed together.
- A library that uses the card catalogue can participate in a central and cooperative cataloguing scheme. This reduces the burden on the staff.

- The cards are hard and tough, so the durability of the card catalogue is more than that of other catalogues.

Disadvantages

- The card catalogue occupies a large space in libraries.
- The growth and complexity associated with the card catalogue call for greater maintenance costs and make it administratively unmanageable. It is difficult to detect the lost card taken out by some careless and thoughtless reader.
- Due to inherent defects associated with the structure of a card catalogue, it is possible for a single person to monopolise a considerable number of trays at a time, precluding its use simultaneously by other users.
- It is not portable, and hence, the users need to go to the library to consult it. This naturally leads to a waste of time, particularly if the library does not possess the documents of their interest.
- The speed of search is slower as compared with book form and sheaf form of catalogue.

Computer-Produced Book Form

This type of book catalogue was produced with the help of a computer. The structure, extent of information about the document, typography, etc., varied from that of the conventional physical forms of catalogues. The available printout used to be in the form of a line printer output. Many institutes of repute, like the LC, used to provide services like abstracting and indexing services, including the production of catalogues using a computer.

Advantages

- The cost of production of multiple copies was less because this catalogue was first produced by creating a master copy from which additional copies could be reproduced.
- The maintenance cost was low since the whole catalogue display is recreated at internals, which facilities the

complete catalogue that can be reorganized as and when necessary.

- At a time, one entry could be referred to in a card catalogue, whereas this catalogue presents an entire page displaying a number of entries.
- The computer-produced book catalogue represents both the bibliographic information of a catalogue and the organisation.

Disadvantage

- Problems might arise in displaying current additions and changes in the cataloguing database.

Microform Catalogue

In a microform catalogue, entries are greatly reduced and printed upon a film or fiche. The microform cannot be read by naked eyes. A suitable microform reader that magnifies the reduced images on the film or fiche and projects them onto a screen is necessary to consult a microform catalogue. A microform catalogue may either be in the form of a microfilm or in the form of microfiche. Microfilm can be on a single reel, but generally, it is housed in a cassette containing two reels so that the film can be wound forwards or backwards within the container at the time of consultation. Microfilm readers usually allow the rotation of images by 90°. On the other hand, microfiche is a transparent card-type format. A reduction of nearly 42 × 42 indicates the width and height of the micro images, are 1/40 that of the original. The micro-image area is correspondingly 1/1600 that of the original, giving 200 frames per card.

Advantages

- Microform catalogues are compact and occupy less space in libraries. The space requirements of microform catalogues arise mainly because of space for microfilm or microfiche readers.
- At a time, several records can be viewed.
- They are portable and accessible to users depending upon the number of copies of catalogues and machines

available. Multiple copies of these catalogues can be prepared easily and inexpensively.

- These catalogues are very easy to use and maintain. COM catalogues are much cheaper than printed book catalogues produced the computers.

Disadvantages

- It is not easily updated, and rearrangement of information is difficult on a live catalogue.
- Unless the file is updated, the deleted material still remains.
- Psychologically, the users do not feel comfortable operating the equipment.
- It cannot be used without a microform reader.
- It also requires special care and protection.
- Medium and small libraries might not be benefited from this catalogue as microform readers/printers are costly.

MARC and Online Catalogue

There has been a lot of change in cataloguing practice with the increasing use of computers, information communication technology and network communications. Cataloguing standards have been rationalised to suit the changing cataloguing practice, universally accepted and adopted. In a machine-readable catalogue, entries are rendered in a format that permits input and storage on magnetic tape or magnetic disc for manipulation in a computer. MARC format, UNIMARC and Common Communication Format (CCF) are standard formats. Some communication formats are different from physical formats. Access to the catalogue entries may be 'offline' or 'online'. 'Offline' means that the computer can be used only at certain times. There are three major computer-produced physical forms of library catalogues that are relevant to offline access. These are:

Printed form: Entries are printed in a conventional book format and are available in multiple copies.

Card form: Each entry is transferred to one or more standard catalogue cards filed just like a conventional card catalogue.

Microform: Entries are transferred to microfiche and are used with appropriate microform readers.

In these forms, they are no more than the conventional catalogue forms. The only difference is their mode of production.

Advantages

- A computer-readable catalogue can be kept updated with speed and efficiency.
- It can search for any bibliographical element, such as author, subject, publisher and price.
- It is user-friendly, and new access points and search capabilities can be added as and when necessary.
- It can easily be multiplied.
- Union catalogue amongst several libraries by electronic communication is possible.
- It is easy to construct provided the cataloguer has expertise in the technique, and the user feels very easy and has instant access to the pool of information.
- It facilitates an extensive search facility and possesses all the best qualities of both DDC and CC.
- Interchange of catalogue records has led to greater consistency, uniformity and standardisation in catalogue records.

Disadvantages

- Users should be trained in computerised systems to fully exploit the capability of a machine-readable catalogue.
- Both the users and the library need to be trained to use the online catalogue.
- Interruption in power supply, breakdown of computer system and lack of proper knowledge of the users to operate the system poses problems for its best use.

CD-ROM Catalogue

It is a MARC-based compilation of bibliographic records distributed on CD-ROMs supported with software. CD-ROMs are optical discs, and with the help of laser beams, they can be written and recorded. It is an offline format, like the microform, that provides excellent search facilities. The introduction of offline, computer-produced books and the computer output microform (COM) catalogue was a milestone in the history of library catalogues in terms of production and maintenance. It reveals many of the problems in card catalogue production and effective maintenance. Besides, many cumbersome tasks fundamental to card catalogues were eliminated with the use of computers and machine-readable records.

Advantages

- This type of catalogue is used because of its fine quality of portability and transportability.
- It provides the best possible combination of large data-storage capacity, less production and high-speed computer-based search.
- Union catalogues could be prepared for sale purposes with the production of CD-ROMs.

Disadvantages

- Since it is an offline medium, it faces all the problems of conventional forms of offline catalogues.
- In comparison with online retrieval, CD-ROM is slow.

Comparative study of physical forms of a catalogue: After studying above sections, readers can comprehend the comparative study of different physical forms of catalogues effectively.

Unit 7
Formats and Standards in Cataloguing

Format

A machine-readable bibliographic record is defined as a collection of information pertaining to a single document and is stored in a machine-readable form as a self-contained and unique logical structure. Such a record is arranged according to a particular format. Format conveys the notion of a formalised framework or structure, which will hold records of varying content according to a certain set of rules or conventions controlling the representation of data. These rules may be unique to a system or shared with other systems.

Bibliographic Record Formats

Bibliographic record formats are used to describe the arrangement or structure of computer-readable records of bibliographic items. The essential components of a bibliographic record format are:

1. A description of the document itself in relation to the author, title, publisher, etc.;
2. Choice of elements to use as approach points for retrieval of the record;
3. A unique record identifier of the document; and
4. Descriptors representing the subject matter of the document selected from a standard list of subject headings or thesaurus.

Types of Formats

Formats can be of two types, as defined below.

Internal/Local Format: Internal formats are so called because they are internal/local to a software system. They can be changed specifically as per the needs of the local system and do not have to conform to any external standards. For the internal format (the identifiers used and their records structure), system designers can adopt any conventions they wish. Rules for input are more restricted, constrained by existing cataloguing codes and practices and need to be compatible with other systems or a standard exchange format. Their main aim is economy and efficiency in processing, while the ability to convert, if necessary, from the local format to an exchange format is an extra advantage. This conversion can be done by a computer program.

Exchange/Communication/Interchange Format: Exchange formats are also known as interchange/communication formats. Exchange formats are used for the exchange of records between systems. Systems should be sufficiently flexible to cope with the needs of many different software systems. Ideally, they should facilitate the exchange of data to be used in a wide range of bibliographic applications, from the production of traditional catalogue cards to records in databases used for online access. A major problem for the designer of an exchange format is the lack of international agreement on standards for constructing bibliographic records.

Exchange Formats of Bibliographic Records: Structure and Content

Bibliographic data formats adopted for the exchange of data consist of three basic components. They are:

1. *A Defined Physical Structure*: Rules for the arrangement (on a computer storage medium) of data to be exchanged. It may be linked to a container or carrier into which data may be placed. The carrier remains constant, although the data change from record to record.

2. *Content Designator*: Codes to identify the different data elements in the record, such as author, title, scale of map, starting data of journal, etc.
3. *Rules*: The content of the records governed by rules for the formulation of the different data elements, very closely tied up with the content designator. The data elements separately identified by the codes in the exchange format must be defined, not only in terms of content but also in form, if the records are to be suitable for use by another agency.

Structure of Bibliographic Records

Records in automated systems may be of fixed length or variable length. Fixed-length records in a file must contain the same field, and any given field must always be of the same length from one record to another. If a field is repeatable, it must be repeated the same number of times in each record. Bibliographic records do not fit naturally into the fixed-length pattern. This has resulted in the need to develop various bibliographical standards for bibliographical control.

Bibliographic Standards

The basic need for bibliographic standards is to have bibliographical control, which facilitates comprehension and transfer of bibliographic data between bibliographic agencies at national and international levels. It is highly necessary to develop and design a suitable and feasible standard record format uniformly acceptable to all agencies involved in the exchange of information. Bibliographic standards are thus standards that provide a common and basic level of information necessary to help all library users find the resources they need. Simultaneously, standards provide choices for individual libraries to build upon the base level and improve the quality of the shared data. Some of the standards have been discussed in the subsequent sections.

International Standard Bibliographic Description (ISBD)

Introduction

The International Standard Bibliographic Description (ISBD) is a set of rules produced by the International Federation of Library Associations and Institutions (IFLA) to create a bibliographic description in a standard, human-readable form, especially for use in a bibliography or a library catalogue. The International Standard Bibliographic Description (ISBD) dates back to 1969, when the International Federation of Library Associations and Institutions (IFLA) Committee on Cataloguing (subsequently renamed the Standing Committee of the IFLA Section on Cataloguing, now known as the Standing Committee of the IFLA Cataloguing Section) sponsored an International Meeting of Cataloguing Experts. This meeting produced a resolution that proposed the creation of standards to regularise the form and content of bibliographic descriptions. As a result, the Committee on Cataloguing put into motion work that ultimately would provide the means for a considerable increase in the sharing and exchange of bibliographic data. This work resulted in the concept of the International Standard Bibliographic Description (ISBD).

The first of the ISBDs was the International Standard Bibliographic Description for Monographic Publications [ISBD (M)], which appeared in 1971. In 1975, the Joint Steering Committee for Revision of the Anglo-American Cataloguing Rules proposed to the IFLA Committee on Cataloguing that a general International Standard Bibliographic Description (ISBD) suitable for most common types of library resources [ISBD (G)] should be developed. The ISBD (G) was published in 1977. The ISBD (M) was then revised to align it with the ISBD (G), and the 'First standard edition revised' was published in 1978. A preliminary consolidated edition of the International Standard Bibliographic Description (ISBD) was published in 2007, and the consolidated edition was published in 2011, superseding earlier ISBDs for monographs, older monographic publications, cartographic materials, serials and other continuing resources, electronic resources, NBMs and printed music. In 2022, International Federation of Library Associations and Institutions (IFLA) published the 2021 update to the 2011 consolidated edition, which includes expanding International Standard Bibliographic Description (ISBD) to include unpublished resources, integrating stipulations for the application of ISBD to the description of component parts, clarifying cartographic resources stipulations as well as the added examples and updates to the Areas and Glossary sections. IFLA's ISBD Review Group is responsible for maintaining the International Standard Bibliographic Description (ISBD).

Purpose of International Standard Bibliographic Description (ISBD)

One of the original purposes of the International Standard Bibliographic Description (ISBD) was to provide a standard form of bibliographic description that could be used to exchange records internationally. This would support IFLA's Universal Bibliographic Control (UBC) program. The ISBDs seek to serve the following primary purpose: First, and of greatest importance, they are intended to make it possible to interchange records from different sources. Secondly, as subsidiary purposes, the ISBDs have assisted in the interpretation of records across language barriers since bibliographic items in each record can be easily identified through specialised punctuation and its place for the record so that records produced for users of one language can be interpreted by users of other languages. Thirdly, they have facilitated the conversion of bibliographic records to electronic form. Fourthly, the ISBD was to provide a standard form of bibliographic description that could be used to exchange records at the international level. It would support IFLA's program of UBC.

Structure of an ISBD Record

The ISBD defines nine areas of description. Each area, except area 7, is composed of multiple elements with structured classifications. Elements and areas that do not apply to a particular resource are omitted from the description. Standardized punctuation (colons, semicolons, slashes, dashes, commas and periods) is used to identify and separate the elements and areas. The order of elements and standardized punctuation make it easier to interpret bibliographic records when one does not understand the language of the description.

0: Content form and media type area

1: Title and statement of responsibility area, consisting of
   - Title proper
   - Parallel title
   - Other title information
   - Statement of responsibility

2: Edition area

3: Material or type of resource-specific area (such as the scale of a map or the numbering of a periodical)

4: Publication area, production area, distribution area, etc.

5: Material description area (such as the number of pages in a book or the number of CDs issued as a unit)

6: Series area

7: Notes area

8: Resource identifier and terms of availability area (such as ISBN and ISSN).

ISBD and Functional Requirements for Bibliographic Records (FRBR)

In the early 1990s, the IFLA Section on Cataloguing, with the cooperation of the Section on Classification and Indexing, set up the IFLA Study Group on the Functional Requirements for Bibliographic Records (FRBR). One immediate consequence of this development was the decision to suspend most revision work on the ISBDs. While the FRBR Study Group pursued its charge to 'recommend a basic level of functionality and basic data requirements for records created by national bibliographic agencies'. In 1998, the FRBR Study Group published its final report after its recommendations were approved by the IFLA Section on Cataloguing Standing Committee.

ISO 2709

Bibliographical information plays an important role in information retrieval for the research community, particularly in the field of science and technology. But during the bibliographical information exchange, certain problems arise. Even more problems arise when the information interchange is on magnetic tape or CD-ROM. Different international organisations, such as UNESCO/PGI, UNISIST, ICSU-AB, IFLA and ISO, have taken many steps to standardise bibliographic exchange formats. The process of standardisation follows a set of codes given by the International Standard Organisation (ISO). ISO 2709 is an ISO standard for bibliographic descriptions, titled information and documentation—format for information exchange. It is maintained by the Technical Committee for Information and Documentation.

Purpose of ISO 2709

The major purpose of ISO 2709 standardisation is to:

- Permit the exchange of bibliographic records between groups of libraries and abstracting and indexing services;
- Permit a bibliographic agency to manipulate bibliographic records received from both libraries and abstracting and indexing services;
- Serve as the basis of a format for an agency's own bibliographic database by providing a list of useful data elements; and
- Assist the development of individual systems.

Basic Structure

ISO 2709 describes a generalised structure specially designed for communication between the data processing systems and not intended for use as a processing format within systems. However, this standard was designed specifically for recording and processing data on magnetic tapes, and its structures can be used for other data carriers. An ISO 2709 record has four sections:

1. **Record maker/label:** The ISO 2709 format, also known as MARC, is a standard bibliographic information view. The record maker in the ISO 2709 format has a fixed structure and comprises 24 characters. It is the

only portion of the record that is fixed in length. The record label includes the record length and the base address of the data contained in the record. It also has data elements that indicate how many characters are used for indicators and subfield identifiers.

2. **Directory:** The directory provides the entry positions to the fields in the record, along with the field tags. A directory entry has four parts and cannot exceed nine characters in length. These are (i) Field tag (three characters), (ii) Length of the field, (iii) Starting character position of the field, and (iv) Implementation-defined part (Optional).
3. **Data fields:** A string containing all field and subfield data in the record. There are three kinds of fields in the ISO 2709 record, including (i) Record identifier field: Identifying the record and assigned by the organisation, (ii) Reserved fields: Supplying data that might be required to process the record, and (iii) Bibliographic fields: Containing data and a field separator.
4. **Record separator:** A single character.

Note that although tags are often displayed as labels on bibliographic fields, and each bibliographic field has an associated tag, the tags are stored in the directory, not in the bibliographic field.

Advantages of ISO 2709

- It provides a small number of mandatory data elements, which are recognised by all sectors of the information community as essential in order to identify an item.
- It gives mandatory data elements that are sufficiently flexible to accommodate varying descriptive practices.
- It also provides several optional elements, which may be useful to describe an item according to the practices of the agency, which creates the record.

- It provides a mechanism for linking records and segments of records without imposing on the originating agency any uniform practice regarding the treatment of related groups of records or data elements.

MARC and MARC 21

A MARC record is a Machine-Readable Cataloguing record. It is a standard format for the storage and exchange of bibliographic records and related information in the machine. Here, machine-readable means that one particular type of machine, a computer, can read and interpret the data in the cataloguing record, and a cataloguing record means a bibliographic record or the information traditionally shown on a catalogue card. MARC 21 was designed to redefine the original MARC record format for the twenty-first century and to make it more accessible to the international community. The record includes (not necessarily in this order):

1. ***Description of the Item***: Librarians follow the rules of AACR (second edition), 2002 revision, to compose the bibliographic description of a library item. It includes the title, statement of responsibility, edition, material-specific details, etc.
2. ***Main Entry and Added Entries***: AACR-2R also contains rules for determining 'access points' to the record (usually referred to as the 'main entry' and 'other added entries') and form these access points or retrieval points.
3. ***Subject Headings***: The librarian uses the SLSH, the LCSH or some other list of standard subject headings to select the subjects under which the item will be listed.
4. ***Classification or Call Number***: The librarian uses DCC or LCC schemes to select the class/call number for an item. The purpose of the class/call number is to place items on the same subject together on the same shelf in the library.

MARC 21

In 2000, the British Library, after consultation with the UK library and information community, unanimously decided to move from UKMARC, the national cataloguing format maintained by the British Library since 1975, to the MARC 21 bibliographic format developed by the LC and the National Library of Canada after merging their respective national formats. Thus, MARC 21 has become the format favoured by other national libraries and by online bibliographic utilities and their end-users. This format is supported by the majority of library systems. It offers participation in an international bibliographic community following common standards and the advantage of copy cataloguing at a much-reduced cost and with no need to maintain conversion programs. The British Library undertook to support libraries and other organisations, including overseas users of UKMARC, in preparing their implementation of MARC 21. There are five types of MARC 21 formats. These are:

***Format for Bibliographic Data*:** It provides details for the creation and design of bibliographic records. It describes the records and provides access to them. It defines the different data elements in terms of codes, tags and indicators for processing the records.

***Format for Authority Data*:** Authority format provides codes and code values for accepted and used headings for authority control. It includes personal and corporate names as well as subjects and their subdivisions.

***Format for Holdings Data*:** The format includes codes, tags and indicators that provide holdings information of single-part and multi-part items as well as serial items. It enables interfacing the automated system with the union catalogue or interlibrary loan system.

***Format for Classification Data*:** It includes codes and indicators for classification data in an LC scheme and DDC. It provides details of classification schedules, helping in assigning and validating class numbers.

Format for Community Information Data: It is suitable for coding community non-bibliographic information. One might be interested in creating a database for experts in an area for which there are details in this format. Similarly, the format provides details for organisations, events, programmes or services most commonly used in cataloguing in libraries.

Importance of MARC/MARC 21

MARC format is most necessary to any type of library for:

- Prevention of duplication of work,
- Better sharing of bibliographic resources and
- Bibliographic control at the international level.

USMARC

The USMARC formats are standards for the representation and communication of bibliographic and related information in machine-readable form. A USMARC record involves three elements: The record structure, the content designation and the data content of the record. The structure of USMARC records is an implementation of national and international standards, such as Bibliographic Information Interchange (ANSI Z39.2) and Format for Bibliographic Information Interchange on Magnetic Tape (ISO 2709). The content designation, the codes and conventions established to explicitly identify and further characterise the data elements within a record and to support the manipulation of those data, is defined in the USMARC formats. USMARC formats are communication formats primarily designed to provide specifications for the exchange of bibliographic and related information between systems. They are widely used in a variety of exchange and processing environments. As communication formats, they do not mandate internal storage or display formats to be used by individual systems. USMARC formats, particularly the bibliographic and authority formats, were developed to enable the LC to communicate its catalogue records to other institutions. The formats have had a close relationship to the needs and practices of the US libraries.

UKMARC

The UKMARC format was developed primarily to facilitate the production of the printed British National Bibliography (BNB) and thus closely reflects the cataloguing practice of the British Library in its interpretation of AACR2 and other standards. A distinction can, however, be drawn between the UKMARC format as a national format and its use by the national library in preparing records for the national bibliography, and the UKMARC manual seeks to make such a distinction. MARC is an acronym for Machine Readable Cataloguing. The MARC format was primarily developed as a convenient way of storing and exchanging bibliographic records. It has since been extended to include non-bibliographic forms of library material, such as maps and music scores. There is also a MARC format for the storage and exchange of authority records.

In 1969, the British National Bibliography (BNB) introduced a MARC tape service for current British books, and a machine-readable version of the weekly printed BNB was published. UKMARC primarily reflected the requirements of BNB but was gradually being developed to cater for use by the wider information community. By 1975, when the first edition of the UK MARC Manual was published, UKMARC had become a national communications format, and its use in the production of records for BNB represented just one particular application of the format.

UNIMARC

UNIMARC is a family of bibliographic metadata schemas with formats for descriptive information, classification, authorities and holdings. UNIMARC was the brain child of IFLA. It was conceived as a tool for an international network. Although the record structure, which became ISO 2709, was accepted early on during the very first cooperative project between LC and BNB.

Despite cooperation, several versions emerged, such as UKMARC, INTERMARC and USMARC, whose paths diverged owing to different national cataloguing practices and requirements. Since the early 1970s, an extended family of more than 20 MARC formats has grown up. Differences in data content mean editing is required before records can be exchanged. One solution to the problem of incompatibility was to create an international MARC format (UNIMARC) that would accept records created in any MARC format. So, records in one MARC format could be converted into UNIMARC and then be converted into another MARC format. The intention was that each national agency would need to write only two programs—one to convert into UNIMARC and one to convert from UNIMARC—instead of one program for each other in MARC format. For example, INTERMARC to UKMARC, USMARC to UKMARC, etc.

So, in 1977, IFLA published the universal MARC format (UNIMARC), stating that "The primary purpose of UNIMARC is to facilitate the international exchange of data in machine-readable form between national bibliographic agencies". This was followed by a second edition in 1980 and a UNIMARC Handbook in 1983. All focused primarily on the cataloguing of monographs and serials and took advantage of international progress towards the standardisation of bibliographic information reflected in the ISBDs.

Purpose of UNIMARC

(i) The primary purpose of UNIMARC is to facilitate the international exchange of bibliographic data in machine-readable form between national bibliographic agencies.

(ii) UNIMARC may also be used as a model for the development of new machine-readable bibliographic formats.

(iii) UNIMARC is intended to be a carrier format for exchange purposes. It does not stipulate the form, content or record structure of the data within individual systems.

(iv) UNIMARC does provide recommendations on the form and content of data when it is to be exchanged. Records are usually structured in exchange tape format as the last stage in any conversion process after form, content, and content designators have been converted to the UNIMARC standard.

(v) It facilitates the description, retrieval and control of bibliographic items. This is achieved by providing a structure for recording bibliographic information, which is input by reference to international standards.

Scope of UNIMARC

The scope of UNIMARC is to specify the content designators (tags, indicators and subfield codes) to be assigned to bibliographic records in machine-readable form and to specify the logical and physical format of the records. It covers monographs, serials, cartographic materials, music, sound recording, graphics projected and video materials, rare books and electronic resources.

The UNIMARC Format

The UNIMARC format, like any other version of MARC, involves three elements of a bibliographic record:

1. **Record structure:** The record structure is designed to control the representation of data by storing it in the form of strings of characters known as fields.
2. **Content designation:** Certain conventions are followed in order to identify the data elements within records. Such elements, which include author, title and subject access, are further characterised wherever necessary.
3. **Data content:** The content is the data that is stored in the fields within the record. Data can be coded data or bibliographic data.

Common Communication Format (CCF): CCF is a structure format for creating bibliographical records and for exchanging records between groups of information agencies and libraries. The purpose of the CCF is to provide a detailed and structured method for recording a number of mandatory and optional data elements in a computer-readable bibliographic record for exchange purposes between two or more computer-based systems.

The rapid growth of international bibliographic exchange formats, including ISO's well-known format for bibliographic information interchange on magnetic tape (ISO 2709) and the lack of compatibility amongst them, poses problems to libraries and other information services to exchange records with one another. Hence, the necessity arose for each of these organisations to agree upon a common standard format for easy exchange purposes. As such, to study the desirability and feasibility of establishing optimum compatibility between existing bibliographic exchange formats led to the convening of the International Symposium on Bibliographic Exchange Formats with the initiation by the UNESCO General Information Programme in April 1978 in Taormina, Sicily. The Symposium was organised by UNISIST International Centre for Bibliographic Description in collaboration with the International Council of Scientific Unions Abstracting Board, IFLA and ISO. As a direct result of the Symposium, an ad hoc group was constituted to develop the CCF.

Need for CCF

The need for CCF is of paramount importance if two or more organisations wish to exchange records with one another. It cannot be achieved unless these organisations agree upon a common standard format for exchange purposes. If there is a single national standard exchange format, information interchange with that country is possible, with the exchange greatly facilitated both technically and economically. But, on the other hand, if each nation's standard format is different from all others, then it will be more problematic and complex to have international information interchange among national bibliographic agencies because of the number of computer programs that must be written to accommodate the translation of records from one format to another.

Scope of CCF

The CCF is designed to provide a standard format for three major purposes:

- To permit the exchange of bibliographic records between groups of libraries and the abstracting and indexing services.
- To permit a bibliographic agency to use a single set of computer programs to manipulate bibliographic records received from both the libraries and the abstracting and indexing services.
- To serve as the basis of a format for an agency's own bibliographic database by providing a list of useful data elements.

Uses of CCF

The uses of CCF have been accommodated in the following ways:

- By specifying a small number of mandatory data elements recognized by all sectors of the information community is essential in order to identify an item.
- By providing mandatory data elements that are sufficiently flexible to accommodate varying descriptive practices. A section entitled 'USE' for each field and subfield indicates whether the use of that data element is mandatory or optional.
- By providing a number of optional elements, which might be useful to describe an item according to the practices of the agency that creates the record.
- By providing a mechanism for linking records and segments of records without imposing on the originating agency any uniform practice regarding the treatment of related groups of records or data elements.

Structure of CCF

The record structure of the CCF comprises a specific implementation of the international standard ISO 2709. Each CCF record comprises four major parts:

Record label: Each CCF record begins with a fixed-length label of 24 characters to provide parameters to process the record.

Directory: The directory is a table containing a variable number of fourteen-character entries. The table is terminated by a field separator character.

Data fields: A data field consists of indicators, one or more subfields and a data field separator.

Record separator: The record separator (Character 1/13 of ISO 646) is the final character of the record. It follows the field separator of the field data field of the record.

Features of CCF

- It can be used to produce catalogue cards as all the necessary data elements are incorporated.
- It is user-friendly and rather catalogue friendly, for no cataloguing rules are imposed.
- It is a flexible and very popular format among UN organisations and international bodies.
- It provides basic data elements and a facility for optional elements and private fields, thus enabling an agency to incorporate new standard elements considered important.
- It facilitates a library and bibliographic agency to use a computer program for the exchange of data.
- Some of the mandatory data elements are flexible and can accommodate varying descriptive practices.
- It is a simple set of data elements that can be used at any bibliographic level and are dissociated from cataloguing codes.
- It is the logically defined record structure that uses the fourth element of the ISO 2709 directory to denote the bibliographic level and filed occurrence.

Indian Standards

Standardisation of record format has not received due attention in Indian libraries. At the national level, the Indian standards institution, now renamed as Bureau of Indian Standards (BIS), had evolved a standard for bibliographical references in 1963 for use in non-computerised systems. However, it could not keep track of the development in the media and forms of documents in the following years. A revision of the standard appeared in 1979, wherein ISBD was suggested as a substitute format to be adopted by agencies willing to do so. It was a format incomplete and inadequate in many respects. The sixteenth Indian Standards Convention of ISI, held in Bhopal in October 1975, discussed the issue of standardisation of bibliographic information in the context of machine-readable records. Continued efforts taken by ISI in this direction resulted in the design and publication of a standard IS: 11370-1985 titled 'Guide for data element and record format for computer-based bibliographic description of different kinds of documents' in July 1986. The structure of this format conforms to ISO 2709-1981.

Unit 8

Cataloguing of Non-Book Material

Introduction

A library is a centre for the communication of ideas and knowledge. It is also a repository of records of human civilisation, serving as an information-clearing house to the community. The librarian must organise and order the flow of information so as to maximise the use of the resources of a library. In the present era of scientific and technological advancement, the sources of knowledge are not confined to conventional print media only. The impact of ICT has directly led to the spread of non-print materials. These documents are responsible for the communication of recent information and new knowledge. As a result, libraries around the world have acquired large collections of such materials. These materials need to be collected, organised and disseminated at the right time. The information loses its dynamism if not communicated timely. The nature of non-print material demands a separate treatment for their organisation, which will be discussed in the subsequent sections.

Non-Book Material (NBM)

NBMs are materials that do not come within the definition of a book, periodical or pamphlet and require special holdings, such as audio-visual materials, microforms or computer files and electronic resources. It is generally understood to be any resource material that is not a printed book but contributes to the learning process. The NBMs require special treatment in terms of bibliographic description in order to exploit information from those formats. Webster's Third New International Dictionary defines non-book being something 'other than a book; being a manuscript, microfilm, map on other library holdings that is not a book'.

Types of NBM

There are various types of NBM, which are mentioned as follows:

1. ***Cartographic Materials***: Ariel chart, leaf, atlas, chart, globes, map, plan, etc.
2. ***Manuscripts***: Item (for collection of manuscripts), box, etc.
3. ***Motion Pictures and Video Recordings***: Film cartridge, video cassette, video disc, etc.
4. ***Graphic Materials***: Art original, art reproduction, art print, photograph, etc.
5. ***Music***: Score, condensed, chorus score, etc.
6. ***Sound Recordings***: Sound disc, soundtrack, sound cassette, etc.
7. ***Computer Files***: Data files, program files, etc.
8. ***Three-Dimensional Artefacts***: Art original, game, model, etc.
9. ***Microform***: Postcard, slide, transparency, etc.

Utilities of NBM

Following are some of the utilities of NBM:

- NBM as storage media provides potential alternative access to information and has enormous information storage capacity with low cost.
- Data damage is drastically reduced with NBM, and information can be retrieved and transferred speedily and accurately.
- Their durability provides the benefit of repetitive use of the information without deterioration or loss.
- Presently, there is a trend towards compressing information carriers so that they occupy less space

and make storage and distribution easy. Books are 'space eaters' whereas NBM are 'space savers'.

- They have the quality of security, accessibility, portability, reliability, economy, easy retrieval and easy updating.
- Rare books can be stored in microform.

Constraints of Using NBM

Listed below are some constraints in using NBM:

- In a paper-oriented society, majority of the people are still not acquainted with microform or the screen display of information, and thus, they are not quite reconciled to this change.
- Special methods of handling materials are troublesome to operate. Hence, special awareness programs for users are very much essential.
- Reading NBM sometimes puts strain on the eyes.
- Acquiring equipment for the operation of NBM and its maintenance and storage facilities amounts to a high cost.
- Unlike books, NBMs are not issued for use at home.
- The cost of microfilming may not be justified if the record has a short retention schedule with little or no reference. It requires special storage devices for the NBM.
- Special types of equipment are required to retrieve information from different types of materials. For example, a microfilm reader or reader/printer is required to retrieve information from a microform.
- High obsolescence of equipment due to technology adds to the cost.

Problems of Cataloguing NBM

New media materials, due to their inherent peculiar format, very frequently pose serious problems in their arrangement and cataloguing and retrieval of information contained in them.

Hence, the cataloguer might encounter the following possible problems.

- Information might be more difficult to obtain from the documents to be catalogued than conventional documents having a title page.
- Information collected from one source in the NBM might differ from that obtained from another source of documents.
- It might be harder to reach the cataloguing decisions about the choice of an access point, that is, determining the heading or choosing the person who is chiefly responsible for the intellectual content of the document, that is less experienced in books and serials' matter.
- Information about the physical description of different types of NBM definitely creates more problems for cataloguers than conventional documents.
- It is not possible to obtain information through the naked eyes as it requires special equipment.

Cataloguing NBM

AACR-2 specifies sources of information to be used in describing a publication. In the case of a printed monograph, for example, such sources include the title page, the verso of the title page, etc. Of these, the source of bibliographic data must be given first preference as the source from which a bibliographic description is prepared is called the chief source of information. The rules identify a chief source of information for each type of material.

Punctuation Marks

One of the significant features of the ISBD is a set of prescribed punctuation. The prescribed punctuation mark precedes each element in the description and signifies the nature of that element. The prescribed punctuation marks are used as a device of recognition for both machine and human manipulation of bibliographic records. Specific and detailed rules with regard to prescribed punctuation are given in each chapter in AACR-2.

Besides, some punctuation marks necessary for NBM have been mentioned below:

1. **Parentheses '( )':** Used to enclose physical details of accompanying material and to enclose the number of frames of microforms.
2. **Plus sign '+':** Precedes a statement of accompanying material and indicates the northern hemisphere when giving the declination of the centre of a celestial chart.
3. **Square brackets '[ ]':** Encloses information taken from outside the prescribed source and encloses the general material designation.

Areas of Description

AACR-2 prescribes detailed rules for each area of description. The general rules are presented in AACR-2R Unit 1, and rules for specific types of materials are given in Units 2 to 12. In presenting data in the bibliographic description, information taken from the chief source of information is preferred. If the required information is unavailable or insufficient from the chief source, other sources are used. Rules for each area are enumerated in Units 2 to 12. Information taken from outside the prescribed sources is enclosed in brackets.

Structure of Description

The bibliographic description of NBM follows the same norms as for books and other materials. The main structure of the bibliographic entry comprises the heading, the description and the subject description. The structure of the bibliographic description according to AACR-2R is given below.

First level (1.0D1): This level was designed for minor-item and for entries in catalogues with a policy of minimum description. The bibliographic elements to be included are shown in the following schematic illustration.

"Title proper/First statement of responsibility, if different from the main entry heading in the form of a number or if there is no main entry heading. Edition statement. Material (or type of publication) specific details first publisher, etc., date of publication, etc. Extent of item – Note(s) – Standard number."

Second level (1.0D2): This level was designed for the standard range of items found in the library and for entries in catalogues with a policy of standard description. The following elements are included:

> Title proper [General material designation] = Parallel title: other title information/First statement of responsibility, Each subsequent statement of responsibility. – Edition statement/First statement of responsibility relating to the edition, – material (or type of publication) specific details, – first place of publication, etc.: First publisher, etc., Date of publication, etc. – extent of item: other physical details; Dimensions. – (Title proper of series/ Statement of responsibility relating to series, ISSN of series; Numbering within the series. Title of sub-series, ISSN of sub-series; Numbering within sub-series) – Note(s). – Standard number. This level might appropriately be used in medium sized library.

Third level (1.0D3): It includes all the rules applicable to the item being catalogued. This level represents full description and is recommended for items that, in the context of the catalogue, are considered to be important and rare. All elements set forth in the rules applicable to the item being described are included. This level is appropriate for large libraries and research collections.

General Material Designation (GMD)

GMD prescribes the broad class of publication to which the item belongs. For example, sound recording, music, map, film-scripts, microform, motion picture and machine-readable data files will be replaced by computer files, etc. This is an optional addition in AACR-2. The use of GMD is essential in the case of NBMs, and it may not be preferred by the libraries for book-form materials.

Anglo American Cataloguing Rules (AACR)

AACR was an international library cataloguing standard. First published in 1967 and edited by C. Sumner Spalding, a second edition (AACR2), edited by Michael Gorman and Paul W. Winkler, was issued in 1978, with subsequent revisions

(AACR-2R) appearing in 1988 and 1998. All updates ceased in 2005.

Published jointly by the American Library Association (ALA), the Canadian Library Association, and the UK Chartered Institute of Library and Information Professionals, the rules were designed for the construction of library catalogues and similar bibliographic tools. The rules cover the physical description of library resources as well as the provision of name and title access points.

AACR2 was issued in several print versions, including a concise edition and an online version. Various translations were also available. Principles of AACR included cataloguing based on the item 'in hand' rather than inferring information from external sources and the concept of the 'chief source of information', which is preferred where conflicts exist.

Resource Description and Access (RDA)

RDA is a standard for descriptive cataloguing initially released in June 2010, providing instructions and guidelines on formulating bibliographic data. Intended for use by libraries and other cultural organisations, such as museums and archives, RDA is the successor to AACR2. RDA emerged from the International Conference on the Principles and Future Development of AACR held in Toronto in 1997. It is published jointly by the ALA, the Canadian Federation of Library Associations and the Chartered Institute of Library and Information Professionals (CILIP) in the UK. Maintenance of RDA is the responsibility of the RDA Steering Committee (RSC). As of 2015, RSC is undergoing a transition to an international governance structure, expected to be in place in 2019. RDA is a package of data elements, guidelines and instructions for creating library and cultural heritage resource metadata that are well-formed according to international models for user-focused linked data applications. The underlying conceptual models for RDA are the FRBR, Functional Requirements for Authority Data (FRAD), and Functional Requirements for Subject Authority Data (FRSAD) maintained by IFLA. These models will be compliant with the

Library Reference Model, the IFLA standard that consolidates them.

Objectives and Principles for the Design of RDA

The objectives and principles set out in this section govern the overall design of RDA as a standard for resource description and access. They address matters of Scope, Formulation, Currency, Comprehensiveness, Consistency, Clarity, Rationality, Currency, Compatibility, Adaptability, Ease and Efficiency of Use, Format, Generalisation, Specificity, Non-Redundancy, Terminology, Reference structure, etc.

The Key Features of RDA

The first key feature is that RDA will be designed as an online product for use in a Webenvironment Functional Requirements for Authority Records. This will allow different views of the rules to be presented. For example, to present a concise version of the rules or rules of particular interest to, say, those cataloguing music.

The second key feature is that the structure will be aligned more directly with the FRBR and Functional Requirements for Authority Records FRAR models. This more flexible framework will help address the challenges of describing digital resources. The produced data should also be more readily adaptable to newly emerging, more efficient database structures.

The third key feature is that instructions for recording data will be presented independently of guidelines for data display. This will provide more flexibility, enabling the records to be used in various online environments with different structures of syntax for data storage or display.

The final key feature is that RDA will contain clear general instructions written in plain English. The instructions will be supplemented by detailed rules or references to other standards as needed, and they will be backed by guidance on the principles behind the rules. This will enable the code to be used more readily beyond the library world. Together, these changes will pave the way for improved catalogue design and a greater user focus.

FRBR and Its Relationship with RDA

The acronym 'FRBR' stands for Functional Requirements for Bibliographic Records. FRBR was developed by an IFLA Study Group (1992–97), and it continues to monitor the application of FRBR and promote its use. FRBR includes a conceptual model of entities, relationships and attributes; identifies specific user tasks that bibliographic records are intended to fulfil—find, identify, select, obtain; and recommends a set of elements for inclusion in national bibliographic records. FRBR provides the conceptual foundation for RDA. RDA includes the FRBR terminology when appropriate (for example, use of the names of bibliographic entities: 'work', 'expression', 'manifestation' and 'item'), will use the FRBR attributes as the basis for specific data elements to be included in bibliographic descriptions, will address FRBR relationship and will use the FRBR user tasks (find, identify, select and obtain) as the basis for defining a set of mandatory data elements. RDA will also use FRAD as the basis for instructions on authority control. Each section contains general guidelines and a chapter for each entity. Each chapter is associated with an FRBR user task. The chapters on recording attributes and relationships for concepts, objects and events are placeholders for completeness in mapping to FRBR and FRAD and may be developed further in future releases of RDA. The instruction on recording attributes and relationships for places will not initially go beyond the scope of Unit 23 of AACR2.

EXERCISE UNIT 5 – UNIT 8

1. What do you understand by library catalogue?
2. Discuss the need for and objectives of a library catalogue.
3. Highlight some of the important functions of a library catalogue.
4. Discuss the qualities of a library catalogue in detail.
5. Differentiate between a library catalogue and an index.
6. Discuss how ICT has improved the role of a library catalogue?

7. What do you mean by an author catalogue? Discuss its advantages and disadvantages.
8. What do you understand by an alphabetical-subject catalogue? Discuss its advantages and limitations.
9. Compare a dictionary catalogue with a classified catalogue.
10. Discuss the criteria for the selection of the best physical form of a catalogue.
11. What are the different outer forms of a library catalogue? Discuss any three of them in detail, along with their respective advantages and disadvantages.
12. What is a microform catalogue?
13. What is the full form of MARC?
14. Discuss types of formats in a library catalogue?
15. Discuss International Standard Bibliographic Description (ISBD). Throw some light on its purpose and structure.
16. Discuss the structure of MARC 21 in detail.
17. What is the purpose and scope of UNIMARC? Highlight its structure.
18. What are the uses of CCF?
19. What are the utilities of NBM?
20. Highlight some of the problems encountered while cataloguing NBM.
21. Discuss AACR-2R in detail. Highlight its genesis and structure in detail.
22. What do you understand by RDA?

Unit 9
Basics of Subject Indexing

Subject Indexing: Definition

The term 'index' came from the Latin word 'indicare', which means 'to point out, to guide, to direct, to locate'. An index indicates or refers to the location of an object or idea. It is a methodically arranged list of items or concepts along with their addresses. The process of preparing an index is known as indexing. According to the British Standards, an index is "a systematic guide to the text of any reading matter or to the contents of other collected documentary material, comprising a series of entries, with headings arranged in alphabetical or other chosen order and with references to show where each item indexed is located". An index is, thus, a working tool designed to help the user to find his way out of a mass of documented information in a given subject field or document store. It gives subject access to documents irrespective of their physical forms, like books, periodical articles, newspapers, audiovisual documents, and computer-readable records, including web resources.

A subject can be defined as any concept or combination of concepts representing a theme in a document. Subject indexing term is defined as the representation of a concept in the form of either a term derived from natural language or a classification symbol. This is done first by establishing the subject content, or in other words, the content of concepts in the document. Thereafter, the principal concept presented in the subject content is identified, and finally, the concepts are expressed in the indexing language. This process of representing the theme of a document in the form of indexing terms is referred to as subject indexing.

Purpose of Subject Indexing

The first objective refers to the need to locate individual items, and the second refers to the need to collocate materials on the same subject and related subjects. A subject is a set of interrelated component ideas in which each component idea is related directly or indirectly to other component ideas. A subject of a document is amenable to structuring into a subject heading. It is a kind of linear structuring of subject surrogates and some criteria for formatting or modelling it into an accessible procedure. The purpose of subject indexing is to:

- Satisfy the subject approach to information;
- Identify pertinent materials on a given subject or topic;
- Enable the enquirer to find materials on related subjects;
- Link-related subjects by a network of references;
- Prescribe a standard methodology to subject cataloguers/indexers for constructing uniform subject headings;
- Bring consistency in the choice and rendering of subject entries, using standard vocabulary and according to the given rules and procedures;
- Be helpful to users in accessing any desired document(s) from the catalogue or index through different means of such an approach;
- Decide the optimum number of subject entries and thus economise the bulk and cost of indexing; and
- Provide a user-oriented approach in naming the subjects through any vocabulary common to a considerable group of users, specialists or laymen.

Difference between Cataloguing and Indexing

There has always been confusion about the distinction between 'subject cataloguing' and 'subject indexing'. Basically, cataloguing is the process of creating the bibliographic description of a document as a whole entity, and subject cataloguing and classification assign subject labels that together describe the overall topic of the document. Indexing involves delving into a document to analyse its contents at a much deeper level to provide access to many of its concepts at greater depth. Although most articles in a periodical issue and many books are listed under only one or two subject headings, a back-of-the-book index contains hundreds of subject terms associated with the content of an individual book. Subject cataloguing usually refers to the assignment of subject headings (bibliographic description) to represent the overall contents of whole documents (such as books, reports, periodicals, etc.) within the catalogue of a library. Subject indexing is a term used more loosely. It may refer to the representation of the subject matter of the parts of whole documents as in the case of a back-of-the-book subject index. Thus, a library may enter a book under the subject heading 'roses' in its catalogue to indicate its overall subject matter. The detailed contents of the book are only revealed by the back-of-the-book subject index. The process by which the subject matter of documents is represented in databases—printed or electronic form—is referred to as 'subject indexing', whether overall documents or their parts are discussed.

Need and Purpose of Indexing Principles

- To set out the general directions for the consistent application of subject indexing techniques;
- To serve as a useful guide for developing new indexing techniques and to develop one that already exists;
- To facilitate the evaluation of indexing systems;
- To provide a theoretical rationale for particular standards or guidelines for designing a subject indexing system and its application;
- To promote understanding of different subject indexing systems by identifying commonalities underlying them and providing a structure for their comparison; and

- To determine how the subject headings are established and applied.

Indexing Principles

Indexing principles may be stated as follows:

1. ***The User as the Focus***: The wording and structure of the subject heading should match what the user will seek in the index.
2. ***Unity***: A subject index must bring together, under one heading, all the documents that deal principally or exclusively with the subject, whatever the terms applied to it by the authors and whatever the varying terms applied to it at different times. It must use a term that is unambiguous and does not overlap in meaning with other headings in the index.
3. ***Common Usage***: The chosen subject heading must represent common usage or, at any rate, the usage of the class of users for whom the documents on the subject within which the heading falls are intended. Whether a popular term or a scientific one is to be chosen should depend on the approaches of the users.
4. ***Specificity***: The heading should be as specific as the topic it is intended to cover. As a corollary, the heading should not be broader than the topic. Rather than a broader heading, the cataloguer should use two specific headings that will approximately cover it.

Indexing Policy

Indexers must take policy decisions about how many terms should be included in an index entry, how specific the terms should be and how many entries an index should incorporate. Together, this gives a depth of indexing. The depth of indexing describes the thoroughness of the indexing process with reference to exhaustivity and specificity. While taking such a policy decision, indexers should strive for a balance between specificity and exhaustivity and should consider the requirement of the users of the index along with the cost and time factors.

Exhaustivity in Indexing: It is the detail with which the topics or features of a document are analysed and described. In other words, an exhaustive index lists all possible index terms associated with the thought content of a document.

Specificity in Indexing: The specificity describes how closely the index terms match the topics they represent in a document. It is the extent to which the indexing system permits us to be precise when specifying the subject of a document we are processing. Higher specificity leads to higher precision.

Indexing Process

The representation of documents and the knowledge expressed by them is one of the central and unique areas of study within Library and Information Science (LIS) and is commonly referred to as indexing. A common demand in the LIS field is for a set of rules or a prescription for how to index. When this demand is raised, it is usually based on the assumption that it is possible to explain the intellectual operations in the subject indexing process. The indexing process basically consists of two intellectual steps: Conceptual analysis and translation.

1. Conceptual Analysis

This step refers to the identification of different component ideas associated with the thought content of the document and the establishment of the inter relationship between those component ideas. According to Ranganathan, it involves the work in the idea plane carried out in two stages, although these tend to overlap in practice. These include:

(a) **Examining the document and establishing its subject content:** In the first stage of the conceptual analysis of the thought content of the document, it is examined for the establishment of its subject content. A complete reading of the document is often impracticable, but the indexer should ensure that no useful information has been overlooked. While examining the document, the indexer should give particular attention to several places in the document: The title; the abstract, if provided; the list of contents; the introduction, etc.

(b) Identifying the principal concepts present in the subject: In this stage of the indexing process, the indexer identifies the principal concepts in the subject. The second stage is laid over the first stage because the indexer should not go back to the document to look for concepts. Rather, the indexer should look for concepts within the findings of the first step, that is, the natural language representations of the subject content.

2. Translation

During the first two stages, the indexer has established the subject content of the document and identified the principal concepts in the subject. The indexer is hereafter ready to translate the concepts into the indexing language. This step refers to the expression of principal concepts, as identified while analysing the thought content of the document in the language of the indexing system. If the concepts that the indexer has identified during the second stage are present in the indexing language, the indexer should translate the concept into preferred terms.

Indexing Language

An indexing language is a set of terms and devices used to establish the relationship between terms for representing the content of the documents and the queries of the users. It consists of three basic elements: Controlled vocabulary, syntax and semantics. Controlled vocabulary has been defined as a limited set of terms showing their relationships and indicating ways in which they may usefully be combined to provide a subject index to the documents and search for these documents in a particular system. Syntax comprises a grammatical structure or a set of rules that govern the sequence of occurrence of terms/ words in representing the content of the document. Semantics refers to the systematic study of how meaning is structured, expressed and understood while using an indexing language. More discussion on indexing languages can be found in the subsequent units of the book.

Problems in Indexing

An indexer analyses a text and strives to ascertain meaning. Ideally, this analysis anticipates a searcher, in some future time, looking for text with the same meaning. But, the meaning is not fixed at either end of this process. And even if the meaning is relatively unambiguous or stable, the terms used to represent it are not. Thus, most indexing processes encounter the below-mentioned problems:

- Subjects of documents are complex, usually multi-worded, terms, making it difficult to assign index terms.
- Users' requests for information tend to be multidimensional.
- Choice of terms among different categories, including entities, activities, abstracts, properties and heterogeneous concepts (synonymous with semantic factoring).
- Choice of word forms among different forms, including noun versus adjective, singular versus plural, etc.
- Homographs, if neglected, will give rise to reduced relevance. The seriousness of the problem will depend on the coverage of the system.
- Choice of the kind of vocabulary that should be used and syntactical and other rules necessary for representing complex subjects.
- Identification of term 'relationship'—semantic versus syntactic.
- The decision about the exhaustivity level (that is, the depth to which indexing should be done).
- The decision about the specificity level (that is, the levels of generality and specificity at which concepts should be represented).
- Ensuring inter-indexer consistency (that is, consistency in indexing between several indexers) and intra-indexer consistency (that is, consistency in indexing by the same indexer at different times).
- Ensuring that indexing is done not merely on the basis of a document's intrinsic subject content but also

according to the type of users who may be expected to benefit from it and the types of requests for which the document is likely to be regarded as useful.

Quality in Indexing

The quality of indexing depends on two factors: (i) Qualification and expertise of the indexer and (ii) Quality of the indexing tools. In order to achieve quality in indexing, the indexer should have adequate knowledge of the field covered by the documents, they are indexing. They should understand the term of the documents as well as the rules and procedures of the specific indexing system. Quality control will be achieved more effectively if the indexers are in contact with users. An indexer who has contact with the users might be better able to represent the documents in accordance with how the users think. The idea is that the indexer should attempt to determine the subject of the document taking into account the users' questions and information needs. This might help the indexer when a document contains multiple concepts. In such a situation, the indexer can select only those concepts to represent the content of a document that is regarded as the most relevant by a given community of users. Indexing quality can be tested by analysis of retrieval results, such as by calculating recall and precision ratios.

Evaluation of Indexing

Evaluation of an indexing system essentially means measuring the performance of the system, success or failure, in terms of its retrieval efficiency (ease of approach, speed and accuracy) to the users, and its internal operating efficiency, cost-effectiveness and cost benefit to the managers of the system.

Purpose of Evaluation

- To identify the level of performance of the given indexing system;
- To understand how well the given indexing system fulfils the queries of the users in retrieving the relevant documents;

- To compare the performance of two or more indexing systems against a standard;
- To identify the possible sources of failure of the given indexing system or inefficiency to raise the level of performance in the future;
- To justify the existence of the given indexing system by analysing its costs and benefits;
- To establish a foundation for further research on the reasons for the relative success of alternative techniques; and
- To improve the means employed for attaining objectives or to redefine goals in view of research findings.

Evaluation Criteria for Indexing System

It is evident from the history of the experimental evaluation of information retrieval systems that there has been a remarkably coherent development of a set of criteria for the evaluation of indexing systems. These evaluation criteria generate argument, disagreement and heated dispute, but there remains a relatively stable common core, which has, despite its limitations, served us well over the last 50 years. The most important criteria used for evaluating an indexing system are 'Recall' and 'Precision'.

Recall: Recall refers to the index's ability to let relevant documents through the filter. The recall ratio is the ratio of the relevant documents retrieved to the total number of relevant documents potentially available. It measures the completeness of the output. Hence, the recall performance can be expressed quantitatively using a ratio called recall ratio, as mentioned below:

$$\text{Recall ratio} = R/C \times 100$$

where, R = Number of relevant documents retrieved against a search

C = Total number of relevant documents available to that search

Precision: The term 'precision' refers to the index's ability to hold back documents not relevant to the user. The precision ratio is the ratio of the relevant documents retrieved to the number of documents retrieved. It measures the preciseness of the output, that is, how precisely an indexing system functions. If recall is the measure of a system's ability to let through wanted items, precision is the measure of the system's ability to hold back unwanted items. The formula for the calculation of the precision ratio is as follows:

Precision ratio = R/L × 100

where, R = Total number of relevant documents retrieved against a search

L = Total number of documents retrieved in that search

Other Important Criteria

- **Resolution factor:** The proportion of total items retrieved over the total number of items in the collection.
- **Pertinency factor:** The proportion of relevant items retrieved over the total number of retrieved items. This factor was popularly named the precision ratio in the subsequent evaluation studies.
- **Recall factor:** The proportion of relevant items retrieved over the total number of relevant items in the collection.
- **Elimination factor:** The proportion of non-retrieved items (both relevant and non-relevant) over the total items in the collection.
- **Noise factor:** The proportion of retrieved items that are not relevant. This factor is considered the complement of the pertinency factor.
- **Omission factor:** The proportion of non-relevant items retrieved over the total number of non-retrieved items in the collection.

Unit 10
Indexing Languages

Indexing language is an artificial language made up of expressions connecting several kernel terms and adopted to the requirements of indexing. The function of an indexing language is to do whatever a natural language does and, in addition, organise the semantic content through a different expression providing a point of access to the seekers of information. An indexing language is a system for naming subjects and has a controlled vocabulary. The vocabulary of an indexing language may be verbal or coded. A classification scheme uses coded vocabulary in the form of notation, and authority lists use verbal vocabulary. It is a prerequisite to understanding the features of the language used for the representation of the subject content of the documents in terms of their linguistic structures and functions, to study the structure of indexing language. Thus, some areas of linguistics are of common interest to information scientists.

Natural Language versus Indexing Language

The differences between the natural language and indexing language are furnished below:

Natural Language	Indexing Language
A natural language is a set of codes and their admissible expression used to communicate ideas in speech and writing in our day-to-day life.	An indexing language is a set of codes and their admissible expression used for representing the content of the documents as well as queries of users.

Natural Language	Indexing Language
A natural language is 'natural' in the sense that it grows freely in the lips of human beings, totally free from any control.	An indexing language is 'artificial' in the sense that it might depend upon the vocabulary of a natural language, though not always. But its syntax, semantics and orthography would be different from the natural language.
A natural language is developed to communicate ideas among human beings in their day-to-day life.	Indexing language is developed and used for special purposes, such as for the representation of the thought content of the documents.
A natural language is a free language, and there is no control on synonyms and homographs.	An indexing language is a controlled language. There is a restriction in using the words/terms in indexing language. Synonyms and homographs are controlled.
There is no standardisation of terms/words.	Terms/words are standardised.
Natural language provides auxiliaries, like prepositions, conjunctions, etc.	Such auxiliaries are not available in an indexing language.

Structure of Indexing Language

Like natural language, an indexing language consists of three elements: (a) Vocabulary (not free vocabulary, but controlled vocabulary), (b) Syntax and (c) Semantics. All the structured indexing languages are based on careful subject analysis.

Controlled Vocabulary: An indexing language operates with a controlled vocabulary. An indexing language having controlled vocabulary attempting to indicate the relationship between terms in the index vocabulary is systematically structured. The vocabulary of an indexing language is either verbal or coded. Subject heading lists and thesauri come within the purview of verbally controlled vocabulary. A classification scheme employs coded vocabulary in the form of its notation.

Syntax: The etymological meaning of syntax is 'putting things together in an orderly manner'. In the context of an indexing language, syntax refers to a set of rules or grammar that governs the sequence of words in a subject heading or notation in a classification number. Most subjects treated even in modern macro documents are of compound nature. It means that the name of a subject can no longer be represented by a single word or term. When the number of terms are used to represent the subject coextensively, syntax is necessary to put the terms in the most helpful and known searchable order.

Semantics: Semantics refers to the systematic study of how meaning is structured, expressed and understood in the use of an indexing language. Various types of semantic relationships are evident in an indexing language. These relationships include equivalence relationships, hierarchical relationships, and associative relationships. The meaning of the term can be derived from its hierarchy. A semantic relationship is a document-independent relationship. The syntactical rules of an indexing language are also used to resolve the meaning of the term in a subject heading (consisting of a string of terms) through the determination of context.

Attributes of an Indexing Language

Indexing language is designed for a special purpose. It serves three purposes: Representing the subject content of documents, organising a searchable file and representing the subject content of the queries of the users while searching the index file. A positive search result is achieved only when the content representation of the document by the indexer and that of the queries by the searcher match. This matching of the file is very much dependent on the organisation of the index file in a predetermined order and the awareness of the users of it. Various attributes of an indexing language, like vocabulary control, concept coordination, multiple access, syndetic devices, relation manifestation, and structural presentation, play very important roles in the successful organisation of the index file and subsequent matching of the index and queries of the users. These have been discussed below:

Vocabulary Control: The vocabulary of an indexing language is controlled for standardisation of terms, that is, one concept should be denoted by only one term. This is done by controlling synonyms, near-synonyms and word forms and by distinguishing among homographs.

Concept Coordination: The contents of most documents today cannot be represented by only one term. Because of the use of multiple terms and multiple relationships among terms to represent the content of the document, it has become imperative to make available standard guidelines for the coordination of concepts denoted by the terms.

Multiple Access: The syntactical rules of the given indexing language help determine the order of significance in a linear representation of the subject of a document. It provides only a single access in the searchable index file. The rigidity of the significance order may not meet the approaches of all the users of the index file. In order to satisfy the approaches of all the users, indexing languages have introduced the mechanism for multiple index entries by rotating or cycling the component terms representing the subject of the document.

Syndetic Device: Syndetic device is an organisational framework in which related subjects are linked together in a classificatory structure either through cross references or inversion of headings.

Relation Manifestations: The range of an indexing language is not simply a matter of vocabulary. Provision for rules of syntax is to be made for the expression of relationships between the terms comprising the vocabulary. These relationships between different retrieval systems are of two types: (i) Paradigmatic relationship, also called semantic or generic relationship, which usually finds expression in the organisation of the vocabulary itself; and (ii) Syntagmatic relationship, in which, in addition to the expression of paradigmatic relationships, rules and facilities are provided for the coordination of terms from the vocabulary in order to express more complex meanings.

Structural Presentation: The basic objective of an indexing language is to provide a subject approach to the contents of documents to the users. It is generally agreed that a user-oriented approach may not be confined to a specific subject only. This situation calls for structuring the indexing language so systematically that the semantic network of concepts and relationships between concepts are displayed in it. All the indexing languages display such relationships in one way or another, and thus, all of them are structured. A classification scheme displays such relationships by notation, whereas a verbal indexing language, like a readymade list of subject headings and thesaurus, displays such relationships by the relationship indicators BT (Broader Term) and NT (Narrow Term).

The Two Vocabularies Control

The term 'vocabulary control' refers to a limited set of terms that must be used to index documents and search for these documents in a particular system. It may be defined as a list of terms showing their relationships and indicating ways in which they may be usefully combined to provide a specific subject of a document. A certain degree of structure is introduced in a controlled vocabulary so that terms whose meanings are related are brought together or linked in some way. The opposite, an uncontrolled vocabulary (that is, free vocabulary), is an unlimited set of terms drawn from natural language.

Objectives of Vocabulary Control

The basic objective of controlled vocabularies is to provide a means for organising information. Through the process of assigning terms selected from controlled vocabularies to describe documents and other types of content objects, the materials are organised according to the various elements that have been chosen to describe them. Controlled vocabularies serve five purposes:

1. *Translation*: Provide a means for converting the natural language of authors, indexers, and users into a vocabulary that can be used for indexing and retrieval.
2. *Consistency*: Promote uniformity in term format and the assignment of terms.
3. *Indication of Relationships*: Indicate semantic relationships among terms.

4. *Label and Browse*: Provide consistent and clear hierarchies in a navigation system to help users locate desired content objects.
5. *Retrieval*: Serve as a searching aid in locating content objects.

Types of Indexing Languages

As mentioned in the previous sections of this unit, the controlled vocabulary of an indexing language is of two types: Verbal and coded vocabulary. A classification scheme employs coded vocabulary, while authority lists use verbal vocabulary. These are discussed below:

Classification Schemes

A classification scheme employs coded vocabulary in the form of its notation. Libraries have long been using notational schemes of library classification to organise information resources on the shelves and provide means for locating information resources in the bibliographical tools, such as catalogues, bibliographies, abstracting and indexing documents. We know that classification is a mental process of grouping entities in order of their degree of likeness and separating entities according to their degree of unlikeness. All class designations of subjects are the names of subjects, irrespective of whether they are in terms of class numbers or verbal specifications. The assignment of class designation in the notational plane is called the class number, and the preparation of tools used for this purpose is classification schemes. Modern classification schemes, such as DDC, UDC, LCC, CC, etc., were devised several decades ago or more. Though they have been modified and improved over the years, their main objectives remain unchanged. The web version of DDC (twenty-second edition), Web Dewey, includes all updates since its publication in 2003, plus supplemental data.

Subject Heading Lists

A subject heading list contains the preferred subject access terms (controlled vocabulary) that are assigned as an added entry in the bibliographic record, which works as an access point and enables the work to be searched and retrieved by the subject from the library catalogue database. Subject heading has been defined as a word or group of words (phrase) indicating a subject under which all materials dealing with the same theme is entered in a catalogue or bibliography or arranged in a file. A vocabulary control device depends on a master list of words/terms that can be assigned to documents. Such a master list of terms is referred to as a list of subject headings. A subject heading list is an alphabetical list of terms and phrases, with appropriate cross-references and notes, that can be used as a source of subject headings to represent the subject content of a document. A list of other semantically related terms or phrases is displayed under each term or phrase. A printed list of subject headings incorporates the thoughts and experiences of many librarians of various types of libraries.

General Principles for Assigning Subject Headings

The rules for subject headings in a dictionary catalogue were formulated by Charles Ammi Cutter in 1876 in his book *Rules for a Printed Dictionary Catalogue*. The impact of Cutter's principles on the construction and maintenance of subject headings is still discernible today. Both the LCSH and the SLSH adopted Cutter's principles in assigning subject headings for a document. The general principles that guide the indexers in the choice and rendering of subject headings from the standard lists of subject headings are discussed below:

Specificity: The principles of specific and direct entry require that a document be assigned directly under the most specific subject heading that accurately and precisely represents its subject content.

Common Usage: This principle states that the word(s) used to express a subject must represent common usage. There may be problems in the selection of subject headings when the same concept is expressed by two or more terms.

Uniformity: The principle of uniform heading is adopted in order to bring consistency in the use of subject headings. A subject heading list must be very precise and exact.

Consistent and Current Terminology: The principle states that the term(s) chosen as subject headings should be both consistent and current, as has already been said regarding the justifications for uniform headings.

Form Headings: Refer to the words or phrases that represent the literary or artistic form (such as essays, poetry, fiction, etc.). These words or phrases follow a subject heading and are indicated by a dash. These words or phrases are used to make the subject more specific.

Cross-Reference: Cross-references direct the user from a term/phrase not used as a heading to the term/phrase that is used and from broader and related topics to the one chosen to represent a given subject.

Subject Authority File

A subject authority file consisting of subject authority records ensures uniformity and consistency in subject heading terminology and cross-references. The process of creating subject authority records and maintaining subject authority files is called subject authority control. Subject authority control is exercised at two levels: Central and local. At the central level, a central agency (such as the LC) maintains the subject authority file (in card or machine-readable form) or subject heading list (in print form) and makes changes to existing headings and cross-references as well as adds new ones. At the local level, a library creates local subject authority records only for headings that have not yet appeared as established headings in a subject heading list, along with the needed maintenance information.

Thesaurus

Thesaurus is a form of controlled vocabulary that seeks to dictate semantic manifestations of metadata in the indexing of content objects. A thesaurus serves to minimise semantic ambiguity by ensuring uniformity and consistency in storing and retrieving the manifestations of content objects. A thesaurus serves to guide both an indexer and a searcher in selecting the same preferred term or combination of preferred terms to represent a given subject. ISO 25964, the international standard for information retrieval thesauri, defines a thesaurus as a "controlled and structured vocabulary in which concepts are represented by terms, organized so that relationships between concepts are made explicit, and preferred terms are accompanied by lead-in entries for synonyms or quasi-synonyms".

A thesaurus is composed of at least three elements: (i) A list of words (or terms); (ii) The relationship amongst the words (or terms), indicated by their hierarchical relative position (such as parent/broader term, child/narrower term, synonym, etc.); and (iii) A set of rules on how to use the thesaurus.

The term thesaurus has been derived from Greek and Latin words, which mean 'a treasury', and it has been used for several centuries to mean a lexicon or treasury of words. Modern usage might be said to date from 1852, when the first edition of Thesaurus of English Words and Phrases was published by Peter Mark Roget. A thesaurus (plural: thesauri) with which we are concerned is meant for information retrieval and is used as a valuable vocabulary control device for indexing and searching in a specific subject area.

Purpose of Thesaurus

A thesaurus is a semantic network of terms. Its purposes are:

- To provide a map of a given field of knowledge, that is, how concepts or ideas about concepts are related to one another, which helps an indexer or a searcher understand the structure of the field;
- To provide a standard vocabulary for a given subject field, which will ensure that indexers are consistent when they are making index entries to an information storage and retrieval system;
- To provide a system of references between terms, which will ensure that only one term from a set of synonyms is used for indexing one concept;
- To provide a guide for users of the system so that they choose the correct term for a subject search;
- To locate a new concept in a scheme of relationships with existing concepts in a way that makes sense to users of the system;

- To provide classified hierarchies so that a search can be broadened and narrowed systematically;
- A desirable purpose, which it would be premature to say is being achieved, is to provide a means by which the use of terms in a given subject field might be standardised.

Basic Thesaural Relationships

Basic thesaural relationships or the semantic relationships in a thesaurus refer to two types of relationships: (1) Hierarchical relationship and (2) Non-hierarchical relationship.

Hierarchical Relationship

Hierarchical relationships are based on degrees or levels of superordination, where the superordinate term represents a class or a whole, and subordinate terms refer to its members or parts. This relationship is of four types: Genus-species (generic) relationship, whole-part relationship, instance relationship and polyhierarchical relationship.

Genus-species (generic) relationship links genus and species and represents the basis of the scientific taxonomic system. For example, the relationship between vertebrates and mammals.

Whole-part relationship covers situations in which one concept is inherently included in another, regardless of context, so the terms can be organised into logical hierarchies, with the whole treated as a broader term. For example, the central nervous system and the spinal cord.

Instance relationship identifies the link between a general category of things or events, expressed by a common noun and an individual instance of that category, often a proper name. For example, mountain range and the Himalayas.

Polyhierarchical relationship occurs when some concepts belong, on logical grounds, to more than one category. For example, a piano being a keyboard and string based musical item has polyhierarchical relationship with three broader terms viz: musical instrument, keyboard musical item and string based musical instrument.

Non-Hierarchical Relationship

Relationship between terms other than hierarchical is called non-hierarchical relationship, which may further be grouped as equivalence (or preferential) relationship and associative relationship.

Equivalence (or preferential) relationship refers to the relationship between preferred and non-preferred terms in which each term is regarded as referring to the same concept. When the same concept can be expressed by two or more terms, one is selected as the preferred term. A cross-reference to the preferred term should be made from any 'equivalent' entry term. Reciprocity in the equivalence relationships is expressed by the relationship indicators, including USE, which leads from a non-preferred (entry) term to the preferred term, and UF or USED FOR, which leads from the preferred entry term to the non-preferred term(s). Four basic types of equivalence relationships are as follows: (a) Synonyms, (b) Lexical variants, (c) Near-synonyms and (d) Generic posting.

Synonymy occurs when a concept can be represented by multiple terms having the same or similar meanings. For example, birds and birdie.

Lexical variants differ from synonyms in that synonyms are different terms for the same concept, while lexical variants are different word forms for the same expression. For example, bridge (game) and bridges (structure).

Near-synonyms are terms whose meanings are generally considered different but which are treated as equivalents for the purposes of a controlled vocabulary. For example, sea water and salt water.

Generic posting is a technique in which the name of a class and the names of its members are treated as equivalents, with the broader class name functioning as the preferred term. For example, 'Waxes UF Plant waxes' and 'Plant waxes USE Waxes'.

Associative relationship covers associations between terms that are neither equivalent nor hierarchical, yet the terms are semantically or conceptually associated to such an extent that the link between them is made explicit in the thesaurus on the grounds that it might suggest additional terms for use in indexing or retrieval. The associative relationship used in thesauri is indicated by the abbreviation RT (Related Term). As a general guideline, whenever one term is used, the other should always be implied within the common frames of reference shared by the users of the thesaurus. Either of the following types of terms can be linked by associative relationship: (a) Those belonging to the same category and (b) Those belonging to different categories.

(a) Those belonging to the same category: Relationships are needed for terms belonging to the same category in various special situations, primarily to guide the user in locating the desired term. Each of the terms belonging to the same category has its own particular meaning. But the boundary between them is often confused with common usage, so a user checking one of them in the index should be informed of documents indicated by others. For example, ship and boat.

(b) Those belonging to different categories: It is possible to establish many grounds for associating terms belonging to different categories. RT references are often made between etymologically related terms, that is, terms that contain the same root but do not represent the same kind of thing. For example, temperature control and thermostat.

Thesaurofacet

Thesaurofacet is a thesaurus and faceted classification for engineering and related topics. It was developed from the English Electric Company's Faceted classification for Engineering and its first edition was published in 1958. Thesaurofacet came about when the third edition of Faceted Classification for Engineering, published in 1961, was ready for revision. This system was used to organise documents belonging to the libraries of the corporation of English Electric. However, with the growing trends in science and technology and the need for using computer techniques and post-coordinate indexing, a decision was taken in 1967 to commission Jean Aitchison, a member of the Classification Research Group, to review the indexing needs of the company and the result of that review was the compilation of a new and improved fourth edition of the faceted classification system called Thesaurofacet, published in 1970. In the fourth edition, the alphabetised index to the classification scheme was replaced with a thesaurus.

Thesaurofacet covers the whole field of science and technology, but subjects are treated in varying depths, and only engineering and allied fields are covered exhaustively. Full subject coverage includes engineering and fields directly related to engineering, such as computers, measurement and testing, physics and management. Relevant management-related concepts were borrowed from the 'Classification of Business Studies' developed by the London Graduate School of Business Studies.

Thesaurofacet is considered a multi-purpose retrieval language tool because it has classification schedules and a faceted thesaurus. The classification comprises main classes and facets and a notation system that consists of letters in upper case and numbers from 2 to 9. The faceted thesaurus is the key to the uniqueness of the tool because it offers the user options to identify topics within the system. Because both are linked, each term in the system appears twice, once in the schedule and once in the thesaurus, with a notation that links the two parts together. However, the information given about the term in the thesaurus is not the same information given about that term in the schedule. The two parts of the system are complementary and should be used conjunctively and not separately. Finally, Thesaurofacet can be used to arrange books on the shelves and arrange entries in the subject catalogues. Further, the index terms are intended for indexing and searching.

Classaurus

Classaurus is a faceted hierarchic scheme of terms with vocabulary control features. It is a system of terms having separate hierarchic schedules of the elementary categories—discipline, entity, property and action—together with their respective species/types, parts and special modifiers. Also, there are separate schedules for the common modifiers: Form, time, environment, and place. Each of the terms in these hierarchic schedules is enriched with synonyms, quasi-synonyms, etc. The hierarchic schedules constituting the systematic part is supplemented by an alphabetical index of chain entries. Classaurus is used in the formulation of subject headings in general and, in particular, subject headings according to the Postulate-based Permuted Subject Indexing (POPSI) language. For the construction of a classaurus, the POPSI language itself provides guidelines. A set of programs have been developed to construct a classaurus using, as input, subject headings formulated according to POPSI language, which are enriched with certain codes to denote the different elementary categories, their species, parts, special modifiers and other common modifiers of different kinds. The resulting classaurus has hierarchic schedules, but terms in an array are arranged only alphabetically. It has two parts: Systematic part (modifiers, entities, etc.) and alphabetical index part (synonyms, antonyms, etc.).

Library of Congress Subject Headings (LCSH)

LCSH is the list of headings produced from the subject authority file maintained by the United States LC for use in bibliographic records and published annually. It is popularly known by its abbreviation as LCSH and is sometimes used interchangeably with the phrase subject authority file. LCSH is a multidisciplinary vocabulary that includes headings in all subjects, from science to religion to history, social science, education, literature, and philosophy. It also includes headings for geographic features, ethnic groups, historical events, building names, etc. LCSH is the most widely used subject vocabulary in the world. It is the model for many other vocabularies in English and other languages and has been translated into numerous languages. The strongest aspect of LCSH is that it represents the subject headings of the LC, the national library of the United States and one of the richest national libraries in the world.

The LCSH is used quite widely as a controlled vocabulary for catalogues and bibliographies all over the world. Andrea Crestadoro is usually given credit, who, for the first time in his book, *The Art of Making Catalogues* published in 1856, pointed out that the cataloguer should provide a standardised guide to the subject content of a book by giving it a heading. In 1895, the first standard list of subject headings, entitled List of Subject Headings for Use in Dictionary Catalogues produced by a committee of the ALA, of which C.A. Cutter was a prominent member, was based on Cutter's principles. It went through three editions (1895, 1898 and 1911). In 1910–1914, when the LC began publishing its list under the title 'Subject Headings Used in the Dictionary Catalogs of the Library of Congress', it was found unnecessary to continue the ALA list. LCSH was basically designed to represent the subject and form of books and serials in the LC collection. Now, it is not only considered as worldwide authority for subject headings in the English language but has also been translated into several other languages. Later renamed LCSH, this list has been updated in many editions. It is available in various formats, including hard copy, microfiche, CD-ROM and online through the Web (locis.loc.gov).

Types of Subject Headings in LCSH

Subject headings in LCSH can be constructed in a number of ways. The prominent ones have been elaborated below:

Single-word headings: A single-word heading is usually a noun representing objects, things, persons or concepts. For example, Skating, Electrometallurgy, etc.

Adjectival phrase headings: Adjectival phrase headings start with a modifier followed by a noun or noun phrase. The modifier may be an adjective, or it may be a noun used as an adjective. For example, Administrative Law, Dental Records, Spanish Literature, etc.

Conjunctive phrase headings: Conjunctive phrase headings refer to those that are composed of two or more nouns, with or without modifiers, connected by 'and' or ending with 'etc.'. Headings of this type are established only when a work being catalogued discusses a relationship between two topics from both perspectives and in such broad terms that the relationship could not be described using a main heading with a subdivision. For example, Wit and Humour, Libraries and Society, etc.

Prepositional phrase headings: Prepositional phrase headings are used to enable the subject cataloguer to express single but complex ideas for which there is no one word. For example, Photography in Psychiatry, Radioisotopes in Cardiology, etc.

Inverted headings: Inverted headings serve the alphabetico-classed function of subordinating specific descriptors under their broad generic categories. Proverb, Korean, Education, Elementary, etc. Names of geographic features have traditionally been inverted in order to place a significant word in the initial position instead of the generic word. For example, 'Lake Eric' is formulated as Eric, Lake so that the distinguishing part of the name, 'Eric' appears first.

Proper name headings: Any proper name can be used as a subject heading when that proper name becomes the subject of a work. Names are not, however, all included in the LCSH. The only ones appearing in the LCSH are those that are used as pattern headings, as examples or that need special subject subdivisions or instructions printed under them. For example, Bermuda Islands, Shakespeare, William, 1564–1616, Canadian Psychological Association.

Subdivisions in LCSH

LCSH requires extensive use of subdivisions to combine different concepts into a single subject heading. Subject subdivisions are words or phrases that can follow a subject heading and are listed below the subject heading and indicated by a dash. These words or phrases are used to make the subject more specific. Complex topics are represented by subject headings, followed by subdivisions. Some subdivisions are printed in LCSH, but a greater number of subdivisions may be assigned according to the rules specified in the Subject Headings Manual (2008). The LC has published a separate alphabetical listing of various subdivisions that can be used after any listed subject heading unless otherwise specified. Subdivisions fall into several broadly defined categories: Topical and chronological subdivisions specific to particular headings, form subdivisions, geographic subdivisions, free-floating subdivisions and subdivisions under pattern headings. Valid subdivisions are marked in bold letters. Primary subdivisions are preceded by a single dash. Secondary subdivisions, that is, subdivisions of subdivisions, are preceded with a double dash. Each category is described below:

Topical subdivisions: Topical subdivisions are used under the main headings or other subdivisions to limit the scope of the concept expressed by the heading to a special subtopic. Such headings are displayed by a long dash in LCSH; if two subdivisions are used, there are two long dashes. For example, Women—Employment; Automobiles—Motors—Carburettors.

Chronological subdivisions: Chronological subdivisions are used to limit a heading, with or without subdivision, to a particular time period. For example, Philosophy, French—Eighteenth Century. Specific topical subdivisions and chronological subdivisions printed under the names of countries and other jurisdictions or regions may be used with them.

Form subdivisions: Form subdivisions are used to indicate the form in which the material on a subject is organised and presented, and as such, are added as the last element to any heading. For example, Art—Bibliography—Periodicals.

Geographic subdivisions: For geographic subdivisions, headings with the code may have added place names that are not specifically listed in LCSH. For example, Labor Supply—France.

Free-floating subdivisions: There are a number of identical (or nearly so) subdivisions that can be applied in specifically defined situations to primary headings and won't have separate authority records for each heading and subdivision combination. The five broad groups of free-floating subdivisions are: General; under classes of persons and ethnic groups; under names of corporate bodies, persons and families; under place names; and entries controlled by pattern headings.

Entry Structure in LCSH

All preferred primary subject terms and subjects with subdivisions are listed in boldface type, while those only in the entry vocabulary (that is, references interfiled with the main headings) appear in normal typeface. Each entry in the LCSH is accompanied by all or some of the following:

Headings: Subject headings displayed in the LCSH consist of single-word or multiple-word headings.

Class numbers: LC classification numbers are included in LCSH for many primary subject terms and some subject subdivisions.

Scope notes: This is a note under the subject heading that explains and clarifies what is and is not meant in the definition of the term and in its use as a subject heading. It specifies the range of applications for a heading or draws distinctions between related terms. Scope notes may follow in separate paragraphs.

Reference structure: References associated with the headings are then listed in groups under codes, like USE = Use this heading instead of another, UF = Used For (do not use this heading); BT = Broader Topic (less specific), NT = Narrower Topic (more specific), etc.

Merits and Deficiencies of LCSH

The strongest aspect of LCSH is that it represents the subject headings of a national library, one of the richest national libraries in the world. The administrative and managerial machinery of the LC has made it possible for LCSH to stand out as an undisputed leader in almost all aspects of library development. In addition to the printed version, LCSH is now available in different formats: Microfiche, revised quarterly; CD-ROM, revised quarterly; and online through the LC Internet node. A number of bibliographic utilities allow searching by LCSH. The prominent examples are the Research Libraries Information Network (RLIN) and Washington Library Network's own online catalogue with access by subject, often with sophisticated search options. Most of these libraries use LCSH for subject cataloguing.

With all these strengths and reputation, the LC has yet to publish a statement of principles for its subject cataloguing system. Without a proper theoretical foundation, it has become a mammoth tool rather becoming difficult to use. The principles that underlie the system must be inverted from practice and policy statements.

Very often, LCSH is criticized for its outdated terminology, illogical syntax and general inefficiency in precise subject retrieval. Its limitations are that it would meet the subject cataloguing requirements only for macro documents. Its use as a bibliographic list, therefore, cannot be extended to index micro documents.

Conscious of all these drawbacks, more intensive efforts are underway at the LC to modernise its subject heading system and systematize the existing tool. Many of its new features recently introduced represent steps in this direction. For the foreseeable future, LCSH gives every sign of retaining its vitality and prominence for subject access to library collection.

Sears List of Subject Headings (SLSH)

The SLSH, now in its nineteenth edition (2007), is an abridged version of the LCSH, named after the first compiler Minnie Earl Sears (1873–1933). It emerged in response to demand from small and medium-sized libraries for a list of subject headings that Sears compiled. Each edition strives to keep in mind current needs and users' approaches to subject access. The SLSH is still a living manifestation of the principles of subject cataloguing put forth by C.A. Cutter (1837–1903). The reforms of the SLSH began in its fifteenth edition with the display of headings and their relationships using standard abbreviations, namely NT, BT, RT, UF, USE, and SA, instead of the confusing x, xx and 'see also' for codified instructions. The thesaurus format conforms to the ANSI/NISO Standards for Thesaurus (1993). Nevertheless, the Sears List remains an index for pre-coordinated indexing instead of a true thesaurus. Its terminology is modern, although with an American bias. It is widely used today in and outside the US by small and medium-sized libraries.

Like LCSH, subject headings in the SLSH consist of various forms, ranging from a single word to different kinds of complex descriptive phrases of single concepts in two or more words to complex and compound subjects. SLSH is guided by general principles, such as 'Specific and Direct Entry', 'Common Usage' and 'Uniformity', in the formation of its subject hidings as discussed under Section 10.7.2.1 of this unit. There are four types of subject headings in SLSH:

Types of Subject Headings in SLSH

Topical headings: Topical subject headings refer to the words or phrases for common things and concepts that represent the content of the document.

Single word heading: The single noun is the most desirable form of subject heading if it is specific enough to fit the document in hand and the needs of the library. For example, Mythology, Neopaganism, etc.

Phrase heading: A phrase heading comprises two or more words representing the subject of a document, such as LCSH, adjectival phrase headings (for example, Computer animation, Open access publishing, etc.), conjunctive phrase headings (for example, gods and goddesses, anarchism and anarchists, etc.), etc.

Form headings: Form refers to the form of exposition of the content of the document, such as Almanacs, Dictionaries, Directories, Encyclopaedias, Gazetteers, etc. These headings are assigned to individual documents as form subdivisions.

Geographic headings: SLSH prescribes the documents on geographic areas, countries, cities, etc., under the names of the places. The SLSH does not provide the full list of places. The geographical headings United States, Ohio and Chicago (III) are provided only as examples.

Subdivisions in SLSH

The purpose of subject subdivisions is to subdivide topics that are broad in scope or have much written about them. Subdivisions provided by the SLSH indicate a specialised aspect of a broad subject or point of view. There are different types of subdivisions, including topical, geographic, chronological and form subdivisions. Subdivisions are compounded under a given topic. Examples of the different types of subdivisions [form, key (like LCSH pattern headings), special topic, time and geographic] refer to the heading 'United States—History—1861–1865,

Civil War—Medical Care'. The subdivisions in SLSH usually follow the standard order of [Topical]—[Geographic]—[Chronological]—[Form].

Form subdivisions are used to indicate the physical form of the exposition of the document. For example, Bibliography.

Topical subdivisions provide the aspect of a subject or point of view presented in a particular document. For example, Oceanography—Research.

Key headings in SLSH, like LCSH, serve as patterns for the subdivisions and may be used under all headings of the same type. Some of these 'key headings' are Shakespeare, William, 1564–1616 (to illustrate subdivisions under any author); President—United States (to illustrate subdivisions that may be used under presidents, prime ministers, governors, and rulers of any country, state, etc.).

Chronological subdivisions, that is, time divisions, which apply most frequently to history, define a specific chronology for the primary topic. For example, Europe—History—1789–1900. If a chronological period has a given name, this name is included in the heading following the dates. For example, United States—History—1600–1775, Colonial period.

Geographic subdivisions provide the geographical aspect of a broad subject. Two forms of geographic divisions are evident in the SLSH: (a) Area—Subject, such as Chicago (III)—Census; and (b) Subject—Area, such as Geology—Bolivia. Parenthetical instructions are provided with those headings that may be subdivided by place. For example, Folklore.

References in SLSH

References in the SLSH are grouped into three main categories: Specific 'See' references, specific 'See also' references, and general references. With the fifteenth edition of SLSH in 1994, 'See' and 'See also' references and the complementary 'x' and 'xx' were replaced by the thesaurus symbols UF/USE, BT, NT, RT and SA as explained in previous sections.

Specific 'See' References: The UF symbol stands for 'Used for' and designates the preferred terms or phrases from which 'see' references are made. The most frequent and helpful varieties of See references direct the users from synonyms or near-synonyms, variant spellings, etc.

Specific 'See also' References: A 'See also' reference connects a heading to a related heading or headings designated in the SLSH as Narrower term(s) (NT(s)) and Related term(s) (RT(s)) if the library has material listed under both headings and normally move downward from a general term to a more specific term(s). For example, Indoor gardening See also Terrariums; Window gardening.

General References: The symbol 'SA' stands for 'See also' and introduces a general reference, which refers to one heading to an entire category or class of headings rather than an individual heading. Here, a general explanation or direction is given instead of a long list of individual headings. For example, SA furniture of particular countries, like American furniture; types of furniture and names of specific articles of furniture, like Tables, Chairs; etc.

Filing Order in SLSH

Filing of entries of SLSH follows the ALA Filing Rules (1980). All headings are interfiled, disregarding all punctuations. Headings with modifiers given in round brackets and phrase headings appear intermingled with those with dashes and commas. Although this straightforward alphabetical arrangement may appear to be less logical than the one used with punctuations, the increasing use of computers in libraries and the wish to adhere to standard rules have prompted the practice to adhere to standard rules that have prompted the editors of SLSH to adopt the ALS Rules for Filing.

Merits and Deficiencies of SLSH

SLSH is comparatively simpler to use than LCSH. The rules and principles are fairly explicit in their directions, containing scope notes and specific instructions for their use. If followed consistently, SLSH will provide a useful reference guide for the user and library reference staff.

The major inadequacies in SLSH and LCSH are that these subject heading lists are not backed up by theoretical foundations intrinsic to subject indexing. With the growth of knowledge throwing forth new subjects and intricate facet and phase relations, these enumerated subject heading lists are not equipped to respond to new challenges in subject cataloguing.

Unit 11

Indexing Techniques

Different Types of Indexing Techniques

There are two broader types of indexing techniques: Derivative indexing and assignment indexing. Derived indexing is a method of indexing in which a human indexer or computer extracts from the title and/or text of a document one or more words or phrases to represent the subject(s) of the work for use as headings under which entries are made. It is also known as extractive indexing. In derivative indexing, terms to be used to represent the content of the document are derived directly from the document itself. Here, no attempt is made to use an indexer's own knowledge of the subject or other guides, but only the information that is manifested in the document is used. Examples of derivative indexing are keyword indexing, citation indexing, automatic indexing, etc.

Assigned indexing is also known as 'concept indexing' because it involves identifying concept(s) associated with the content of each document. It is a method of indexing in which a indexer selects one or more subject headings or descriptors from a list of controlled vocabulary to represent the subject(s) of a work. The indexing terms selected to represent the content need not appear in the title or text of the document indexed. Here, an indexing language is designed, and it is used for both indexing and searching. Some notable examples of assignment indexing are chain indexing, PRECIS, POPSI, classification schemes, etc.

Pre-Coordinate Indexing System

Pre-coordinate indexing systems are conventional systems mostly found in printed indexes. In this type of system, a document is represented in the index by a heading or headings comprising a chain or string of terms. These terms, taken together, are expected to define the subject content of the document. All indexing systems are, by nature, coordinate indexing. The purpose of using a combination or coordination of component terms is to describe the contents of the documents more precisely. Many subjects can be expressed in a single term, such as Libraries, Cataloguing, Management, etc. Others are expressed as a combination of these, such as Cataloguing in libraries, Management of libraries, etc. When the indexer assigns subject headings representing such compounds and arranges entries in a series of classes according to the subject content of the document, the resulting system is referred to as a pre-coordinate indexing system. Here, the indexer coordinates the component terms representing compounds at the input stage, that is, at the time of indexing in anticipation of the users' approach. Most of the classification schemes allow a measure of coordination, either by including compound subjects or by providing facilities for creating them out of simple elements. The same is true for readymade lists of subject headings like SLSH and LCSH. Such classification schemes and lists of subject headings can therefore be regarded as pre-coordinate indexing languages.

Chain Indexing

Chain indexing or chain procedure is a mechanical method to derive subject index entries or subject headings from the class number of the document. It was developed by Dr. S.R. Ranganathan. He first mentioned this in his book *Theory of Library Catalogue* in 1938. In chain procedure, the indexer or cataloguer is supposed to start from where the classifier has left. No duplication of work is to be done. They need to derive subject headings or class index entries from the digit-by-digit interpretation of the class number of the document in the reverse direction to provide the alphabetical approach to the subject of the document. According to Ranganathan, chain indexing is a "procedure for deriving class index entry (that is, subject index entry) which refers from a class to its class number in a more or less mechanical way." Chain indexing was originally intended for use with CC. However, it may be applied to any scheme of classification whose notation follows a hierarchical pattern.

A chain is a string of terms organised in a particular sequence based on the classification scheme that the chain adopts. The concept of 'chain' is the foundation of chain indexing. A chain is deemed to be a structural manifestation of a subject. The term 'structure', in this context, refers to the parts constituting a subject and their mutual interrelationship. It is a modulated sequence of sub-classes or isolated ideas. The sequence of terms is pre-coordinated according to the syntactical rules of the given classification scheme. Chain indexing is a method of deriving subject headings from the chain of successive subdivisions leading from general to specific levels needed to be indexed.

The concept of 'chain' becomes operative only after the concept of a set of 'links' about the structure of the subject is conceded. A chain should comprise a link of every order that lies between the first and last links of the chain. The different types of links in the chain indexing system are discussed below:

- **Sought links (SL):** Sought links denote the concepts (at any given stage of the chain) that the user is likely to use as access points.
- **Unsought links (USL):** Unsought links denote the concepts that are not likely to be used as access points by the user.
- **False links (FL):** False links are those that do not really represent any valid concept. Mostly, these are connecting symbols or indicator digits.
- **Missing links (ML):** Missing links represent the concepts that are not available in the preferred classification scheme. These are inserted by the indexer by means of verbal extension.

Steps in Chain Indexing

The following steps are followed in chain indexing for deriving different types of subject headings:

1. **Construction of the class number of the subject of the document:** Classify the subject of the document by following a preferred classification scheme. A class number constructed according to a scheme for notational classification will form the basis for applying the rules for the chain procedure for deriving subject headings.
2. **Representation of the class number in the form of a chain:** Represent the class number in the form of a chain in which each link comprises two parts: Class number and its verbal translation in standard term or phrase used in the preferred classification scheme.
3. **Determination of links:** Determine different kinds of links, including sought links (SL), unsought links (USL), false links (FL) and missing links (ML).
4. **Preparation of specific subject heading:** Derive specific subject heading for the specific subject entry from the last sought link and move upwards by taking the necessary and sufficient sought links in a reverse rendering or backward rendering process.
5. **Preparation of subject reference headings:** Derive subject reference heading for the subject reference from each of the upper sought links. This process continues until all the terms of upper sought links are exhausted and indexed.
6. **Preparation of subject reference entries:** Prepare subject reference entries or 'see also' references from each subject reference heading to its specific subject heading. When a subject heading starts from the last sought link, denoting space, time or form, prepare 'See' references instead of 'See also' references from subject reference heading(s) to a specific subject heading.

7. **Preparation of cross-references:** Prepare cross-references (that is, 'see' references, if any) for each alternative and synonymous term/heading used in the specific as well as subject reference headings.
8. **Alphabetisation:** Merge specific subject entries, subject references (that is, 'see also' references) and 'see' references and arrange them in a single alphabetical sequence.

Advantages of Chain Indexing

- A major advantage of chain indexing is that it ensures the collocation of a subject's aspects scattered in the classification scheme (that is, distributed relatives) because the last link in the class number is always the first link in the chain of subject index entries.
- It offers general and specific information to all information seekers by deriving subject headings from the chain of successive subdivisions that leads from the general to the most specific level.
- It is more or less a mechanical system, and it is economical too.

Disadvantages of Chain Indexing

- **Too much dependency on classification schemes:** Chain indexing could be effectively operative only if they are backed up by a good structured classification scheme.
- **Disappearance of chain:** The chain disappears in each stage of deriving subject reference entries, and thus, it results in the loss of full context of the content of the document.
- **Lack of specificity:** Chain indexing provides only one specific entry, and others are subject references.
- **Unsuitability for computerisation:** The formation of a 'Chain' is very much a human intellectual operation, which is beyond the capability of the computer to manipulate.

- **Running from pillar to post:** It makes direct access to the specific subject heading possible only for those who know the specific subject heading for the given document, but in most cases, access to a specific subject heading was possible at the cost of running from pillar to post since only one entry is a specific subject entry, and others are cross-references in the chain indexing system.

Preserved Context Index System (PRECIS)

PRECIS is an acronym for Preserved Context Index System or Preserved Context Indexing System. PRECIS is a computer-assisted pre-coordinate subject indexing system developed by Derek Austin in 1968 as a result of long research that the Classification Research Group (CRG) undertook to give a new general classification for information control. In 1969, British librarians Derek Austin and Peter Butcher issued the PRECIS—a rotated subject index system published by the Council of the British National Bibliography. This appears to be the first published report on an innovative method for adding subject data in the form of descriptors to the computerized MARC record. This system is considered the most important development in the alphabetical approach to subject specification in recent years.

The system aims at providing an alphabetical subject index that can cater to the variant approaches of the users along with their context. In order to achieve this objective, the system arranges the components of a document into a significant sequence. Thus, all the important components in the string are used as approach points. Simultaneously, the terms are displayed in such a fashion that every term is related to the next term in a context-dependent way. Moreover, the system is amenable to computer operation, which further adds to the advantage of the system as the entries will be prepared and arranged automatically by the computer.

PRECIS is a system of subject indexing in which the initial string of terms, organised according to the scheme of role operators, is computer manipulated in such a way that each sought term in the string functions as the approach term while preserving the full context of the document. Entries are restructured at every step so that the user can determine from the format of the entry which terms set the approach term into its context and which terms are context-dependent on the approach term.

Objectives of PRECIS

- The computer, not the indexer, should produce all index entries. The indexer's responsibility is to prepare the input strings and to give necessary instructions to the computers to generate index entries according to definite formats.
- Each of the sought terms should find index entries, and each entry should express the complete thought content/full context of the document, unlike the chain procedure where only one entry is specific.
- Each of the entries should be expressive.
- The system should be based on a single set of logical rules to make it consistent.
- The system should be based on the concept of open-ended vocabulary, which means that terms can be admitted into the index at any time as soon as they have been encountered in the literature.
- The system must have sufficient references between semantically related terms.

Features of PRECIS

- It is more amenable to automatic manipulation than indexing based on the notational classifications.
- The permuted entries read naturally, which is achieved by the prescribed order of the role operators.
- The terms are linked to a machine-held thesaurus, thereby providing possible 'see' and 'see also' references.
- PRECIS can be adapted to other languages.

- The indexer determines the meaning of the terms, codes the roles and identifies the lead terms, whereas the computer takes care of the permutations.
- Its subject formulation is completely independent of classification and, therefore, exclusively geared to no classification numbers assigned in the MARC record.
- Context is preserved, and it presents the full subject statement at every point of the index entry.

Principles of PRECIS

Two principles are followed in PRECIS:

(a) **Principle of context dependency:** The 'context-dependency' principle may be seen as a combination of context and dependency. When this principle is followed in a PRECIS input string, each term is qualified and sets the next term into its wider context. In other words, the meaning of each term in the string depends upon the meaning of its preceding term. Taken together, they all represent a single context. Each term is hence dependent, directly or indirectly, on all the terms that precede it.

(b) **Principle of one-to-one relationship:** When the terms are organised according to the principle of context-dependency, they form a one-to-one related sequence—each of the terms in the string is directly related to its next term.

Syntax and Semantics in PRECIS

The syntax of PRECIS is based on the role operators, codes and logical rules that act as instructions to the computer. The semantics of PRECIS is handled by linking the terms to a machine-held thesaurus, thereby providing possible 'see' and 'see also' references.

PRECIS Indexing Procedure

1. Analysing the document and identifying key concepts.
2. Organising the concepts into a subject statement based on the principle of context dependency.

3. Assigning codes that signify the syntactical function of each term.
4. Deciding which terms should be access points and which terms would be in other positions in the index entries and assigning further codes to achieve these results.
5. Adding further prepositions, auxiliaries, or phrases that would result in clarity and expressiveness of the resulting index entries.
6. Making supporting reference entries.

Postulate-based Permuted Subject Indexing (POPSI)

The inherent weakness of chain indexing has been its dependence on a scheme of classification. Another weakness was its disappearing chain. In view of this situation, the information scientists at the Documentation Research and Training Centre (DRTC), Bangalore, directed themselves from these limitations; the POPSI is the result of these efforts. It was developed by Ganesh Bhattacharya. POPSI does not depend on the class number but is based on Ranganathan's postulates and principles of the general theory of classification. Dr. Ganesh Bhattacharyya first explained the fundamentals of subject indexing languages with an extensive theoretical background, which ultimately led to the development of a newer version of POPSI, forming part of his General Theory of Subject Indexing Languages (GT-SIL). Bhattacharyya developed the POPSI through logical interpretation of the deep structure of subject indexing language (SIL). POPSI drew attention to the helpfulness of adopting a suitable device for ensuring an optimally effective organising classification through the alphabetisation of verbal subject propositions. It prescribes the use of apparatus words, such as prepositions, conjunctions, participles, etc., as and when necessary to communicate the exact meaning of subject propositions. These words are put in parenthesis, and they are ignored in alphabetisation. Since the POPSI Index of all verbal entries, filing them with one alphabetical sequence in a unipartite index is made easy.

Major Working Concepts of POPSI

(1) **Deep structure of subject indexing languages (DS-SIL):** DS-SIL is the logical abstraction of the surface structures of outstanding SILs, like Cutter, Dewey, Kaiser and Ranganathan. According to the GT-SIL, the structure of a specific SIL has been assumed to be a surface structure of the deep structure of SIL. Any specific subject may belong to any one of the elementary categories (D, E, A, P) and modifiers.

(2) **Elementary categories and modifiers:** These include the following:

(a) **Discipline (=D)** refers to an elementary category that includes the conventional field of study, any aggregate of such fields or artificially created fields analogous to those mentioned above. For example, Physics, Biotechnology, Ocean science, LIS, etc.

(b) **Entity (=E)** refers to an elementary category that includes manifestations having perceptual correlates or only conceptual existence, as contrasted with their properties and actions performed by them or on them. For example, Energy, Light, Plants, Animals, Place, Time, Environment, etc.

(c) **Action (=A)** refers to an elementary category that includes manifestations denoting the concept of 'doing'. An action may manifest itself as self-action or external action. For example, Function, Migration, etc.

(d) **Property (=P)** refers to an elementary category that includes manifestations denoting the concept of 'attribute'—qualitative or quantitative. For example, Property, Effect, Power, Capability, Efficiency, Utility, Form, etc.

(e) **Modifier (=M)** refers to a qualifier used to modify any one of the elementary categories D, E, A and P. It decreases the extension and increases the intension of the qualified manifestation without disturbing its conceptual wholeness. A modifier can modify any one of the elementary categories and two or more elementary categories. Modifiers are of two types:

(i) **Common modifiers**, which refer to space (for example, Libraries in India), time (for example, Libraries in India Nineteenth Century), environment (for example, Desert Birds), and form (for example, Encyclopaedia of Physics); and **(ii) Special modifiers**, which are used to modify only one of the elementary categories.

(3) **Organising classification and associative classification:** According to the GT-SIL, classification is a combination of both organising classification and associative classification. In other words, an indexing system is a combination of both organising classification and associative classification. The tasks involved in creating an organising classification are the categorisation of concepts and their organising in hierarchies. In organising classification, compound subjects are based on genus-species, whole-part, and other inter-facet relationships. Here, classification is used to distinguish and rank each subject from all other subjects with reference to its Coordinate—Superordinate—Subordinate—Collateral (COSSCO) relationships.

(4) **Base and core:** In the context of constructing compound subject heading, when the purpose is to bring together all or major portions of information relating to a particular manifestation or manifestations of a particular elementary category, the manifestation/category is Base. In the case of a complex subject, any one of the subjects can be decided to be the Base subject depending upon the purpose at hand. For example, for a document on 'Eye cancer', 'Eye' is the Base subject in an eye hospital library, and 'Cancer' is considered the Base subject for a cancer research centre. When the purpose is to bring together within a recognised Base all or major portions of information pertaining to one or more elementary categories, the category or categories concerned is the Core of the concerned Base. Core lies within the Base. Which one will be the Base and which one will be the Core depends on the collection or purpose of the library. For example, in DDC, 'Medicine' is the Base, and the 'Human body' and its 'Organs' constitute the Core of the Base.

Features of POPSI

From the operational point of view, the salient features of POPSI may be grouped under three components: Analysis, synthesis, and permutation. The work of 'Analysis' and 'Synthesis' is primarily based on the postulates associated with the deep structure of SILs for generating organising classification. The task of analysis and synthesis is largely guided by the POPSI-table. 'Permutation' is based on cyclic permutations of each term-of-approach, either individually or in association with other terms, for generating associative classification effect in alphabetical arrangement.

Rules of Syntax

The basic rules of syntax associated with POPSI are as follows:

- Discipline is followed by Entity, both modified and unmodified.
- Property immediately follows the manifestation in relation to which it is a Property.
- Action immediately follows the manifestation in relation to which it is an Action.
- A Property can have its own Property.
- An Action can have its own Action.
- A Species/Type immediately follows the manifestation in relation to which it is a Species/Type.
- A Part immediately follows the manifestation in relation to which it is a Part.
- A Modifier immediately follows the manifestation in relation to which it is a Modifier.

Steps in POPSI

The main steps in applying POPSI are as follows:

(1) **Content analysis:** Involves the identification of different component ideas associated with the content of the document with reference to their elementary categories and modifiers.

(2) **Formalisation:** Involves the preparation of the formalized expression of the subject statement obtained on the basis of the results of Step 1 (Content analysis) according to the rules of syntax.

(3) **Standardisation:** Involves deciding the standard term in the formalized expression of the subject statement, especially for the term(s) having synonym(s), if any. This step calls for the use of classaurus.

(4) **Modulation:** Involves the augmentation of the standardized subject proposition by interpolating and extrapolating, as the case may be, the successive super-ordinates of each manifestation using standard terms along with an indication of their synonyms, if any.

(5) **Entry for organising classification:** Involves the preparation of entries for organising classification by inserting appropriate notation for elementary categories, subdivisions and modifiers from the POPSI table. The modulated subject proposition with appropriate notation from the POPSI table, sorted alpha-numerically, will produce an organising classification effect by the juxtaposition of entries in alphabetical sequence.

(6) **Preparation of entries of associative classification:** Involves the preparation of the entries under each approach term by cyclic permutation of sought terms for generating the associative classification effect in alphabetical arrangement.

(7) **Alphabetisation:** Involves arranging all the entries in alphabetical sequence.

Post-Coordinate Indexing

All indexing systems follow the process of concept coordination to describe the contents of the documents more precisely. We have seen in pre-coordinate indexing that component concepts are coordinated according to the order of significance or citation order by following the syntactical rules of the given indexing language. But the rigidity of the citation order appears to be unsatisfactory to meet the varieties of approaches of all the users. The provision for multiple entries in pre-coordinate indexing by rotating or cycling the component terms covers only a fraction of the possible number of the total permutations, and for this, a large portion of probable approach points is left uncovered. Consequently, the searcher has no choice but to follow the rigid citation order specified by the given indexing language. The above-noted problems stemming from the pre-coordination of terms with the rigidity of citation order triggered the development of alternative indexing techniques where the component ideas of a subject are kept separately, uncoordinated by the indexer. Here, concepts/terms are coordinated at the time of searching (that is, at the output stage) by the user. A greater degree of search manipulation is available in a post-coordinate indexing system since the search terms can be coordinated almost in any combination or order to retrieve records of information about the documents as required by the users. The indexing systems based on this basic principle are called post-coordinate indexing or simply coordinate indexing systems. Based on this basic principle, several post-coordinate indexing systems, such as Uniterm, Optical Coincidence Card, etc., were developed. Among the different types of post-coordinate indexing systems, the Uniterm system developed by Mortimer Taube is considered the most popular post-coordinate indexing model.

Pre-Coordinate Indexing versus Post-Coordinate Indexing

The subjects of documents are not simple. Compound and complex subjects deal with multiple numbers of concepts. When there is more than one concept in the document, the order in which we cite the concepts and their relationship to one another becomes important. Both pre- and post-coordinate indexing systems are, by nature, coordinate indexing, but the coordination is done in two different stages. The following table furnishes the points of differences between the two systems:

Pre-Coordinate Indexing System	Post-Coordinate Indexing System
Component terms are coordinated at the time of indexing (that is, at the input stage) in anticipation of the users' approach.	Component concepts (denoted by the terms) of a subject are kept separately and uncoordinated by the indexer, and the user coordinates the concepts at the time of searching.
The most important aspect of this indexing system is to determine the order of significance by following the syntactical rules of the given indexing language.	The rigidity of the significance order is very much absent in this system.
It is non-manipulative. The searcher has no choice but to try to predict the citation order specified by the indexer.	It is manipulative. The searcher has wide options for free manipulation of the classes at the time of searching in order to achieve whatever logical operations are required.
In this indexing system, both the indexer and the searcher are required to understand the mechanism of the system—the indexer for arriving at the most preferred citation order and the searcher for formulating an appropriate search strategy.	This indexing system does not require the indexer and searcher to understand the mechanism of the system. However, the operational aspects need to be understood by them.

Term Entry System and Item Entry System

In the term entry system, we prepare entries for a document under each of the appropriate subject headings and file these entries alphabetically. Here, terms are posted on the item (Term on Item System). In this type of post-coordinate indexing, the number of entries for a document depends on the number of terms associated with the thought content of the document. Searching two files (Term Profile and Document Profile) is required in this system. Uniterm and Peek-a-boo are examples of **Term Entry System and Item Entry System.** It is possible to take the opposite approach and make a single entry for each item, using a physical form that permits access to the entry from all appropriate headings. A system that works in this way is called an item entry system. Here, items are posted on the term (Item on Term System). In this type of post-coordinate indexing, a single entry is made for each item. Item entry system involves the searching of one file (Term Profile) only. The edge-notched card is an example of the item entry system.

Uniterm Indexing

The uniterm indexing system was devised by Mortimer Taube in 1953 to organise a collection of documents at the Armed Services Technical Information Agency (ASTIA) of the Atomic Energy Commission, Washington. Uniterm is a post-coordinate indexing system based on the term entry principle. Here, the component term (uniterm) is independent of all other terms and serves as a unique autonomous access point to all relevant items in the collection. Uniterm is a subject indexing system and its name is a contraction of 'unit' and 'term', referring to its use of single words as the basis of the index, the 'uniterms'. Taube referred to the overall concept as 'coordinate indexing', but today, the entire concept is generally referred to as Uniterm as well.

Uniterm is designed to allow rapid lookups on topic keywords and then cross-reference those keywords across multiple topics in order to find documents that match all of the terms. The result of a uniterm search is a set of accession numbers that can be used to retrieve the matching documents. Uniterm is based on existing accession numbers, so it is technically a post-coordinate system. This is opposed to a pre-coordinate system, where the subject of the document is given a particular number, as in the DDC. Uniterm was among the most popular post-coordinate indexing systems, although some of its success was due to Taube's company winning contracts to index huge technical libraries.

Uniterm Indexing Process

The processes involved in uniterm indexing are as follows:

(1) **Preparation of document profile:** Here, the indexer is required to prepare a card for each incoming document to:

- Assign an accession number or 'address' to each incoming document and record the same on the card;
- Identify the different component terms (uniterms) associated with the thought content of the document;
- Select the uniterms and record them on the card;
- Prepare an abstract for each document and record the abstract on the card;
- Write the bibliographical details of the document on the card; and
- Arrange all the cards as prepared for all incoming documents according to the ascending order of the accession numbers of the documents.

Cards so prepared and arranged according to the ascending order of the accession numbers of the documents are called document profiles.

(2) **Preparation of term profile:** Here, the indexer is required to:

- Prepare a card (term card) for each uniterm;
- Divide each term card into ten equal vertical columns (from zero to nine);
- Record the accession number of the document relevant to the uniterm according to the system of terminal digit posting. The terminal digit of the accession number determines the column of its posting; and
- Arrange all term cards according to the alphabetical order of the uniterms.

Term cards so prepared and arranged according to the alphabetical order of the uniterms are called the 'term profile' of the system.

(3) **Searching:** The process of searching in the uniterm system involves the following operations:

- Searcher identifies the different component terms/uniterms associated with the content of their queries.

- Searcher, after identifying the component terms/uniterms, pulls out the pertinent term cards from the alphabetical deck of the term profile.
- Term cards, thus pulled out, are matched to find the common accession number(s). The number(s) common in all such uniterm cards represent the sum total of the component concept of the specific subject.
- With the help of the common accession number(s), relevant card(s) are pulled out from the document profile, where full bibliographical information of the required document(s) is available.

Advantage and Disadvantage

The main advantage of the uniterm indexing system is its simplicity and the ease with which persons without much knowledge of subject indexing can handle it. The criticisms against the uniterm system centre around: (**a**) **Search time:** Involves much searching time because of the searching of two files—term profile and document profile; and (**b**) **False drops:** The possibility of retrieving irrelevant documents due to false coordination of uniterms. For example, searching with the uniterms 'Teachers', 'Students' and 'Evaluation' might retrieve documents on both the subjects, 'Evaluation of students by teachers' and 'Evaluation of teachers by students', one of which might be irrelevant to a particular user.

Keyword Indexing

Keyword indexing is based on using natural language terminology for generating the index entries. The term 'Keyword' refers to a significant or memorable word (also called 'catchword') that serves as a key in denoting the subject taken mainly from the title of the document (so, it is called title index) and sometimes from the abstract or text of the document. Common words like articles (a, an, the) and conjunctions (and, or, but) are not treated as keywords because it is inefficient to do so. This system is also known as Natural or Free Indexing language. It is to be pointed out here that the concept of keyword indexing is not new, and it existed in the nineteenth century as a 'catchword indexing'. With the introduction of computers in information retrieval in the 1950s, Hans Peter Luhn, an IBM engineer, presented a computer-produced index in 1958 that became known as. Key Word in Context Indexing (KWCI).

KWIC (KWCI)

The KWIC indexing system is based on the principle that the title of the document represents its contents. It is believed that the title of the document is a one-line abstract of the document. The significant words in the title indicate the subject of the document. A KWIC index makes an entry under each significant word in the title, along with the remaining part of the title, to keep the context intact. The entries are derived using terms one by one as the lead term along with the entire context for each entry.

The production of a KWIC index by H.P. Luhn is the earliest example of an automatic index produced using computers to perform repetitive tasks associated with subject indexing. It was a great step forward in the technique of automatic indexing. Utilizing the capabilities of computers, the KWIC method speedily and with a minimum of intellectual effort produces indexes derived solely from the titles of the documents to be analysed. All significant or keywords of titles/title-like phrases are alphabetised mechanically and then printed out, following a format that emphasises the selected word. The computer uses the 'stop-word' list in order to ignore all syntactical words, such as articles, prepositions, etc., and select the remaining words in the title as indexing words. The remaining words of the title are arranged to stand in the context of their original appearance. The use of a 'stop-word list' reduces the volume of the index.

The result of the machine manipulation is an index of key terms printed in alphabetical order, together with the text immediately surrounding each term. Each significant word as an entry point appears in the margin or a designated middle position while the rest of the title is printed on either side. The alphabetical filing is done on the basis of the keyword printed in bold letters.

Advantages and Disadvantages of KWIC

The KWIC method offers the following advantages:

- The detection of formulaic expressions and repeated word patterns
- Simplicity
- Speed
- Maximisation of computer use
- Minimisation of the indexer's role.

The most common type of complaint against the KWIC indexing method is the lack of terminology control as it is entirely dependent upon the title/abstract/text of the document. Apart from this, KWIC has basically two problems: (i) KWIC shows sentences that contain distant dependency in different contexts and (ii) KWIC also shows sentences that have different word order in different contexts. Other disadvantages can be summarized as follows:

- A large number of index entries under a given keyword, which provokes difficulties in searching.
- Lack of significant words in titles (therefore, the title and the abstract are often used as a source for indexing to increase the depth and range of indexing).
- No cross-references, which make it difficult to find synonyms, spelling variants and inflexions in the index.
- Relatively high computing time due to superfluous non-significant index entries.
- No combination of keywords.
- Lack of consistency in the indexing terms because different authors can use different forms of words to communicate the same idea or give different meanings to the same word or phrase.
- References are not grouped under a convenient heading.
- Redundancy of the index.

Variations of Keyword Indexing

Keyword out of context (KWOC): In KWOC, each index word is extracted from its context and printed separately in the left-hand margin, with the unmodified title in its normal order printed to the right.

Keyword augmented-in-context (KWAC) index: In KWAC, the keywords of the title are enriched with additional keywords taken either from the abstract or from the original text of the document and are inserted into the title or added at the end to generate further index entries.

Double KWIC: It is another improved version of KWIC. Double KWIC index is constructed in the following way: (a) The first significant word in a title is extracted as a main index term and replaced by an asterisk (*) to indicate its position in the title. (b) The remaining words in the title are then rotated so as to permit each significant word to appear as the first word of a wrap-around subordinate entry under the main index term. Steps 1 and 2 are repeated until all of the titles of a given bibliographic listing are processed.

Key-letter-in-context (KLIC) index: This type of index only takes fragmented words (that is, key letters), instead of the full word, either at the beginning or at the end of the entry.

Computerised Indexing

Computerised indexing can be defined as the process whereby a computer is used to process a natural language text already in machine-readable form so that indexing terms are allocated to its content without direct human intervention. The features of computerised indexing are as follows:

- Computerised indexing starts with words.
- Word association prompts the linking of target words in a search statement.
- Computers scan text and create an 'inverted file' that associates words in the file with the position in the text.
- Matches words in a search statement against 'inverted files' to identify texts that have words in common.

- Computer algorithms are used to carry out the above operations.
- Humans do the programming and set the parameters for indexing.
- Computation techniques used include word frequency and keyword analysis.
- Computerised indexing cannot replace human or manual indexing but is rather complementary.

Manual Indexing versus Computerised Indexing

Manual Indexing	Computerised Indexing
The human indexer analyses texts and selects terms for indexing.	Computer analysis of texts is carried out by following human instructions in the form of computer programming.
The human indexer interprets and encodes text and makes inferences and judgement in selecting index terms judiciously.	No text interpretation is possible as a computer cannot think and draw inferences like a human indexer.
Semantic, syntactical and contextual considerations govern the selection of indexing terms.	Computer algorithms are drawn to select or exclude a term by following the rules of semantic, syntactical and contextual connotations, like a human indexer.
Disagreement among indexers on the determination of the subject of a document as the process of determination of subjects might vary from one indexer to another indexer.	Determination of the subject of the document is a mechanical process based on what terms appear frequently and/ or prominently in the text—that is, the more frequently a term occurs in a document, the more likely it is that the document is about that term.
Selected index terms are fewer in numbers.	Selected index terms are more in number.
It is time-consuming.	It consumes less time.
It is expensive.	It is less costly.
It is very difficult to maintain consistency in indexing.	Consistency in indexing is maintained.
The relevancy of results is ensured.	The relevancy of results is not always ensured.
It generally maintains a balance in recall and precision.	It generally shows high recall and low precision.

Advantages and Disadvantages of Computerised Indexing

The advantages of computerised indexing are as follows:

- It is as effective as human indexing.
- It is cost-effective compared to expensive human indexing.
- It maintains consistency in indexing.
- Indexing time is reduced.
- It helps searchers find information quickly.
- It can be applied to large volumes of text (for example, indexing webpages).
- Retrieval effectiveness can be achieved.

The disadvantages are as follows:

- It is not flexible.
- It is not precise when looking at unique materials.
- It is not able to adapt to new terminology.
- It is not able to do the conceptual analysis of the content of the document.
- Not a term that occurs several times in a document will always be a significant term.

Components of Computerised Indexing System

A typical computerised indexing system has four major components:

(1) ***Database***: The database acts as the heart of a typical computerised indexing system. Bibliographic databases that deal with metadata of bibliographic entities (for example, author, title, subject, etc.) include two parts. The first part is a sequential file (a combination of fields —> records —> database), and the second is an inverted file (indexes to sequential file). Full-text databases, apart from the above two parts, also include fieldless information entities [source objects in different formats, such as webpages (HTML), PDF files, doc files, etc.].

(2) ***Search Process***: The database determines what can be retrieved, whereas the search mechanism determines how

information stored in databases can be retrieved. The efficiency of the search process is a very important factor for a computerised indexing system. The search process of a typical computerised indexing system provides two sets of retrieval techniques—basic retrieval techniques (Boolean operators: AND, OR, NOT; Relational operators: >, =, <=, and Positional search operators: NEAR, ADJ, NEARX, etc.) and advance techniques (weighted searching, fuzzy searching, etc.).

(3) ***Language of Indexing***: The search mechanism determines which retrieval techniques will be available to searchers, whereas computerised indexing language determines the flexibility in (1) document representation and (2) query representation. Computerised indexing language may be grouped as natural language and controlled vocabulary (classification, subject heading and thesauri).

(4) ***User Interface***: It is a layer of interaction between users and a computerised indexing system. The efficiency of the user interface depends on the mode of interaction, display features, online help, provision of feedback, etc. It is considered the human dimension of a computerised indexing system.

Categories of Computerised Indexing Systems

Since the time of H.P. Luhn (in the 1950s), different computerised indexing systems have evolved to address the information demands of different user groups. These indexing systems may be categorised as follows:

Category I: Online database indexing. These computerised indexing systems allow users to search databases located in remote places. Here, computer technologies are applied to process, store and retrieve records and communication technologies help access records from centralised databases.

Category II: Optical disk-based database indexing. These computerised indexing systems emerged from online IR systems. These IR systems offer a subset of data (bibliographical, numeric, full-text and multimedia) through optical media (like CD-ROM, DVD-ROM, etc.).

Category III: Online Public Access Catalogue (OPAC)-based indexing. An OPAC is an outer/external form of the library catalogue. OPACs are presently considered IR systems with their own characteristic features. For example, an OPAC is essentially local (serves library resources of one or more institutes) but can act as a global information entity by integrating other IR systems, such as CD-ROM databases, e-journals access, Z 39.50-based searching of other library catalogues, etc.

Category IV: Indexing Internet resources. The first three computerised indexing systems deal with structured objects (fields and field values), whereas the last one deals with unstructured information-bearing objects (textual objects without metadata). Internet-based computerised indexing systems are generally based on automatic harvesting devices, such as robots, spiders, crawlers, etc., for finding and gathering information resources available in publicly indexable Internet.

Artificial Intelligence (AI)-Based Indexing System

The application of AI in information retrieval research basically involves processing source text to identify the roles of words and phrases and the relationships between them. The results of this processing are used to identify appropriate indexing expressions. The following indexing system researches based on AI are evident:

1. **Natural language processing (NLP)-based indexing system:** The basic idea is to process the text of documents to generate indexing terms. The methods focus on the lexical level, attempting to identify grammatical classes or parts of speech of individual words together with machine-readable dictionaries to index documents.
2. **Expert system-based indexing system:** Expert systems have been used in information retrieval research in an attempt to replace what is usually referred to as the expert intermediary. The expertise referred to in this case is necessary to construct a search appropriate to the user's needs and the functioning of the system. The components, therefore, include knowledge of

how to interrogate the system, how to identify the appropriate search terms and how to link these terms.

Search Engine

Indexing Internet search engines are special websites that are designed to help people find information stored on other sites. A search engine searches a database of information on the web. It is a tool to help users locate information available via the Internet. There are differences in the ways various search engines work, but they all perform three basic tasks:

- They search the Internet—or select pieces of the Internet—based on important words.
- They keep an index of the words they find and where they find them.
- They allow users to look for words or combinations of words found in that index.

To find information on the hundreds of millions of webpages that exist, a search engine employs special software robots called spiders (other names for these programs are crawler, worm, wanderer, gatherer, etc.), which traverse the web, following links between pages. It builds the list of the words found on websites. When a spider is building its lists, the process is called web crawling. In order to build and maintain a useful list of words, a search engine's spiders have to look at a lot of pages.

Search Engine Categories

Search engines may be divided into the following main categories:

General search engine: It covers a range of services and compiles its own searchable databases on the web. For example, Google, Alta Vista, etc.

Regional search engine: It refers to a country-specific search engine for locating varied resources region-wise. For example, Euro Ferret (Europe), Excite uk (UK), etc.

Meta-search engine: A meta-search engine does not use a crawler for compiling its own searchable database. These search engines utilise databases maintained by other individual search engines. When a query is put before this type of search engine, it forwards that query to other search engines. Examples of such search engines are Dogpile, Ask Jeeves, Inference Find, MetaCrawler, Profusion and Surfwax.

Subject-specific search engine: It does not attempt to index the entire web. Instead, it focuses on searching for websites or webpages within a defined subject area, geographical area or type of resource. For example, Geo index (Geography/ Environmental science), Biochemistry Easy Search Tool (Biochemistry), etc. Because this specific search engine aims for depth of coverage within a single area rather than breadth of coverage across subjects, they are often able to index documents that are not included even in the largest search engine databases. Some examples of subject-specific search engines are Bioweb (Biotechnology), Scirus (Science and Technology) and Medical World Search.

Directory-based search engine: Due to the explosion of information over the Internet, it is felt that the results fetched by search engines are often mixed with unwanted ones. Subject directories, unlike search engines, are created and maintained by human editors, not electronic spiders or robots. Examples of such search engines are Yahoo, Google, LookSmart, Magellan, Open Directory and Project.

Subject/Information Gateway

A subject/information gateway is a website that provides searchable and browsable access to online resources focused on a specific subject. Subject gateway resource descriptions are usually created manually rather than being generated via an automated process. There are two kinds of gateways: Library gateways and portals. Library gateways are collections of databases and informational sites arranged by subject that have been assembled, reviewed and recommended by specialists, usually librarians. These gateway collections support research and reference needs by identifying and pointing to recommended, academically-oriented pages on the web. Some notable examples of library gateways are Librarians' Index to the Internet, Internet

Public Library, Academic Information, WWW Virtual Library, Digital Librarian, Infomine, etc.

Semantic Web

Search engines usually employ statistical methods, like frequency of occurrence of words, co-occurrence of words, etc., that retrieve a number of irrelevant hits against a search on the web. Though some search engines, like Google and Yahoo, use human-edited entries; still, they come up with a large number of wrong hits. Tim Berners-Lee introduced the concept of the Semantic Web to extend the web with semantic information. The idea behind Semantic Web is to develop technologies that make the information more meaningful for machines to process, which, in turn, makes the search and retrieval of information more effective for searchers. The conception of the Semantic Web is characterized by developing tools and technologies like languages, standards and protocols so that the web becomes meaningful.

Taxonomies

Taxonomies can be considered another tool useful for organising web-based information. For example, taxonomies provide an excellent means for organising subject-specific information into an easily navigable format. The utility of taxonomies for displaying web information can also be found when examining Yahoo's site, which uses a taxonomy/subject hierarchy to classify its indexed information.

EXERCISE UNIT 9 – UNIT 11

1. What do you mean by subject indexing?
2. What are the purpose and objectives of subject indexing?
3. How is subject indexing different from cataloguing?
4. What do you understand by indexing principles? Discuss their need and purpose.
5. Highlight the problems faced while indexing.
6. Discuss the criteria for the evaluation of an indexing system.

7. Define indexing language.
8. How is indexing language different from natural language?
9. Discuss in detail the structure of an indexing language.
10. What are the attributes of an indexing language?
11. What are the different types of indexing languages? Discuss in detail.
12. What do you understand by a subject heading list?
13. What are the general principles for assigning subject headings?
14. What do you understand by thesaurus? Discuss basic thesaural relationships.
15. Define thesaurofacet.
16. Discuss LCSH.
17. What are the types of headings in LCSH?
18. Discuss the merits of LCSH.
19. Discuss different types of indexing techniques.
20. What do you understand by chain indexing? Discuss the steps involved in chain indexing.
21. What do you understand by PRECIS? Discuss its objectives and features.
22. Discuss major working concepts of POPSI.
23. Write down the steps involved in POPSI.
24. Differentiate between pre-coordinate indexing and post-coordinate indexing.
25. Define KWIC and KWOK.

Unit 12

Conceptual Changes: Impact of Technology

Knowledge Organisation

Knowledge organisation (KO), organisation of knowledge, organisation of information or information organisation is an intellectual discipline concerned with activities such as document description, indexing, and classification that serve to provide systems of representation and order for knowledge and information objects. According to *The Organization of Information* by Joudrey and Taylor, information organisation "examines the activities carried out and tools used by people who work in places that accumulate information resources (e.g., books, maps, documents, datasets, images) for the use of humankind, both immediately and for posterity". It discusses the processes in place to make resources findable, whether someone is searching for a single known item or browsing through hundreds of resources just hoping to discover something useful. Information organisation supports a myriad of information-seeking scenarios. By examining the trends in scholarly persuasions under the socio-economic and technological influences, we have traced the six stages of KO development with their characteristic features.

1. Antiquity: Lists
2. Middle Ages: Inventories
3. Seventeenth Century: Finding lists
4. Nineteenth Century: Collocating devices

5. Twentieth Century: Automation and codification
6. Twenty-first Century: Social and collaborative tagging

Knowledge Organisation System (KOS)

The term 'Knowledge Organisation System' was coined by the Networked Knowledge Organisation Systems Working Group at the ACM Digital Libraries 098 Conference in Pittsburgh, Pennsylvania. KOS does not include anything more than what KO does, other than its emphasis on the system. In a general way, KOS refers to the semantic tools that present the organised interpretation of knowledge structures. KOS, concept system or concept scheme is a generic term used in KO for authority files, classification schemes, thesauri, topic maps, ontologies and similar works. Despite their differences in type, coverage and application, all KOSs aim to support the organization of knowledge and information to facilitate their management and retrieval. The core elements of most KOSs can be expressed in Resource Description Framework (RDF) with the Simple Knowledge Organization System (SKOS). Many lists of KOSs exist, with BARTOC being the largest and most general one.

KOS: Types

There are different possible systems for organising digital libraries. Their descriptions are given below based on characteristics such as structure and complexity, relationships among terms and historical function. KOSs are grouped into three general categories: Term lists, classification and categorization and relationship groups.

1. *Term Lists*

These include:

Authority files: Authority files are lists of terms used to control the variant names for an entity or the domain value for a particular field. Examples include names for countries, individuals and organisations. The presentation may be alphabetical or organised by a shallow classification scheme. Specific examples of authority files include the LC Name Authority File, SLSH, and the Getty Geographic Authority File.

Glossaries: A glossary is a list of terms, usually with definitions. The terms might be from a specific subject field or those used in a particular work. Examples including the EPA Terms of the Environment, the ALA glossary of LIS, etc.

Gazetteers: A gazetteer is a dictionary of place names. Traditional gazetteers have been published as books or appear as indexes to atlases. Each entry might also be identified by feature types, such as river, city or school. An example is the Geographic Names Information Service, The Columbia Gazetteer of the World.

Dictionaries: Dictionaries are alphabetical lists of terms and their definitions that provide variant senses for each term, where applicable. A dictionary also sometimes provides synonyms and, through definitions, related terms. There was, however, no explicit hierarchical structure or attempt to group terms by the concept.

2. *Classification and Categorization*

These include:

Subject headings: Subject heading lists can be extensive, covering a broad range of subjects. However, the structure of these lists is generally shallow, with a limited hierarchy. The subject headings are pre-coordinated, with rules for constructing headings narrowing down the scope of a concept. Examples include the Medical Subject Headings (MeSH) and the LCSH.

Classification schemes, taxonomies: In general, these types of KOSs provide ways to separate entities into buckets or relatively broad topics. Some examples provide a hierarchical arrangement of numeric or alphabetic notation to represent broad topics. These types of KOSs lack the explicit relationships presented in a thesaurus. Examples of well-liked classification schemes include LCC, DDC and UDC. Subject categories are often used to group thesaurus terms in broad topic sets outside the hierarchical scheme of the thesaurus. Taxonomies are increasingly being used in object-oriented design and knowledge management systems to indicate any grouping of objects based on a particular characteristic.

3. *Relationship Groups*

These include:

Thesauri: These KOSs are based on concepts, and they show relationships between terms. Relationships commonly expressed in a thesaurus include hierarchy, equivalence, and associative (or related). These relationships are generally represented by the notation of broader terms, narrower terms, synonyms and associative or related terms. Associative relationships might be more granular in some schemes. For example, the Unified Medical Language System (UMLS) provides over 40 associative relationships.

Semantic networks: Semantic network is one of the most significant developments in the area of natural language processing technology. Here, the concepts and terms are not positioned as hierarchies but as a network or a web. Concepts are thought of as nodes with various relationships branching out from them. These include specific relationships of whole-part, cause-effect, parent-child, etc., instead of standard BT, NT and RT. Princeton's WorldNet is a grand example of a semantic network.

Ontologies: In general, ontology is the study or concern about what kinds of things exist—what entities exist in the universe. In information technology, ontology is the working model of entities and interactions in some particular domain of knowledge or practices, such as electronic commerce or 'the activity of planning'. We may define ontology as a specification of conceptualisations used to help programs and humans share knowledge. Ontologies are being developed as specific concept models by the knowledge management community.

Planning KOSs

A KOS is planned by going through multiple processes. These are discussed below:

1. Analysing users' needs: For any type of library, print-dominated or digital, the planning process starts from the assessment of users' needs in terms of content and functionality. Everything else, in terms of resources and service programs, grows out of the users' needs. Therefore, apart from the need to organise the in-house collections, planning must be done to establish possible links between contents within and outside the digital library walls. Since KOSs are to act as intermediate authority files, links must always show their relationship to user needs.

2. Locating KOSs: After mapping the user needs decisively, the next task is to locate suitable KOSs, if any, that exist. It is preferable to use an existing KOS because building KOSs is a costly and time-consuming proposition. The value of a KOS comes from its user community when they appreciate it. By creating a control zone, that is, by selecting some objects and excluding others, information professionals use their expertise to bring users to documents that hold a particular value. The selection policy must acknowledge the users' behaviour. In users' assessments, the sources built by learned societies, professional associations or standards groups stand out as more trustworthy than those built in-house.

3. Planning the infrastructure: In the context of the digital library, the physical location of the KOS is a critical factor for deciding upon the architecture of KOS. The position of KOS depends on the physical location—whether it will be held externally or internally. Both have their own advantages and disadvantages. If KOS is held internally, that is, in a controlled zone, classification, thesaurus and ontologies need to be hand-picked cautiously by applying selection criteria, professional expertise and users' feedback. On the positive side, the KOS is under more local control. Therefore, it might be possible to improve the response time by not accessing the KOS over the Internet. If the KOS is to be used behind the scenes, concerns about speed and integration become more important. If the system is available in an open zone on the web, the architecture of KOS, as an external system, requires a script to locate the resource. One must then launch a query against the resource to obtain the piece of information that will serve as the key between the two files. A query might be necessary if the KOS is stored in a database. The script might transfer log-on information (including user ID and password) from the digital library system to the external KOS in order to provide access to the web-enabled database.

4. Change, upgradation and version updation: Like any social or intellectual organisation, an unexpected change in the organisation and content of the system poses problems. Therefore, there should be a planning process to continue behind the scenes to predict and implement changes systematically. Few areas warrant constant review. The software or telecommunications route between the digital library server and the KOS might prove unreliable. The KOS might be obtained from the owner and found tricky when loaded locally. In many cases, this requires licensing that may not be required when the KOS is accessed remotely. If the KOS uses special software, such as a database management system, loading the KOS locally will require a copy of that software, which might involve added costs toward purchase or licensing. Besides KOS installation, there are other systems-related problems, like firewalls and interface design.

There is yet another way of updating KOSs, known as the transaction-based approach, whereby only changed components are transferred by the KOS provider to the library. This, however, requires that the system provider have the necessary infrastructural facilities to effect these transactions on time.

5. Presenting the KOS to the user: KOS architecture must accommodate the character sets of the incoming sources. This is particularly important if a data string, in ASCII or mark-up language, has been used to represent special characters and diacritical marks. Systems developed in Unicode, which generously accommodate all the existing scripts of languages worldwide, have decisively removed the age-old constraints of inter-lingual communications.

The KOS can be exposed to the user in different ways. On the website of the digital library, KOS-related themes or categories may be clustered logically for users' view and interactions. The KOS may be used at a higher level to identify specific portals launched by different user communities. If the content of the digital library includes metadata records, the

KOS may be displayed as index terms on the records or as an independent navigation tool. KOS may also remain transparent.

Semantic Web

The World Wide Web, or the web, is an embodiment of human knowledge. Technically speaking, the web comprises all the resources and Internet users that are using the Hypertext Transfer Protocol (HTTP). The Semantic Web is an extension of the current web designed to help us find, share and combine information more easily through the process of Knowledge Organisation (KO).

The Semantic Web, sometimes known as Web 3.0, is an extension of the World Wide Web through standards set by the World Wide Web Consortium (W3C). The goal of the Semantic Web is to make Internet data machine-readable. To enable the encoding of semantics with the data, technologies such as Resource Description Framework (RDF) and Web Ontology Language (OWL) are used. These technologies are used to formally represent metadata. For example, ontology can describe concepts, relationships between entities and categories of things. These embedded semantics offer significant advantages, such as reasoning over data and operating with heterogeneous data sources.

Semantic Web Activity

The World Wide Web Consortium (W3C), an international consortium, is primarily responsible for the creation and development of web standards and guidelines. With the development of the Resource Description Framework (RDF), Web Ontology Language (OWL), and Simple Knowledge Organisation System (SKOS), the W3C Semantic Web Activity promotes the deployment of technologies for expressing, exchanging and processing metadata in a form processable by machines. The Dublin Core and related vocabularies of the Dublin Core Metadata Initiative (DCMI) represent a crucial contribution to this growing suite of standards. The W3C's Semantic Web Activity has stimulated a new field of integrative research and technology development at the boundaries between database systems, formal logic and the World Wide Web. One facet of the Semantic Web vision is the hope of better organising the vast amounts of unstructured (that is, human-readable) information on the web, providing new routes to discovering and sharing that information.

Simple Knowledge Organisation System (SKOS)

Simple Knowledge Organisation System (SKOS) is a data-sharing standard that bridges different fields of knowledge, technology and practice. SKOS aims to connect dispersed communities and the Semantic Web by transferring existing Knowledge Organisation (KO) models to the Semantic Web technology context. Looking to the future, Simple Knowledge Organisation System (SKOS) occupies a position between the exploitation and analysis of unstructured information, the informal and socially-mediated organisation of information on a large scale and the formal representation of knowledge.

Unit 13

Online Catalogues: Design and Services

Physical Catalogue

Around 4000 years ago, libraries existed in Sumer and other ancient regions. Those libraries stored collections of stone tablets and had their catalogues as well. Early catalogues were mostly inventory lists, all hand-written until libraries started printing their catalogues in book form. The popularity of printed catalogues grew for their easy handling and storage. However, the librarians experienced difficulties in keeping their catalogues up-to-date. Production of printed catalogues was time-consuming, labour-intensive and expensive.

Librarians found a solution in card catalogue. In 1860, Harvard Librarian John Langdon Sibley introduced a card catalogue for public use. Card catalogue stayed as the most effective form of catalogue for a century.

In the early 1960s, the LC developed a machine-readable cataloguing system with a new set of rules for machine manipulation. They did it to transfer their massive bibliographic records into electronic format. Although the development of an online catalogue was not their immediate objective, this initiative paved the way to build an online catalogue with the support of advancing telecommunications computing technology. It took more than three decades for libraries to reach the era of online catalogues.

Descriptive Catalogue

Along with the changes in the physical shapes and media, the rules governing the arrangement of bibliographic descriptive elements have been continuously evolving. The first age of descriptive cataloguing began with Panizzi and included Cutter. Michael Gorman labelled it as 'the age of the single-author code'. Before Anthony Panizzi's *Rules for the Compilation of the Catalogue*, printed in 1841, there had been no serious and successful attempt to construct comprehensive code for cataloguing. Many contemporaries of Panizzi, such as Thomas Carlyle, thought of a catalogue as a simple listing of authors and book titles. They found his rules unnecessary. Charles Ammi Cutter's *Rules for a Dictionary Catalogue*, published in 1876, has a deep impact on the development of cataloguing principles and methodologies. We can trace FRBR's development in Cutter's cataloguing code.

The second age of descriptive cataloguing was 'the era of the committee code', as Gorman called it. The year 1908 was important in cataloguing—the ALA and the Library Association of the United Kingdom published a set of common cataloguing rules.

The third age of descriptive cataloguing began in 1967 with the release of AACR. It was an international (American, Australian, British, Canadian) standardisation of descriptive cataloguing rules, with a philosophy based on the Paris Principles.

Cataloguing Standards

The three cataloguing standards produced during the third age, namely MARC, ISBD and AACR2, are presently being critically reviewed by professional bodies and experts. The MARC format came out after a long trial, with valid promises to carry on bibliographic record sharing at a large scale. The IFLA published a standard specification for bibliographic description (ISBD) in 1971. ISBD was originally constructed as a means of standardising the presentation of descriptive data so that it could be machine-translated into MARC. In 1978, AACR2 reached a historic agreement between the North American and the British library associations and published the two sets of rules as a continuous single-text document. These three standards, which serve as the bedrock of cataloguing as of now, began in the card catalogue environment and embedded specifications well-suited for the physical catalogue of 5′ × 3′ cards.

Electronic Catalogue

Michael Gorman considered that the confluence of a need (national and research libraries throughout the world needing less expensive and more current cataloguing) and a means (automation and, more specifically, the MARC format) that has brought us nearer to UBC than anyone would have been dreamt possible thirty years ago.

In the early 60s, the LC had developed a schematic design to help transfer its card catalogue records into a newly installed computer. The design provided a way to pass on coded instructions to the computer, made of numbers, letters and special characters, along with bibliographic data. This was how MARC began. During the span of four decades, the LC, with collaborators, enriched MARC in terms of document types and contents. They enhanced its structural design to accommodate requirements of all kinds of recorded knowledge—from prehistoric artefacts to Web publications.

Online Catalogue

The definition of an online catalogue is simple. It is a catalogue in electronic (machine-readable) format accessible online. The term ‘online’ means ‘connected to a computer network or accessible by computer’. The recent technological boom has empowered libraries to exploit computer and communication facilities to their best advantage and implement MARC standards for the interchange of bibliographic information between databases. Besides an institutional will, what the libraries need most is the knowledge and skill to develop MARC-compliant databases addressing local as well as global requirements.

Next-Generation Catalogue

The technology of Web 2.0 has opened up alternative ways to develop many different search models for bibliographic databases. Quite a few successful catalogue systems are already visible online, though still in the experimental stage. They:

- Give the patron a simple search interface that allows the user to enter vague, broad and simple searches;
- Allow the patron to drill down through the large result list, narrowing it down by whatever criteria they choose, until it is as precise as they want, to sort the results list so that the most relevant items are at the top of the list; and
- Are tolerant of misspellings and unusual word choices in the patron's search.

The list shows what patrons desire to get and what the next-generation catalogues can provide. Next-generation catalogues give patrons the same tools they already enjoy on websites. Since library databases are generally built in compliance with MARC, they look beyond integrated library systems and will have little problem working with a variety of systems.

Online Catalogue: Definition

An online catalogue is a library catalogue consisting of a collection of bibliographic records in machine-readable format. In other words, it is a machine-readable catalogue, by definition, and something more. It needs to be maintained in a dedicated computer that provides uninterrupted interactive access via terminals or workstations in direct, continuous communication with the central computer. In short, it is a catalogue in an electronic (machine-readable) format accessible online. The term 'online' means 'connected to a computer network or accessible by computer'. For example, when you are connected to the Internet, you are online. When you search British Library Catalogue, you search an online database. An online database needs two common record formats: A physical format and a logical format. The common physical format serves as a vehicle to carry records of bibliographic data to remote computers. The common logical format, on the other hand, ensures that the recorded data are stored and interpreted correctly at remote ends.

MARC

MARC standards are a set of digital formats for the description of items catalogued by libraries, such as books, DVDs and digital resources. Computerized library catalogues and library management software need to structure their catalogue records as per an industry-wide standard, that is, MARC, so that bibliographic information can be shared freely between computers. The structure of bibliographic records almost universally follows the MARC standard. Other standards work in conjunction with MARC. For example, AACR/RDA provide guidelines on formulating bibliographic data into the MARC record structure, while the ISBD provides guidelines for displaying MARC records in a standard, human-readable form.

The key to the machine-readability is the common record format. MARC follows a physical structure and a set of control mechanisms for enabling the machine to identify and process the data elements whenever needed. This physical data structuring scheme, originally developed as a carrier of MARC data, is now being used as a standard, nationally (ANSIZ39.2) and internationally (ISO2709), by other communication formats for bibliographic information interchange, like UNIMARC, CCF, national MARCs, etc. They all are implementations of the ANSIZ39.2/ISO2709 standard.

MARC-Compliant Database

MARC database and MARC-compliant database are not the same. A MARC database contains a sequential file of hierarchically arranged records following ANSIZ39.2/ISO2709 specifications and MARC-defined content designation for every field in every record. On the other hand, a MARC-compliant database may be a relational, or a different model, holding records comprising elements equivalent to MARC fields by definition. A database compliant with MARC can transform its records into MARC communication format and exchange records with any MARC database or with another MARC-compliant database, while a database not compliant with MARC cannot do so.

Resource Sharing Initiative

In the manual environment, libraries had no other option but to invest a huge staff and time in creating catalogue entries of their own for every document they acquire. When MARC files became available, individual libraries with no computer facility started buying computer-printed cards from the LC. In due course, more and more libraries installed computers. Those who designed their databases in compliance with MARC preferred to download MARC from the LC or from other bibliographic utilities, like OCLC, WLN, RLIN and A-G Canada. The agencies extended their online services based on their high-power mainframe systems against fee-plus-communication costs. Output was a magnetic tape containing bibliographic information tagged in a modified MARC 21 format. The academic institutions, having sufficient funds and sophisticated library software, joined bibliographic utilities. They enjoyed the benefit of sharing their collective resources by downloading and contributing MARC records. With the advancement of information technology, computer systems are getting more powerful, affordable and friendlier day by day. Libraries have found automated systems are cost-effective and efficient, and resource sharing is the key to solving the problem of unleashed proliferation of information and ever-increasing information price.

Importance and Advantages of MARC

It is important for the implementing agencies to note the plus points of MARC, particularly MARC 21, and its advantages over other bibliographic exchange formats, like UNIMARC, CCF, and national MARCs. These points have been elaborated below.

MARC is a collaborative effort. The MARC scheme, with its massive structure and exceedingly ambitious planning for upgrading its capabilities, depends on the active participation of expert agencies. Primarily, the LC is responsible for the creation and upkeep of the scheme. The National Agricultural Library, National Library of Medicine, United States Government Printing Office and National Library of Canada, together with the LC, serve as sources of authoritative cataloguing and provide most of the codes and standards used for MARC cataloguing.

MARC is one of the very few international schemes that sustain the tempo of development and continuously update its resources. It stands current and serves as a reliable processing instrument for machine-readable cataloguing. The LC made no revisions in MARC specifications unilaterally. Two committees were set up to review and update MARC 21 format documentation. One is the MARC Advisory Committee, and the other is the Machine-Readable Bibliographic Information (MARBI) Committee of the ALA.

MARC 21 embraces all media of documents in its scheme. In 1970, the Library of Congress issued specifications for magnetic tapes containing monographic records in MARC II format, as they named it. The first document published with USMARC in the title appeared in 1990. After a decade, a revised edition of the USMARC format for bibliographic data, MARC 21, was produced in collaboration with the British Library and the National Library of Canada. As its variant name suggests, the revised format aims to meet the challenge of the twenty-first century.

There is hardly anything in MARC that falls outside the scope of standardisation. Being a bibliographic information interchange format, MARC, in principle, does not dictate the use of any particular standard but allows its users to follow any one of the available standards or authorities, especially for data rendering, choice of access points, codes, classifications and choice of subject heading, name authorities, etc. MARC Program for Cooperative Cataloguing (PCC), as an international cooperative effort, emphasises greater flexibility in tailoring the local cataloguing practice to local needs and priorities while maintaining relative standards.

MARC databases are multiplying. The LC, the official depository of US publications, is a principal source of cataloguing records for US and international publications. The OCLC shared database, another enormous source of MARC records, available online for downloading against fees. Apart from these, many public and institutional libraries in the US, Canada, Britain and Australia offer MARC records, often at no cost. The population of MARC databases is growing fast. In India, under government patronage, MARC 21 implementations are in progress in a number of libraries, including the National Library of India. The increase in accessibility of MARC records tends to boost MARC implementations in turn.

Schematic Design

In the early 60s, the LC developed a schematic design to help transfer its card catalogue records into a newly installed computer. The design provided a way to pass on coded instructions to the computer, made of numbers, letters and special characters, along with bibliographic data. The computer requires all those for identifying cataloguing data elements and reproducing LC catalogue cards and tapes for distribution among the member institutions. This was how MARC began. The communication format of the MARC records, in the beginning, was suitable for encoding the bibliographic elements of books in Roman script. During the span of four decades, the LC, with collaborators, enriched MARC in terms of document types and contents. They enhanced its structural design to accommodate the requirements of all kinds of recorded knowledge—from prehistoric artefacts to web publications.

Union catalogues comprising MARC records can be generated and maintained efficiently by using MARC 21 holding format. MARC 21 bibliographic format offers full coverage of bibliographic elements related to every possible type of document. Its integrated design allows records of varied types and sizes to be kept together and searched together.

Bibliographic and Other Related Formats

For efficient management of bibliographic data in a networking environment, five separate formats are defined to handle five types of data: Bibliographic, holdings, authority, classification and community information.

1. Bibliographic format: MARC 21 Format for Bibliographic Data is central to the MARC system. It is an integrated format defined for the identification and description of different forms of bibliographic material, no more restricted to monographs as it was but extends specifications in detail for encoding elements of documents of any description, shape and material type, such as books, serials, computer files, maps, music, visual materials, websites, databases and mixed materials.

2. Holding format: The format for holdings data serves as a subset of bibliographic format. It contains that portion of format specifications that a library might require for encoding data elements pertinent to the holdings and physical location of the items the library holds.

3. Authority format: This is a format of the authority record. Libraries maintain the files of records as cataloguing tools. Authority records help input consistently and uniformly personal and corporate names and subject headings, which serve as preferred access points in records. Format specifications for encoding these bibliographic elements standardise the textual representations of these bibliographic elements and ensure data consistency—a precondition for effective search.

4. Classification format: MARC 21 Format for Classification Data contains format specifications for encoding classification numbers and their descriptive terms. It serves as an in-house tool for maintaining consistency in library classification and helps catalogue search by class numbers and browsing books on shelves.

5. Community information format: Format for community information provides format specifications for records containing house-keeping information, events, programs, services, etc., required for running circulation system and other library management programs.

Implementing MARC

The people working with MARC standards, directly or indirectly, stand responsible for the success and failure of MARC in playing its primary role, which is to develop sharable bibliographic resources. The software developers building MARC utility programs, the database vendors distributing

MARC records and the professionals cataloguing MARC records must know MARC adequately to do their part responsibly. In implementing a MARC-compliant library automation system, it is important that the people at the top acquire a clear-cut understanding of MARC to support their decision-making and help them see that:

- Their library management package is demonstratively MARC-compliant and includes efficient MARC utility programs.
- MARC data files, whenever downloaded from external sources, hold no substandard records.
- MARC cataloguers work proficiently, adhering to MARC specifications.

Metadata

Metadata is 'data that provides information about other data', but not the content of the data, such as the text of a message or the image itself. There are many distinct types of metadata, including:

- **Descriptive metadata:** It provides descriptive information about a resource. It is used for discovery and identification. It includes elements such as title, abstract, author and keywords.
- **Structural metadata:** It is the metadata about containers of data and indicates how compound objects are put together. For example, how pages are ordered to form chapters. This metadata describes the types, versions, relationships and other characteristics of digital materials.
- **Administrative metadata:** It provides the information to help manage a resource, like resource type, permissions and when and how it was created.
- **Reference metadata:** It provides information about the contents and quality of statistical data.
- **Statistical metadata:** Also called process data, it describes processes that collect, process or produce statistical data.

- **Legal metadata:** It provides information about the creator, copyright holder and public licensing, if provided.

Metadata is not strictly bound to one of these categories, as it can describe a piece of data in many other ways. In 2004, NISO defined METADATA as "Structured information that describes, explains, locates, or otherwise makes it easier to retrieve, use or manage information objects". It is machine-understandable and supports a wide range of operations.

Cataloguing Metadata Tools

There are many metadata tools for cataloguing networked resources, and many of them are dependent on the nature and type of resources. The typology of metadata can be mapped in the following way:

- Data structure: Dublin Core, MODS, CDWA, VRA and LOM
- Data content: AACR2, RDA, FRBR, CCO and CDPDCMBP
- Data value: LCSH, AAT, TGN, LCTGM, ULAN and W3CDTF
- Data format: XML, SGML and MARC
- Data presentation: ISBD, CSS and/or XSLT

Here, we briefly introduce the core sets of metadata developed particularly for online cataloguing, namely AACR/ RDA and MARC, and two more related standards, namely ISBD and FRBR.

AACR

AACR is a content standard for bibliographic description and access. It covers not just books but all other print formats as well. Rules for each category of material specify what fields should be used and what data to include in each field. Text strings were originally intended for printed catalogue cards. The key principles of AACR are:

- One principle entry per resource,
- Catalogue from item in hand, and
- The chief source of information.

It all began with the publication of UK and US editions in 1967. The unified second edition, consistent with ISBD specifications, was published in 1978. The major breakthrough was achieved in 1997 at the Toronto conference on AACR2. Next year, the FRBR was brought out. In 2005, RDA was developed. AACR2, in its first part, deals with bibliographic descriptions: General rules, resource-specific rules, and rules regarding analytical entries. The second part deals with the choice and construction of access points.

RDA

RDA stands for 'Resource Description and Access', the new standard that replaced AACR2. The primary purpose of using RDA is to analyse the knowledge resource being described and determine the type of content; its carrier form; other resources it relates to; persons, families or corporate bodies, it relates to concepts, events and places to RDA rules apply to all content types and all media types.

The aims of RDA are as follows:

- Should be easy to use and interpret;
- Should be applicable to an online, networked environment;
- Should provide effective bibliographic control for all types of media;
- Should encourage use beyond the library community;
- Should be compatible with other similar standards;
- Should have a logical structure based on internationally agreed principles;
- Should separate content and carrier data.

RDA timeline: The RDA Prospectus was issued along with a draft of some chapters in 2005. During the next two years, further drafts of chapters on description and access were issued. At the 2008 IFLA conference, a screenshot demo was presented. The launch of the online product was scheduled in early 2009.

MARC

MARC is a communication and exchange format that provides a structure for encoding the content of bibliographic and authority data. The MARC format was developed in the late 1960s as a tagging scheme for exchanging catalogue records on magnetic tape. It remains the standard way to represent such data. At present, MARC is steadily being converted (slowly) to modern computing formats, such as Unicode, Extensible Markup Language (XML) (discussed earlier as well), etc.

ISBD

The ISBD is a set of rules produced by IFLA to describe a wide range of library materials within the context of a catalogue. One of the original purposes of the ISBD was to provide a standard form of bibliographic description that could be used to exchange records internationally. This would support IFLA's UBC program.

ISBD timeline: ISBD was developed by IFLA from 1969 onwards. The consolidated edition of the ISBD was published in 2007. It superseded earlier separate ISBDs published for monographs, older monographic publications, cartographic materials, serials and other continuing resources, electronic resources, non-book materials and printed music. IFLA's ISBD Review Group is responsible for maintaining the ISBD. ISBD defined seven areas of description, their sequential order and associated punctuations: (1) Title; (2) Statement of Responsibility; (3) Edition; (4) Resource-specific information; (5) Publication details; (6) Physical description; (7) Series information; and (8) Notes and standard identifiers (optional).

FRBR

FRBR is a product of the logical progression of thought, initiated one and half a century ago, on how to organise the catalogue in this challenging information age.

FRBR timeline: FRBR was prepared by IFLA in 1998. From 1992 to 1995, the IFLA Study Group on FRBR developed an entity-relationship model as a generalised view of the bibliographic universe intended to be independent of any cataloguing code or implementation.

FRBR aims: The idea behind the FRBR conceptual model is that the catalogue is not seen as a sequence of records but rather as a network of connected data. FRBR clarifies how catalogues should function and illuminates what information is of the most value to the users of the catalogue.

OPAC

OPAC, or simply a library catalogue, is a digital database of materials held by a library or group of libraries, such as text files, e-books, journals, etc. Patrons can use the online library cataloguing software to find out any item under the control of a library. It displays the query search results in an easy-to-understand format to enable patrons to find digital material quickly. Online catalogues have largely replaced the analogue card catalogues previously used in libraries. For all practical purposes, we may define OPAC as a computer terminal at the user end, providing a friendly interface for searching, retrieving and viewing the machine-readable cataloguing data in eye-readable text format. Web 2.0 technology helped decouple the user interface from the back-end systems that support all internal operations of a library, including the management of databases and services.

OPAC in Next-Generation Web Catalogue

There are quite a few next-generation library interfaces now available on the Internet. Those are still in their early stages of development but have already demonstrated the revolutionised ways in which libraries can interact with users. These interfaces are easy-to-use, look impressive and take a sophisticated approach to find information and put the details on view helpfully. Some of the most innovative projects, like Endeca, Encore, Extensible Catalogue, Aqua Browser Library and Koha, are now working in several forward-looking institutions.

Search Tools

Basic expectations from a web-based interface are that it should provide the user with search results in order of relevancy ranking, facets (automatically generated terms that can be clicked to narrow results), corrections of misspellings and suggestions to alternative search terms. To meet these expectations, the new generation library interfaces offer relevance ranking; faceted navigation; search result clustering; breadcrumb trails; and a faster, more friendly search environment. Each has its strengths. By critically examining the key concepts, features and techniques associated with these tools, librarians should be able to identify the essential elements of a successful search interface that libraries can adapt to their systems.

Relevance Ranking

Whoever searches the Internet often becomes used to the idea of relevance ranking, where the best and most interesting items rise to the top of their hit list. This is because all the giant search engines on the web, like Google and Yahoo!, work this way. Relevance ranking works satisfactorily when it comes through careful refinement of the formulae that determine the ordering of results. One must develop skills to achieve a good relevance ranking. With relevance ranking, users might expect to get a large result set. That does not make them upset. They know, by looking up the top of the first page, where the most relevant information should be found. In fact, most users do not notice how big the result set is. In spite of the great advantage of relevance ranking, users might often need to sort the search hits by title, author, date or some other elements. The provision of sorting by elements of users' choice is another attractive feature of the new OPAC.

Faceted Navigation

A well-constructed faceted navigation scheme will allow users to quickly drill down from a broad set of results to a manageable group of results. The search interface selects the facets from metadata associated with the items in the body of information. Names, subject headings, publication dates and other fields from a structured record provide good opportunities for generating facets. There has been considerable interest in the faceted application of subject terminology, an alternative way of applying the LCSH. This system has been designed to be more amenable to interfaces that employ faceted navigation.

Clustering

Clustering results by subject, author, genre format or date can allow users to easily refine a search with one click of the mouse. New methods of browsing—via peer recommendations, subject taxonomies or related websites—have emerged. Result clustering, like faceted navigation, aims to give the user a fast and easy way to narrow results. While faceted navigation usually relies on metadata terms, clustering operates by analysing the raw text of the items in the result set to create labels representing each group or cluster. From the user's perspective, faceted navigation and clustering look much the same. With both, you click through succession to progressively narrow the results down to a manageable number.

Breadcrumbs

Breadcrumb links, also known as contextual links, are a type of navigation aid for web pages. They provide a textual representation of a site's structure, usually a vertical hierarchy of a site. For example, on e-commerce websites, breadcrumb links often have the following format:

Home > Category > Subcategory > Product

Breadcrumb links can help users' take some steps back toward home when needed. A new link appears with each step through the site and persists until the user safely exits. Breadcrumbs are especially helpful in search environments that use faceted navigation. New breadcrumbs show each facet that's been selected to narrow the search.

Search Result Data

Key challenges for these new interfaces include the need to extract data from the library service environment and provide up-to-the-minute status information on each item in the library's collection. For example, 'on circulation'. Librarians need to construct search interfaces that include the catalogue of hybrid collections that might include a large portion of the electronic content to which they subscribe. Both the nature of information requirements and information-seeking behaviour have changed in the twenty-first century. Some of the new-generation OPAC are paving the way toward providing more immediate and seamless access to diverse content collections, giving equal footing to both the digital and print collections.

Search View Print Facility

The below-mentioned software are capable of performing Search/View Print:

Book Where: WebClarity Software Inc.'s Book Where product allows users to simultaneously search and retrieve metadata from over 1900 pre-defined databases located around the globe. Bibliographic and media records can be found in seconds and exported in a wide variety of formats, including MARC 21, FINMARC and UNIMARC. www.webclarity.info

FRBR Display Tool-Free: The FRBR Display Tool sorts the bibliographic data found in a set of MARC records into hierarchical displays by grouping the bibliographic data using the FRBR concepts of 'Works', 'Expressions' and 'Manifestations'. Possible uses for the FRBR Display Tool include experimenting with the collocation and sorting of search result sets into the FRBR categories to test concepts and applying FRBR to local data to evaluate its consistency for FRBR-type development. www.loc.gov/marc/frbr/tool.html

MARCView ™: MARCView™ is an easy-to-use program to view, search, and print any MARC 21, USMARC, CanMARC, UNIMARC or MARCXML bibliographic or authority file. Records are formatted for easy viewing and printing. Navigation to any record in the file is instantaneous. Searches can specify field, subfield, both or neither. www.systemsplanning.com/marc

MarciveWeb SELECT: It enables librarians to search 10 million records from LC, NLM, NLC, GPO, A/V Access (R) and other sources and obtain customized MARC 21 bibliographic records, catalogue cards, smart barcode labels, book labels and MARC 21 authority records. www.marcive.com

Copy Cataloguing

Copy cataloguing is done using the following:

Impact/ONLINE CAT: It is a Windows-based cataloguing system that provides users with the ability to search multiple databases of MARC 21 bibliographic, authority and community information records. Features include a MARC Editor with built-in MARC validation and the ability to download records to the local hard drive. www.autographics.com

Connexion: This is a robust suite of full-service online cataloguing tools and services backed by OCLC's 35+ years of cataloguing experience. Its enhanced features provide unparalleled flexibility for libraries and other allied institutions. Connexion lets you create and edit high-quality bibliographic and authority records and then share them with the entire OCLC cooperative, which benefits libraries around the world.

OCLC-MARC Record Delivery: Various WorldCat services generate bibliographic records in the OCLC-MARC format. OCLC makes copies of these records available for you to import to your local system to keep your local holdings in sync with your holdings in WorldCat. Downloading records on a regular basis makes it easier for your systems staff to manage and upload them into your OPAC.

Surpass Copycat: Surpass Copycat is a Windows-based Z39.50 copy cataloguing tool that allows users to find and download free MARC records from the Internet. It searches multiple libraries simultaneously, such as the LC, public libraries, medical libraries, statewide union catalogues and more. Over 100 libraries come pre-configured. Copycat also features 'scan and search' that allows the user to simply scan the EAN/ISBN barcode from the back of the book they wish to catalogue to instantly launch a search for that book. www.surpasssoftware.com/copycat.htm

WorldCat Cataloguing Partners: OCLC records delivery in coordination with your vendor orders through a collaborative effort with materials vendors. Corresponding OCLC MARC records are delivered with the materials you order through participating vendor partners. Additionally, your library's holdings are set automatically in WorldCat.

Converter

MARC RTP – Free: MARC RTP will read files of bibliographic records in MARC format and convert them to a format the user designs. The program can also produce a human-readable listing or summarise the structure of a file of records. www.loungebythelake.com/marcrtp/

MARConvert™: MARConvert™ handles special problems or unusual requirements in converting records into or out of MARC 21, USMARC, CanMARC, UNIMARC or MARCXML. It will also convert MARC records to another character set, such as ANSEL, Latin-1, Unicode or UTF-8. It operates in both interactive mode and batch mode for converting multiple files. It works on Windows 95/98/NT/2000/XP. www.systemsplanning.com/marc/mvd.asp

MARCMaker – Free: MARCMaker is developed by the LC that generates the MARC record structure from the preformatted text. It runs under DOS or Windows 95/98/ME/ 2000. (www.loc.gov/marc/makrbrkr.html#download) (www.loc.gov/marc/makrbrkr.html)

USEMARCON Plus: (The Universal MARC Record Converter – Free) Like the original USEMARCON program, the USEMARCON Plus program enables libraries to create rules-based systems to convert records between national MARC formats. It also allows users to create and modify rule files used to achieve MARC conversions in order to meet specific local requirements. www.bl.uk/services/bibliographic/usemarcon.html

Validator

Cooperative of Indic Language Library Authorities (CILLA): The CILLA service provides quarterly book lists for Bengali, Gujarati, Hindi, Panjabi, Tamil and Urdu materials suitable for public library audiences. This cooperative service enables library authorities to purchase materials more easily and in confidence for languages where they do not have a local specialist. The supply of MARC records also enables library authorities to gain efficiencies in cataloguing.

Cataloguing Calculator – Free: The Cataloguing Calculator finds variable and fixed MARC fields (bibliographic and authority data), language codes, geographic area codes, publication country codes, AACR2 abbreviations, LC main entry and geographic Cutter numbers. http:// home.earthlink.net/~banerjek/calculate/

InfoWorks Link Checker: InfoWorks Link Checker is designed for librarians to quickly check URL links in MARC 21 records and works with flat MARC files containing URLs. InfoWorks Link Checker can also check multiple links simultaneously by applying the multiple threading technology. www.itcompany.com/linkcheck.htm

InfoWorks Spelling Checker for Database Maintenance: It locates spelling errors and cleans up bibliographic databases. It works with flat MARC files in any integrated library system. InfoWorks Spelling Checker for database maintenance allows users to define which languages and fields to check and provides both batch and interactive checking. It includes a special dictionary for library use and allows users to build custom dictionaries. www.itcompany.com/checkerd.htm

Unit 14

Overview of Web Indexing, Metadata, Interoperability and Ontologies

Web Indexing

Web indexing, or Internet indexing, comprises methods for indexing the contents of a website or the Internet as a whole. Individual websites or intranets may use a back-of-the-book index, while search engines usually use keywords and metadata to provide a more useful vocabulary for Internet or onsite searching. With the increase in the number of periodicals that have articles online, web indexing is also becoming important for periodical websites.

Web index is a tool used for searching web documents, like individual websites or collections of websites or collections of webpages and so on. It is a browsable list of terms or sections leading towards further reading/resources to the desired topic or subject. Sitemap is an example of a web index.

Indexing is an intellectual activity where the indexer determines what concepts are worth indexing. The entries and arrangement of these entries are equally important. There is a view that web indexing and traditional indexing are best done by individuals skilled in the art of indexing. It requires imagination and formal knowledge of the subject. However, there are automated ways of doing web indexing. Search engines use a program called 'spider' or 'crawler' to extract the search terms from individual webpages. These spiders or crawlers collect the terms and store the terms inside a local database of a search engine and use it as a search index. These terms are either extracted from the 'meta tag' or from the contents of the webpage. Normally, indexes are used for web browsing. The terms in the sitemap of a website are directly hyperlinked to the topical webpage or the topic itself within the webpage. An index performs the following three important tasks:

1. It describes the relationships among subjects. These include hierarchical and other relationships that exist amongst the subjects.
2. Once stored in the database, it can be used as a source of meaningful metadata for searching. Search engines use index terms stored in such a type of database. An index provides visibility to all the available literature. Sometimes a user does a search but cannot express the exact search phrase. In such a case, a good index brings material related to what they are looking for with the help of related terms or concepts.
3. It is not only useful from the searchers' point of view but also from the author's point of view. An index focuses on the content of the document and demonstrates the inconsistencies in the treatment of the topics. Hence, it is an aid for authors to review the writing for completeness of the content.

Types of Web Indexes

Web indexes are of the following types:

1. *Hyperlinked A–Z Indexes*

A hyperlinked index is a kind of back-of-the-book index. It is arranged alphabetically (A–Z). Normally, in a back-of-the-book index, the terms or phrases are listed with the appropriate page number or section number. In the web environment, an A–Z index is a webpage or a group of pages. Each entry in the webpage is hyperlinked to a topic or, to be more precise, to the anchor tag of the resource. The list may also contain synonymous terms linked to the same resource.

2. *Meta-Tag Keyword Indexing*

Meta-tag is used in Hypertext Markup Language (HTML) documents for page description, keywords and other metadata. It is used in the header section of the web. The content of the tag is not visible on a web browser. Metadata is normally referred to as 'data about some object'. The object could be anything. The data about the object reflects the properties of the object. Some examples of objects in a bibliographic database are Title, Author, Place, Publisher, etc.

Metadata

Metadata is information about an informational resource. The document can be a webpage, image, dataset or other resource. Metadata is valuable towards the storage and retrieval of documentary resources. Structured metadata makes objects easily discoverable. In library parlance, catalogue is known as metadata, which provides descriptive information about an object or resource available in the library. The resource can be physical or electronic. Metadata is a tool used to locate an object or document. There are various metadata schemas. Some of them are as follows:

- AACR2
- MARC 21
- Government Information Locator Service (GILS)
- Encoded Archive Description (EAD)
- Dublin Core

Hence, metadata is 'data about data'. It is a structured set of data that describes the various characteristics of an object or document.

Purpose of Metadata

Metadata is used for various purposes. It is used to:

- Retrieve a document,
- Define the structure of a document and its future maintenance,
- Store the preservation conditions, and

- Preserve the additional information regarding the handling and usage of a document.

Types of Metadata

As discussed above, it is a common practice to use metadata for easy retrieval. But the application of metadata has a much deeper role to play in an electronic environment. Based on their roles, metadata are classified into the following types: Administrative metadata, technical metadata, structural metadata, descriptive metadata and preservation metadata.

Administrative metadata: When a document is created, several kinds of information are also generated with it. This information is valid and useful during the whole lifespan of the document. These data are stored as administrative metadata. Administrative metadata is related to the life cycle of the document. It includes information regarding serials in the digital environment concerning ordering, acquisition, maintenance, licensing, rights, ownership and provenance.

Technical metadata: The technical metadata stores information regarding the file type and associated content type and how it should be rendered. It stores information regarding how the bytes should be read or, in other words, how the file should be read. Apart from this, it also stores information regarding the size or the extent of the file. This information is very useful for playing the file. Further, it is also useful for digital preservation, particularly for migration and refreshing of the document. Technical metadata is helpful in checking the intactness of the object.

Structural metadata: Structural metadata or the structural map of an object explains different components and their role. This handles various sections and subsections of the documents and their corresponding relations and roles.

Descriptive metadata: The metadata used for describing the documents in the library is descriptive metadata. AACR2 or MARC 21 are good examples of descriptive metadata. In library parlance, we call it descriptive cataloguing. Descriptive metadata stores information regarding title, author, place and publisher and so on. This metadata set is important for identifying and locating the documents. For document location over the web, a Uniform Resource Identifier (URI) is used.

Preservation metadata: One of the most important metadata sets used for digital longevity is preservation metadata. Digital preservation is the process of increasing the longevity of documents from physical deterioration. The deterioration of digital objects is against time, technology, media and transfer. In order to secure the document and its original features, libraries, archives and museums need some kind of documentation in the form of metadata. Preservation metadata stores the preservation conditions of a document and its original features at the time of its digital provenance. Preservation Metadata: Implementation Strategies (PREMIS) is the standard metadata set used for digital preservation purposes.

Ontology

The term 'ontology' is derived from the Greek '*onto*' (meaning being) and '*logia*' (meaning written or spoken discourse). It is part of metaphysics, a branch of philosophy. Ontology studies the existence of entities and their relationships. The relationship is derived due to grouping the entities based on formed groups. These groups are formed due to the likeness or similarities of characteristics or attributes of individual entities. The relationship is depicted in the form of a hierarchy and subdivisions. In other words, it is the conceptualisation of the world based on entities and their mutual existence as studied in Philosophy.

However, ontology is also studied in computer science and information science. In computer science, ontology is the formal representation of a concept or a set of concepts within a specific domain of knowledge and their relationships. For example, organisms are classified into two categories, that is, Plantae and Animalia. Then, Animalia is further classified into Chordata and Non-Chordata. Chordata is further classified into Protozoa, Coelenterate and so on. This is the taxonomy of the animal kingdom.

One of the important parts of ontology is the definition of classes and their properties. A class represents a group of concepts or objects with the same kind of properties. Properties can be defined as distinguishing features for the identification of a class or an individual object. Hence, it can be stated that the use of ontology is the use of classification for web documents. The term classification is also known as taxonomy.

Web Ontology

Presently, search engines search over stored indexes in their databases with a pattern match algorithm. This search lacks representation of the concept with the search term. This inherent problem is not due to any difficulty with search engines. Rather, it is due to the representation of data on a webpage using HTML, the language of the web. Hence, a mechanism is visualized to represent the data of webpages using another language, that is, Extensible Markup Language (XML) with a standard data description framework called Resource Description Framework (RDF). It is understood that each individual webpage can be considered an entity and will have its attributes or characteristics. Based on this property, the pages can be grouped, and further, they can form relations with other webpage(s) or groups of webpages. This develops a kind of web-based ontology, also known as web ontology for web documents, but the original idea of ontology remains the same. This framework uses standard vocabulary, like Resource Description Framework Schema (RDFS) and OWL, for describing the concepts and their relationships with other concepts. The search engines extract the data from the webpage and preserve the relationship with the data so that meaningful results can be generated.

Types of Web Ontologies

1. *Generic Ontologies*

Generic ontologies cover a large spectrum of knowledge domains. They define concepts at a very broad level. A generic ontology represents broad concepts and their relationships. These ontologies are easy to reuse. Generic ontologies represent a class of libraries that can be used with different problem domains and environments. These ontologies are like an umbrella ontology that can be further used for more specific purposes in conjunction with more specific ontology. These ontologies provide a mechanism for interoperability among different related ontologies. However, generic ontologies have the following key features:

- Generic ontologies are created from thesaurus, term dictionary or classification schemes and so on.
- It provides logical concreteness and suitability for information interchange.
- These ontologies don't provide any informational explanation for the content used.
- It is suitable to be used with more than one discipline or domain of knowledge.
- Normally, this kind of ontology lacks sound principles of development, or in other words, they follow a popular approach.

2. *Core Ontologies*

With regard to ontological content, there are two schools of thought. One claims that content depends highly on the context, and hence, any prepared ontology can work and only work with the same content or concept. However, the other school suggests that there are ontologies that follow minimal standard vocabulary. The vocabulary used is from philosophy or cognitive science. Hence, the used vocabulary is domain-independent or, in other words, is only dependent on philosophy and cognitive science. But the content it represents belongs to a specific domain of knowledge. This kind of ontology is known as core ontology. The core ontology has been used to reach an agreement on the types of entities (and their relationships) needed in a community of practice. It is being used to dynamically negotiate the intended meaning across a distributed community. Hence, the key features of core ontology are as follows:

- It specialises in a foundational or top-level ontology.
- It has been built through a well-motivated methodology that nonetheless avoids the reuse of a foundational ontology.
- It has 'built-in' (but explicit) criteria for well-foundedness.

3. *Domain-Specific Ontologies*

These ontologies are developed keeping specific objectives in mind, like defining various components, describing specific functionality and so on. Often specific ontologies are required based on a specific knowledge sphere, area, field, region or realm. Such ontologies are known as domain-specific ontologies. For example, the ontology of an organisational chart can be considered domain-specific ontology.

4. *Task-Oriented Ontologies*

In a more complex system, the operations are broken into different levels like top level, middle level and innermost level. Each level may have its own objectives as defined by the system analyst. Therefore, each level performs its individual task and transfers the output to the next level. A conceptual framework of the described system is known as task-oriented ontology. Like other ontologies, it also consists of taxonomy and axioms. Axioms are rules for reasoning, principles or constraints among concepts. Hence, a task-oriented ontology has three parts: Lexical level, conceptual level and symbol level.

Lexical level: At the lexical level, task ontology provides human-friendly understanding in terms of which users can easily describe their own tasks. It provides comprehension for human readability and descriptiveness.

Conceptual level: At the conceptual level, task ontology simulates the various problem-solving processes at the conceptual level and demonstrates the possible solutions through the rules or reasoning. It provides operationality only at the conceptual level rather than the implementation or execution level.

Symbol level: This level provides operationality at the implementation or execution level. The ontology makes the system run the task description by translating it into instructions.

Interoperability

The term interoperability means working in collaboration. In a distributed service environment, different resources work together to produce a common service or goal. It is very common to understand different modules or services of an object/product. It is not desirable to know how each module or service is functioning. But all should be able to work together in collaboration to produce one service or product. The individual module or service must have enough common ground so that exchange of individual output can be shared without any error or misunderstanding. This requires the standardisation of individual output according to some specifications. Standardisation provides a common platform for the exchange of communication or services. Several definitions are given for interoperability. According to National Information Standard Organisation (NISO), "Interoperability is the ability of multiple systems with different hardware and software platforms, data structures, and interfaces to exchange data with minimal loss of content and functionality."

Need of Interoperability

In library parlance, the concept of interoperability has been used since long time. The use of MARC 21 bibliographic standard or any other bibliographic standard, in conjunction with ISO 2709 or MARC format or MARC XML format, provides the facility to exchange bibliographic data among libraries. This exchange can be used in various ways, like generating a single platform-based search facility for a number of libraries, reusability of the library catalogue and so on.

The most important use of interoperability is seen in the telephone industry. Irrespective of operators, one can make phone calls or send messages. This is because of adherence to one kind of standard. Similarly, emails can be sent across different service providers because of Simple Mail Transfer Protocol (SMTP).

Another example of interoperability is seen in the field of industry. In medicine, it is very important to record the case histories. Hence, an efficient Electronic Health Record (EHR) system is required. If different hospitals record case histories under their individual specifications, then communication and exchange of case studies among hospitals will become impossible. Hence, it is the need of the hour that medicine comes out with a standard for maintaining and managing EHR systems so that such systems can communicate among themselves.

Interoperability and Web Search

Interoperability plays a major role in web parlance. The web is an unorganised and distributed environment. Information over the Internet is presented in HTML format. In order to improve upon the search results of search engines, the use of metadata schemas is thought of. But soon, it was realised that there is a plethora of metadata standards. Though Dublin Core metadata elements given by World Wide Web Consortium (W3C) evolved as a de facto standard for describing web documents, but other standards have also made a mark over the scenario, like MARC 21, GILS, e-Government Metadata Standard (e-GMS), Encoded Archival Description (EAD), Geospatial Metadata (GEO) and so on. It has been continuously observed and felt that search engines should come up with some kind of interoperability model so that cross-standard search is possible. This concept is known as federated searching.

Currently, search engines read data from the meta-tag of an HTML document or an XML file, which describes the resource in RDF. RDF is used for defining ontologies in order to describe web resources, and it has a broader scope than the former.

Methods for Achieving Interoperability

1. *Mapping/Matching*: Mapping is one of the methods used for achieving interoperability. Mapping means relating or corresponding one-to-one between the entities of two sets. Mapping between two ontologies means establishing correspondence between each entity of ontology A against entities of ontology B with respect to their meanings. The mapping does not lead to creating a new set of entities. Rather, it only produces correspondence.

2. ***Alignment***: Ontology alignment is a process of bringing different ontologies into mutual agreement. This process involves bringing ontologies together. For instance, redundancies are removed, and logical elements are kept. Hence, the process requires the transformation of the involved ontologies. However, any element expected in the mutual ontology might also be included. Therefore, alignment might bring a completely new picture of ontology.
3. ***Transformation***: Transformation leads to a complete change in the original ontology. The change might occur in terms of elements, attributes or concepts. Hence, the resultant ontology would be a completely new ontology based on the previous one. However, the degree of change in the structure or semantics might vary depending on the situation. The process of transformation may be additive or subtractive depending on the needs of the original.
4. ***Translation***: It often happens that ontology is to be used in different environments. The change of environment can be subject domain, software or language. In such a situation, the original ontology needs to be changed according to the new environment. However, it is expected that the conceptual meaning or semantics of the original will not change and will remain as close as possible to the original.
5. ***Merging/Integrating***: When two or more ontologies are merged together and form a new ontology, it is known as the merging or integrating of ontologies. This process leads to the formation of a completely new ontology based on the previous one.

Protocols for Interoperability

The Internet is a source of many online resources containing documents in different formats, like text, graphics, audio and video. Individual resources hosting these documents might follow different metadata standards. These documents are to be searched using a search engine. Hence, a cross-platform mechanism has been established in the form of protocols to search different resources in one stroke. The whole system is a distributed system and completely untamed. Developing search agents for such a system is a big challenge. The use of protocols allows users to search several data sources with a single effort, irrespective of the metadata standard used. Z39.50 (ZEE Thirty-nine point five zero), Open Archive Initiative and Protocol for Metadata Harvesting (OAI-PMH) and Search/Retrieve via the web or URL (SRW/U) are developed for this purpose. Two protocols are widely used over the Internet for cross-domain search:

(1) Z39.50 and ZING (2) OAI-PMH

Z39.50 and ZING: The core of interoperable searching is the use of protocols. The use of Z39.50 is well accepted and the oldest in library services. This protocol was developed to search OPACs of different libraries. In due course of time, the protocol evolved with several applications, like searching the deep web (databases over the Internet), publishers' catalogues, digital repositories and so on. The protocol performs real-time information retrieval from the source. The next generation of the Z39.50 protocol is ZiNG (Z39.50-International: Next Generation), maintained by the LC.

OAI-PMH: This is also an HTTP-embedded protocol used extensively for interoperable searching and retrieval. The protocol is simple and developed for searching across digital repositories. OAI-PMH intermediary (service provider or search agent) harvests metadata in anticipation from the distributed resources and offers search to the clients. Harvesting means extracting metadata from different resources and storing it inside one's own database. Searching is done by an intermediary service provider using its own harvested metadata. However, any request for the searched document is directed to the resource or repositories.

EXERCISE UNIT 12 – UNIT 14

1. What do you mean by KO?
2. Discuss the types of KOSs.

3. Discuss the processes involved in planning KOSs.
4. Define Semantic Web.
5. What do you understand by Semantic Web activity?
6. What do you mean by SKOS?
7. What do you mean by a descriptive catalogue?
8. What do you mean by cataloguing standards?
9. Define online catalogue. How is it different from a physical catalogue?
10. Discuss MARC in detail.
11. What are the advantages of MARC?
12. Define metadata.
13. What do you understand by the term 'metadata'? Discuss its types and cataloguing tools.
14. Write the full forms of ISBD and FRBR.
15. What do you understand from OPAC? What are its uses?
16. Define breadcrumbs.
17. Define web indexing. Discuss its various types.
18. What do you understand by ontology? What are its types?
19. What is interoperability? Discuss its need and methods.
20. Write a note on protocols for interoperability.

PART 2
DOCUMENT PROCESSING (PRACTICE)

Unit 15

Introduction, Structure and Organisation

Introduction

Library classification or book classification or bibliographic classification is the process of arranging, grouping, coding and organising books and other library materials (such as serials, sound recordings, moving images, cartographic materials, manuscripts, computer files, e-resources, etc.) on shelves or entries of a catalogue, bibliography and index according to their subject in a systematic, logical and helpful order by way of assigning them call numbers using a library classification system, so that users can find them as quickly and easily as possible. The call number serves a dual purpose: It determines the place of a book on the shelf and co-locates books on the same topic next to each other. In a modern library, documents, such as books and other reading materials, are arranged by subject for their location and for browsing. For arranging books, you may devise a homemade system of your own, which is a very difficult and time-consuming process. The other way is to adopt an existing system. There are many universally known and standard classification systems available for this purpose. Well-known among them are the Dewey Decimal Classification (DDC), Library of Congress Classification (LCC), Universal Decimal Classification (UDC), Ranganathan's Colon Classification (CC) and many more.

The DDC, colloquially known as the Dewey Decimal System, is a proprietary library classification system that allows new books to be added to a library in their appropriate location based on their subject. It was first published in the United States by Melvil Dewey in 1876. DDC is the most popular of all the general classification systems used all over the world. From the first (1876) to the fifteenth edition (1952), Dewey Decimal Classification (DDC) was published in one volume of varying sizes. The sixteenth edition (1958), a very important edition, was issued for the first time in two volumes. It made the handling of the growing number of books easy. The second volume was mostly devoted to the index, called the Relative Index.

The eighteenth edition (1971) was issued in three volumes extending the process a bit further. The nineteenth edition, published in 1979, is also in three volumes, which are as follows:

Volume 1	Introduction, Tables
Volume 2	Schedules
Volume 3	Relative Index

The twentieth edition (1989), the twenty-first edition (1996), twenty-second edition (2003) and twenty-third edition (2011) were all in four volumes each. In this unit, we will discuss the nineteenth edition of the scheme.

Nineteenth Edition of Dewey Decimal Classification (DDC)

Different libraries throughout the world are using different editions of DDC depending on the year of their establishment or the time they started classifying their books. The three volumes of the nineteenth edition (1979) comprise 3361 pages, bound in light grey colour. Its bibliographic details are as follows:

> *Dewey Decimal Classification and Relative Index Devised* by Melvil Dewey, Edition 19, edited under the direction of Benjamin A. Custer. Albany, N.Y.: Forest Press, 1979, 3 Volumes.

This complete set should be on your table or can be obtained for reference within the premises of the study centre nearest to you. There is nothing to be afraid of its size, as it is a reference book to be referred to and consulted rather than read from cover to cover or memorised. Dewey Decimal Classification

(DDC) in three volumes is a number-building machine, and you must learn how to use it.

Notation

Notation is a series of symbols, which is used to represent a subject, and it is a very important feature of book classification in a library. Just like every film presents its story and theme through actors, every library classification employs notation to denote classes and subclasses of subjects. Notation may be defined as a systematic series of shorthand symbols to denote classes and their subdivisions and to show the relationship between subjects. It mechanises the arrangement of books in a library. Brevity is implied in notation, but contrary to the popular impression, brevity is not its prime/only concern. It makes the system mechanical.

Properties of Decimal Fractions

All decimal fractions follow a whole number preceded by a decimal point as an indicator. For example, in 10.5, read as 'ten point five', 5 is a decimal fraction and is preceded by a decimal point. Similarly, 0.92 is read as 'zero point nine two' or simply as 'decimal nine two'. Decimal fractions have some mathematical properties (qualities) not possessed by integral (whole) numbers that we ordinarily use in our day-to-day routine. The properties of decimal fractions are discussed below:

1. *Constant Place Value of the Digits*

If we add any digit to the right end of any decimal fraction, the place value of the already present figures does not change. For example, if a decimal fraction 52 is extended by 5 to make it 525, the original place value of the first two digits, that is, 52, remains unaltered. This is due to the fact that every digit in a decimal fraction has its fixed absolute value irrespective of the total number of digits in a decimal sum. This property is the reverse of what it is in the whole numbers.

2. *Superfluity of the Right-End Zero*

By virtue of this property, if any zero is added to the right end of a decimal fraction, its value remains the same. For example, 9.5, 9.50 and 9.500 have the same value. On this account, one needs to be a bit more careful while arranging decimal fractions according to their value. For example, of the two decimal fractions 23 and 1125, the former is of a higher value than the latter.

3. *Ordinal Value of Digits*

As in other classification systems, the number/symbols used here to denote subjects have only ordinal values. They do not possess any cardinal value. Here, the numerals are devoid of any measure of their weight or power or quantity. They only indicate their sequential value, that is, which number will come earlier and which later. In Dewey Decimal Classification (DDC), of the two subjects denoted by numbers, say 953 and 954, it never means that the latter is of any more value or importance than the former or vice-versa. It not only indicates that on the library shelves, the book bearing the class number 954 will come after that of 953 and so on. Similarly, 511 will come earlier than 512 on the shelves, not that it is of less value than 512. And by the same rule, 45 will come earlier than 5 and 301 earlier than 92.

4. *Depiction of Hierarchy Through Notation*

With notation alone, we do not know the importance or value of a subject, but it does help determine its relative status and location among other subjects in the universe of knowledge. Notation also helps determine the relative breadth or depth of a subject and its relationship with other subjects on its left and right sides. Dewey Decimal Classification (DDC) is a hierarchical classification. It means that coordination and subordination of subjects are depicted through notation. For example, of the three subjects denoted by 5, 51 and 515, we say that 51 is subordinate to 5, and 515 is subordinate to 51. In other words, 515 is a part of 51, which, in turn, is part of 5. Thus, the hierarchical order of these figures/subjects will be:

5

51

515

This is only possible if the notation is of decimal fractions.

Basic Plan and Convention of a Minimum of Three Digits

DDC is a universal scheme and is able to classify books in all branches of knowledge. It treats the whole of knowledge as unity and divides it into ten mutually exclusive Main Classes denoted by decimal numbers 0 to 9 as follows:

0	Generalities
1	Philosophy and Related Disciplines
2	Religion
3	Social Sciences
4	Language
5	Pure Sciences
6	Technology (Applied sciences)
7	The Arts
8	Literature (Belles-letters)
9	General Geography and History and Their Auxiliaries

Strictly and mathematically speaking, the numbers denoting Main Classes should have been written as 0.0 Generalities, 0.1 Philosophy and related disciplines, 0.2 Religion and so on. But for the brevity and simplicity of notation, the initial zero and the decimal point are omitted, though these are understood to be there. Thus, in DDC, if you come across a number, say 512, then it should actually be treated as 0.512. We read 512 as 'five one two' and not as five hundred twelve. Similarly, we read 91 as 'nine one' and not ninety-one and 025.4 as 'zero two five point four'. To simplify the ordinal value of these decimal fractions and for their arrangement, there is a convention that no number in DDC shall comprise less than three digits. If any number is less than three digits long, then we add the required number of zeros to make the number of digits three. Hence, in actual practice, the ten Main Classes are denoted as:

000	Generalities
100	Philosophy and Related Disciplines
200	Religion
300	Social Sciences

400 Language
500 Pure Sciences
600 Technology (Applied sciences)
700 The Arts
800 Literature
900 General Geography and History

The above ten divisions are also called the 'First Summary' of Dewey Decimal Classification (DDC) schedules. For a beginner, it is the first practical step to learning the system.

Volume 1: Introduction and Tables

It is comparatively a thin volume containing prefatory material and seven auxiliary tables. It gives a brief history of DDC in 'Publisher's Foreword' (pp. xi–xiii) and has the preface (pp. xv–xviii) by the Chairman of the Decimal Classification Editorial Policy Committee (DCEPC). This preface describes the special features and policies of the nineteenth edition. Then comes the Editor's Introduction (Benjamin A. Custer). It is a very important and useful part of the system in all respects. The Editor's Introduction explains, in detail, the structure of the scheme, its various plans, its fine features and full instructions on its use. It also provides guidance in determining the subject (doing subject analysis) of a book in general (Section 9; pp. i, vi, ix) and, subsequently, in locating the appropriate class number. It also provides rules to further synthesise (extend) a number either from the schedules or the auxiliary tables or both.

Auxiliary Tables

Virtually, the second part of Volume 1 is devoted to the seven auxiliary tables. These are:

1. Standard Subdivisions;
2. Areas;
3. Subdivisions of Individual Literatures;
4. Subdivisions of Individual Languages;
5. Racial, Ethnic, National Groups;
6. Languages; and
7. Persons.

The use of these tables will be explained to you in book unit 5 of book block 1 of this course.

Summaries

This scheme comprises three important summaries, commonly called "Three Summaries of the System" (pp. 471–82, Volume 1). These are three outlines of the scheme in order of their increasing details. The First Summary, also called the Ten Main Classes (p. 471), is the broadest of the first outline of the division of the entire universe of knowledge as per this system. You can remember this summary even on the first reading. On the following page 472, each of these ten Main Classes has further been divided into ten branches called divisions. Hence, there are 10 × 10 = 100 divisions in total. This is called the Second Summary or the 100 Divisions of Dewey Decimal Classification (DDC). It is useful to remember this summary too. An extract from the Second Summary is reproduced below:

The Second Summary of the Main Class 300 Social Sciences, as an example, is as follows:

310 Statistics
320 Political Science
330 Economics
340 Law
350 Public Administration
360 Social Problems and Services
370 Education
380 Commerce (Trade)
390 Customs, Etiquette, Folklore

The Third Summary of Division 330 Economics is as follows:

330 Economics
331 Labor Economics
332 Financial Economics
333 Land Economics
334 Cooperatives
335 Socialism and Related Systems

336 Public Finance

337 International Economics

338 Production

339 Macroeconomics and Related Topics

The Third Summary (pp. 473–82) further divides each of the 100 divisions into ten parts called sections. Hence, there are 100 × 10 = 1,000 sections in all. These 1,000 sections are called the Third Summary. These 1,000 sections enumerate and elaborate the scope of the above 100 divisions. There is no need to remember all these 1,000 sections unless you want to become a super expert.

Volume 2: Schedules

The schedules are a long table of all DDC numbers given in numerical order and showing hierarchical relations of subjects. In other words, it is a series of numbers in order of their increasing ordinal value. It is the core and central part of the DDC system. To understand the correct and efficient use of the schedules, it is necessary to understand various notes and instructions provided under various entries.

Hierarchy

Hierarchy means the sequence of subjects in their successive subordination. Hierarchy also means the arrangement as per the increasing specificity of subjects as we go down the chain. This whole-part relationship or increasing specificity of subjects is shown by the addition of a digit to the number on the left side and the shift of indention of the verbal heading to the right side. For example:

300 Social Sciences

330 Economics

332 Financial Economics

332.4 Money

332.41 Value of money

332.414 Factors affecting fluctuations in value

In the above case, each heading is subordinated to the immediately upper heading. Note the lengthening of the chain by a digit in the number column on the left and the shift in (typographical) indention on the right in the corresponding headings.

Understanding the Schedules

Using the hierarchical principle, the corresponding heading against every number does not describe the full subject but a term most specific to that digit in the chain of numbers. Therefore, to understand the full meaning of every heading in the schedule, it must be read in the context of its immediate upper heading and simultaneously in the still broader context of the whole discipline. Take, for example, a class number:

342.052 Powers, functions and duties

If this entry is taken by itself, one might not understand whose 'powers, functions and duties' this refers to. But if we read it in conjunction with (or in the context of) its immediately upper number in the hierarchy, then its meaning becomes abundantly clear, which is 'powers, functions and duties of the legislative branch of the government'. It can further be read in the context of its still higher number, that is, 342. Then, it will mean 'Powers, functions and duties of the legislative branch of the government in constitutional and administrative law'.

Now, take one more example.

546.342 Simple

One might not understand what the adjective 'simple' stands for here. But reading it in the context of its upper number, that is, 546.34, it means simple salt, which is quite clear. But when you read further in the context of its upper class, that is, 546 Inorganic Chemistry, then it becomes apparent to mean Inorganic Simple Salts.

Volume 3: Relative Index

Volume 3 of the set is devoted to the Relative Index, consisting of 1217 pages. The index is always an important part of any classification system. In Dewey Decimal Classification

(DDC), it is called Relative Index, which is better than other alphabetical indexes and is considered an important and enduring contribution of Melvil Dewey to library classification. Relative Index is a kind of index that not only arranges the concepts and their terms in an alphabetical sequence but also shows the relationship between the terms and the contexts in which the subjects appear in the schedule. It is not only a key to the classified schedules but also makes an independent approach to classification. Thus, it is not an optional but an integral part of DDC.

Transcription of a Class Number

Transcription is the act or process of representing something in a written or printed form. For a class number, transcription may be understood from the following points:

(i) The numbers used in DDC are decimal fractions.

(ii) No class number consists of less than three digits. For example, 5 is written as 500 and 53 as 530.

(iii) When a class number extends beyond three digits, a dot is put between the third and fourth digits, such as 324.3, 362.14, 386.242, etc.

To break the monotony of lengthy numbers and to aid memory, a dot is used after the third digit. This aspect is further explained below.

Dot

It is essential to remember that the dot used is not a decimal point as it might be thought to be. Mathematically, it is absurd. A decimal fraction cannot be divided again decimally. It is simply a psychological pause to break the monotony of numerical digits. It helps ease the transcription, copying and remembering of the class number for a short while. Educational psychologists believe that 324.12 is more easily remembered than 32412. Hence, this dot has no function other than to reinforce memory.

Spaces

If a class number extends beyond six digits, then after every three digits, a space is left. In other words, after the sixth digit, the remaining digits are transcribed in 'groups of three', leaving a space between two groups. This space serves exactly the same purpose as the dot: ease in transcription, copying and remembering of the class number. For example, the number 384.1065 Telegraph Companies is, in actual practice, transcribed in the schedules as:

384.106 5

A space is left between the sixth and the seventh digits (the point is not considered a digit). Similarly, the class number 621.38800287 TV Testing Technique is actually transcribed as:

621.388 002 87

Spaces are left between the sixth and the seventh digits and between the ninth and the tenth digits. Such spaces can be extended to any extent necessary. To repeat, the dot and spaces in a class number are devoid of any substantive meaning. These are not connecting symbols, either.

Numbers in Square Brackets, Obsolete Entries

While consulting or referring to the schedules, you will often come across many class numbers at various levels enclosed in square brackets. For example:

[309] Social situation and conditions
[396] [Unassigned]
[654] [Unassigned]
[511.7] Numerical analysis
[351.721] Fiscal policy

Any number enclosed in square brackets is no longer in use and is currently empty of any heading or meaning. Hence, such a number is not to be used. Such bracketed numbers are of the following five types: (i) Never assigned numbers, (ii) Unassigned numbers, (iii) Left vacant only, (iv) Optional class numbers, and (v) Formerly notes.

Never Assigned Numbers

These are numbers never assigned any meaning/heading in the scheme. Such numbers have always remained vacant so far. For example:

[004] [Never assigned]

[005] [Never assigned]

The number of such entries is decreasing edition after edition. These gaps are helpful in accommodating new subjects.

Unassigned Numbers

These are the bracketed numbers that have remained vacant for long since some previous editions. A heading is given against such a number (unassigned in square brackets). Immediately below that entry, you will find a note stating when the number was used last. For example:

[040] [Unassigned] Most recently used in Edition 16

[313] [Unassigned] Most recently used in Edition 14

[426] [Unassigned] Most recently used in Edition 18

Several such vacant numbers are created and later reused as a result of the constant revision of Dewey Decimal Classification (DDC).

Left Vacant Only

These numbers were left vacant in the nineteenth edition, and their headings shifted and relocated to another number in the same edition. For example:

[329] Political parties and related organisations and processes; Class in 324

[175.83] Reading comics; Number discontinued; class in 175.8

[602.72] Patents; Do not use; class in 608

Optional Class Numbers

These are the optional class numbers in square brackets. Such subjects have been shifted to other numbers. As a policy, if some libraries do not want to disturb their existing numbers, they have been given the option to retain the old numbers. For example, [925] *Scientists*.

Here, as per the footnote on page 1449, *Use is optional; prefer treatment described under 920.1–928.9.

This instruction means that the biographies of scientists may either be placed in 925 and its subdivisions or preferably in 500. Given below is another example of an optional class number in the DDC schedule.

[330.159] Socialist and related schools (Use of this number is optional; prefer 335).

Optional numbers signify that a few subjects can be classified at two places, and DDC leaves it to your choice. For example, the bibliography of a mathematician can be classed under 925.1 or 510.92.

Hence, you need to decide under which number you wish to classify such books. But you must be consistent in using only one number once you have decided upon one of the two choices. It is a policy matter to be decided in advance.

'Formerly' Notes

Linked with one kind of bracketed numbers are the formerly notes appended to some entries. When in the process of revision, a subject (heading) is partially or wholly relocated to a new number, then at the new place, a note is given describing the former number of this newly shifted number. This note is in the form of 'formerly....' printed in italics, enclosed in square brackets and followed by the former number. For example:

002 The book [formerly 001.552]

It simply means that in the previous edition, the class number for the subject 'The Book' was 001.552, and now it is 002.

If an independently existing number is merged into another number, it is indicated by the following device.

418.02 Translation and interpretation

Class here machine translation [formerly 029.756]

It simply means that the subject of machine translation was previously given an independent number 029.756, but in the present edition, it has been merged with 418.02 Translation Techniques in General.

299.934 Theosophy [formerly 147, 212.52]

It means that in the previous edition, 299.934 Theosophy was distributed at two places, that is, 147 (in Philosophy) and 212.52 (in Religion).

Unit 16

Definitions, Notes and Instructions

Introduction

In the seven tables (Volume 1) and more so in the schedules (Volume 2), you will find definitions, notes and instructions under each entry. An entry is a self-contained unit in the schedules and tables consisting of a number or span of numbers, a heading and often one or more notes and number-building instructions, if needed.

These notes are of various kinds and have different functions to perform. They help us understand and interpret the definitions, scope and limitations of a subject covered by an entry. Some notes refer to a more apt number and sometimes to a comparable and related number. But of greater importance are the notes to further extend a number, called 'number building' notes. All these types of instructions have been explained to you in the subsequent sections of this unit.

Understanding these notes and instructions is essential for the classification of documents. Therefore, you must be familiar with these notes and instructions so as to become a good classifier.

Definitions, Explanation and Scope

The scope, connotations and boundaries of a class differ from scheme to scheme. Therefore, invariably all library classification schemes define the boundaries of a class by listing all its subtopics. In other words, every library classification follows the principle: "A class is the sum total of all its enumerated subdivisions" (Ranganathan calls it the Canon of Enumeration).

However, in addition to enumeration, some notes and devices are employed for more explicitness.

Definition of a Class

In the DDC, the definitions of some of the classes or their subdivisions are explicitly stated in verbal terms. The definition given is appended immediately below the heading in the entry. For example, there is a very apt definition of '330 Economics' under the entry, which reads: "The science of human behaviour as it relates to utilization of scarce means for the satisfaction of needs and desires through production, distribution, consumption." Sometimes the scope of a subject is elaborated by a definition-like note.

For example, consider 370.158 Psychological Effects of Education. Its scope is explained as: "Effects on students of school situation, teaching methods, other factors". With this note, the meaning of the entry and the kind of documents to be placed here become clearer.

Though this is a highly valuable feature of the Dewey Decimal Classification (DDC), the definition is not the rule. However, where no definition appears, it is taken from any standard English language dictionary, such as Webster's Third New International Dictionary of the English Language.

Different Types of Notes

Sometimes, instead of formally defining a subject, its scope is explained with illustrations. For example:

330.154 2 Historical school of economic thought

One reads the area covered by the entry as 'School of Roscher, Knies, Hildebrand, Schmoller, Bucher, Knapp'. In another example, the scope of 253 Secular Clergymen and Pastoral Duties (Pastoral Theology) is explicitly explained as: "Priests, ministers, pastors, rectors, vicars, curates, chaplains, elders, deacons, assistants". Sometimes the scope of a subject is explained and illustrated with actual examples, preceded by the word 'Examples'. For instance, note the examples under the following entry:

549.121 Mechanical properties of minerals

Examples: Cleavage, parting, fracture, hardness, specific gravity

Take another example:

025.315 Structure of the library catalogue

Examples: Divided, unified, classified

It is only from the examples that we are sure of the internal structure or form of the library catalogue. These examples are only illustrative and by no means exhaustive. Many more examples of a topic could be cited. On the other hand, the scope is sometimes defined by the exclusion of some topics. For example:

791 Public performances

Other than musical, sports and game performances

It obviously means that arts such as music, games and sports, though they are publicly performing arts, have not been included here, as these, being important subjects, have been given their separate numbers.

Inclusion Notes

Some topics not part of a class are given a standing place with a class. Actually, such topics are not fully developed, and their literary warrant does not demand a full and separate number for them. Hence, these topics are given a standing room (on an ad-hoc basis) in a class with which they might be affiliated. Later, when sufficient literature is produced on the subject, then, as per the policy of DDC editors, these topics may be given a separate number.

For example, see the Inclusion Note in the following entry:

398.47 Ghosts

Including haunted places

It means that logically speaking, any folklore with 'haunted places' as its theme is not a part of the entry '398.47. Ghosts as Subject of Folklore' is not a fully developed subject. Therefore, for the time being (till giving a full number is justified), it is classed at 398.47.

Take another example:

371.104 Relation of teachers to society

Including relation to immediate community; academic freedom; rights, obligations, public status of teachers

The 'including note' in this entry contains many important topics such as relation to the immediate community, academic freedom, right obligations and the public status of teachers. To explain again, the topic of academic freedom has not yet gathered enough literature to justify a separate class for it. Therefore, for the time being, it has been clubbed with other topics under class number 371.104.

'Class here' Notes

Some topics apparently do not seem to be part of a given subject. These are broader or narrower than the topic to which they are attached with the note: 'Class here...'. It means that the place given to them is not very logical, yet it provides a class number to an otherwise unaccommodated topic. For example, note the entry:

576 Microbes; Class here microbiology

It simply means that microbiology, though simply not microbes, is placed with 576 Microbes. Similarly, under:

574.295 Immune reactions; Class here serology

Now, consider the following examples:

370.19 Social aspects of education; Class here educational sociology

370.152 Cognitive processes; Class here intelligence

Principally, there is a lot of difference between the topics listed as scope notes and examples on the one hand and inclusion and 'Class here' notes on the other. Yet, their practical effect is the same.

There can be many examples of such notes. These topics given under notes are also indexed in the Relative Index (Volume 3). It makes their location easy in the schedules.

'Class elsewhere' Notes

'Class elsewhere' notes are in direct contrast to 'Class here' or 'Including' notes. Sometimes a subject, seemingly a part of another subject or related to that, is accorded an independent number. Then there appears a note in various forms. Such a note sometimes refers to a more appropriate class number for the scattered topics of a subject. Such a note is analogous to a 'see' cross reference in an alphabetical list of subject headings. These notes are further discussed below.

'Class...in...' Notes

Consider the example:

523.302 22 Moon pictures and designs
Class charts and photographs in 523.39

It clearly means that 523.302 22 Moon Pictures and Designs does not include charts and photographs of the moon. For the latter, there is a distinct class number 523.39. Similarly, under:

181.4 Indian Philosophy

Class Philosophy of Pakistan and Bangladesh in 181.15

One finds the instruction for the class Philosophy of Pakistan and Bangladesh in 181.15. The relation between these two subjects is obvious, and so is the need for this note. Consider one more example:

177.1 Ethics of courtesy, politeness, hospitality
Class etiquette in 395

There one finds the instructive note: 'Class etiquette in 395'. It means that the topic etiquette should not be mistaken as a part of 177.1 Ethics of courtesy, etc., as 'etiquette', has a separate class number.

'For...see...' Notes

Another kind of note cross refers to a related number. In such a case, it takes the form of 'For...see...' (emphasis theirs) note. For example, note the following entry:

398.356 Scientific and technical themes in folklore
For medical folklore, see 398.353

It means that Medical Folklore has been given (on the basis of its literary warrant) a distinct number of 398.353, which is a broader subject and seemingly includes it. Similarly, see the following example:

181.45 Yoga - Indian philosophy

For physical yoga, see 613.704 6; Hindu yogic meditation, 294.543

The instruction given under the class number for yoga means that related to yoga philosophy are the subjects of yogic (physical) exercise and yogic meditation. Both of them have their separate class numbers as given in the instruction.

'Class comprehensive works in...' Notes

This type of note is appended to a centred entry (explained in section 2.4 of this unit), which is covered by a continuous span of numbers. To assign a single class number to a work covering all the topics, a note gives one number. For example:

181.41–181.48 Hindu-Brahmanical philosophy

Class comprehensive works in 181.4

Similarly, look at:

181.41–181.48 Hindu-Brahmanical philosophy

297.12–297.14 Sources of Islam

Class comprehensive works in 297.1

It means that various sources of Islam are denoted by a span of continuous numbers, that is, 297.12–297.14, but for a book comprehensive of all sources of Islam, the number is 297.1.

Notes Appearing Under Discontinued (Bracketed) Entries

When a number is discontinued in the present edition, then there appears a note indicating its new class number. These notes are again of two types:

(a) Having the Form 'Do not use; Class...'

(b) Having the Form 'Class in...'

Here are some examples of 'Do not use; Class...' type notes:

[221.03] Dictionaries, encyclopedias, concordances of Old Testament

Do not use class dictionaries and encyclopedias in 221.3 and concordances in 221.4–221.5

It means that in the nineteenth edition, the previous number 221.03 for Dictionaries and Encyclopedias of Old Testament has been discontinued and relocated to 221.3 in the present edition.

Under some discontinued, hence bracketed, numbers appear the instructions as to where this subject is to be classed now. For example, see the entry:

[301.56] Educational sociology

Class in 370.19

It simply means that the new number for this topic now is 370.19. This type of note is simpler and more straightforward than the previous form, though their meanings and effects are the same.

Importance of Various Notes

An entry may simultaneously have more than one note; in such cases, no note contradicts the other. The Dewey Decimal Classification (DDC) schedules abound with numerous such definitional, scope and illustrative or 'class here or there' notes. These notes immensely help classify a document correctly and arrive at the correct number. Also, these notes contribute to uniformity in the interpretation of entries and consequently achieve much-desired consistency in the application of DDC in all libraries in all countries. Moreover, there seems to be no consensus on the structure of knowledge and the place of various subjects in the tree of knowledge. The structure of knowledge as outlined and delineated in DDC may not be correct or logical, but these notes help understand the position, boundaries and scope of these subjects as its editors have devised it and wish it to be understood by the classifiers.

Centred Heading/Centred Entry

In the schedules, you will often come across some headings denoted not by one but by a continuous span of numbers. For example:

381–382 General internal and international commerce (Trade)

Here, one topic by virtue of its having many subdivisions has been denoted by a span of numbers 381–382 and their subdivisions. Hierarchy, here, is deliberately broken down. It helps denote the subdivisions of a centred heading by brief class numbers. Take one more example:

220 Bible

221 Old Testament

222–224 Specific parts of Old Testament

Here, instead of denoting the various parts (books) of the Old Testament by hierarchically subdividing 221, these have been denoted by a series of separate sections, that is, 222–224, thus providing ample space (and consequently briefer class numbers) for further subdivisions of the Old Testament.

Such entries occur at all levels of the hierarchy. These are called centred entries or centred headings, as these entries are always printed in the centre of the page and are invariably marked by an equilateral triangle (Δ) on the left-hand margin pointing towards the entry. Some other examples of centred headings are:

251–254 Local church

281.1–281.4 Early church

368.06–368.08 Insurance of specific forms of risks

574.873–574.875 Specific components of cell anatomy and physiology

Hundreds of more such examples can be found in the Dewey Decimal Classification (DDC) schedules. As already said (in the section on 'Class elsewhere' Notes), every centred heading contains a note as to where the comprehensive works on the topic are to be classed, as in practice, a book is denoted by one class number, not by a span of numbers. For example, under 251–254 Local Church, one finds the instruction: "Class comprehensive works in 250, special parochial activities in 259."

To repeat, a centred heading is typographically printed in the centre of the schedule page, denoted by a continuous span of numbers, signalled by a pointing triangle and containing a note giving the class number for comprehensive works on that subject.

It may be noted that every entry denoted by a span of numbers is not a centred entry. For example, 324.274–.279 or 367.91–.99 are not centred headings but merely a group of continuous numbers, which can be further individualised as per instructions.

Number-Building Notes

Any number in the schedules (Volume 2) (and in some cases in Tables 1–7 too) can be further extended by:

(1) Any of the seven Tables 1–7 (in Volume 1)

(2) Any number or part of it in the schedules (in Volume 2)

The extension (called synthesis or number building) can be with or without instructions.

Without Instructions by the Editor

Any standard subdivision in Table 1 can be added to any original or extended number in the schedules, Volume 2. By extending this provision, any number in Table 2 (Areas), in Table 5 (Racial, Ethnic National Groups) and Table 7 (Persons) can be added through the standard subdivisions 09, 088 and 089.

On Instructions Only

Direct use of numbers in Tables 2–7 (Volume 1) can be made only on instructions given in an entry.

Similarly, a number in the schedules can be extended by another whole or part number in the schedules only on instructions given in the form of: "Add to the base number... The number following...". Such kind of instruction is invariably followed by an example given as an illustration.

(a) *Individual 'add to' Instructions*

Such notes are appended to a specific entry. For example, under:

333.31 Land reform

Add 'Areas' notation 4–9 from Table 2 to the base number 333.31

One reads an instruction: Add 'Areas' notation 4–9 from Table 2 to the base number 333.31. Here, this particular number, 333.31, is further added to by some appropriate notation from Table 2.

(b) *Collective Instruction*

Sometimes, an 'add to' instruction applies to a series of numbers occurring on a single page of the schedules. In such a case, all the numbers that have to be further synthesised are marked with an asterisk (*), and at the foot of the particular page, there is another asterisk and a note, giving add-to instructions. This footnote applies to all the asterisk-marked numbers. This is done only to avoid repetition of the same instructions time and again. For example, on page 616 of the schedules, a series of numbers from 494.811 to 495.8 have been marked with an asterisk. Then, at the foot of this page, with another asterisk, there is an instruction reading: "Add to base number as instructed under 420–490". It simply means that all these numbers, if desired, can be further extended, as per instruction given under the class numbers 420–490 (on page 600 of the schedules). These 'add-to notes' are the backbone of the number-building equipment of DDC. And these 'add-to notes' are a major operational asset in the correct use of the DDC. Hence, the majority of the other units of this book block will be devoted to various forms of 'add-notes'. Detailed number-building techniques have been explained in units 5, 6 and 7 of this book block.

Unit 17

Introduction to Three Summaries and Steps in Classifying Documents

Introduction

Dewey Decimal Classification (DDC) is a classification by discipline wherein the universe of knowledge has been divided into major areas of study. These major divisions are disciplines of study. Within each discipline, the classes are divided hierarchically and listed from the general to the specific order. Every page is crammed with the details of classes and their subdivisions listed hierarchically with increasing details as we go down the hierarchical ladder. For example:

300 Social Sciences
330 Economics
332 Financial Economics
332.1 Banks and banking
332.11 Central banks

In many classes, such as those of science and technology, the details are immense and minute. But the progression from the general to the specific or from the whole to the part makes the location of a subject easy. To give outlines of the knowledge for an overview, DDC has provided summaries of classes at various levels. A summary is a list of major subdivisions of a number given at the beginning of the full development of a topic. But the first three summaries are given at the head of the whole classification. The three main summaries are listed at the end of Volume 1 (pp. 471–82). As mentioned above, the summaries maybe divided into two kinds:

(a) Three major summaries of knowledge, that is, ten Main Classes, 100 divisions and 1,000 sections (given in Volume 1).

(b) Lower-level summaries, for example, of a section or a sub-section, given in the densely detailed classes of the schedules (Volume 2).

The three major summaries are technically known as:

(1) First Summary, or ten Main Classes (Volume 1, p. 471).

(2) Second Summary, or 100 divisions (Volume 1, p. 472).

(3) Third Summary, or 1,000 sections (Volume 1, pp. 473-82).

Obviously, the three summaries are in the order of increasing detail. Being a decimal classification, there are ten classes at each step of division. So each summary has been divided by ten.

Ten Main Classes

The term 'Main Class' is vague. Its definition and scope varies from classification system to classification system. In general, it is the first order of classes, that is, the result of the first division of the universe of knowledge. Obviously, the number of Main Classes in a classification system also depends upon the kind of notation employed. The ten Main Classes of DDC and their notations are as follows:

000 Generalities

100 Philosophy and related disciplines

200 Religion

300 Social Sciences

400 Language

500 Pure Sciences

600 Technology (Applied sciences)

700 The arts

800 Literature (Belles-letters)

900 General geography and history and their auxiliaries

Arrangement of Ten Main Classes

As stated earlier, there is nothing logical or philosophical or natural about the number (ten) of the Main Classes that Melvil Dewey created. It all depended on and was constrained by the only ten places provided by the decimal notation. However, a Main Class is always social in character. Their number and scope vary from time to time. New Main Classes emerge as the knowledge progresses. These Main Classes were more or less the academic disciplines in American universities around the 1870s when the scheme was first conceived by Dewey. He borrowed the arrangement of subjects from a contemporary philosopher, W.T. Harris. Hence, it proves that the Main Classes are social in character. It is necessary to memorise these ten Main Classes.

Second Summary of 100 Divisions

Each of the ten Main Classes is further divided into what is called 'divisions'. Thus, there are 10 × 10 = 100 divisions in the DDC. It is also called the Second Summary. The Second Summary of the Main Class 300 Social Sciences, as an example, is as follows:

310 Statistics

320 Political Science

330 Economics

340 Law

350 Public Administration

360 Social Problems and Services

370 Education

380 Commerce (Trade)

390 Customs, Etiquette, Folklore

Similarly, every Main Class has ten divisions. Each Main Class has nine divisions denoted by 1 through 9 preceded by a Generalia division 0 given at the beginning. The sequence of divisions of a Main Class is according to some systematic basis. It will add to your efficiency to memorise these 100 divisions, though it is not necessary to do so.

Third Summary of 1,000 Sections

The Third Summary comprises 1,000 sections. Each of the 100 divisions has been divided into ten sections. Therefore, there are 100 divisions × 10 = 1,000 sections. A section is a 3-digit number. For example, the ten sections of the division 33 Economics are:

330 Economics
331 Labor economics
332 Financial economics
333 Land economics
334 Cooperatives
335 Socialism and related systems
336 Public finance
337 International economics
338 Production
339 Macroeconomics and related topics

It is beneficial to remember some important section numbers, such as 327 International Relations, 954 History of India, etc., from the Third Summary, 'The 1,000 Sections'.

Multi-Level Summaries

Summaries provide an overview of classes and save the time of a classifier in flipping through the pages. At a glance, the classifier is able to select the appropriate class. Such summaries provide a view of the structure of the class. Summaries at lower levels have been carried on in some densely detailed classes. They are called multi-level summaries. These may comprise 4-, 5- or even 6-digit numbers. For example, the summaries of 615 Pharmacology and Therapeutics are given below:

615.1 Drugs (Materia medica)

615.2 Inorganic drugs
615.3 Organic drugs
615.4 Practical pharmacy
615.5 Therapeutics
615.6 Methods of medication
615.7 Pharmacodynamics
615.8 Physical and other therapies
615.9 Toxicology (Poisons and poisoning)

The sub-section 615.7 Pharmacodynamics has its own summary (p. 860, Volume 2):

615.71 Drugs affecting cardiovascular system
615.72 Drugs affecting respiratory system
615.73 Drugs affecting digestive system and metabolism
615.74 Drugs affecting lymphatic and glandular systems
615.75 Antipyretics (Febrifuges)
615.76 Drugs affecting urogential system
615.77 Drugs affecting motor and integumentary systems
615.78 Drugs affecting nervous system

To repeat, the summaries printed in bold face in the centre of the page provide a good overview of the subdivisions of various levels of hierarchy. To arrive at the desired number, by moving down the hierarchy, a classifier does not have to look through every subdivision, nor does they have to flip through every page. These summaries might also be helpful to libraries that prefer broader numbers. Three major summaries and numerous multi-level summaries are of immense help in locating the desired number efficiently.

Steps in Classifying Documents

Classifying documents is both a science and an art. In fact, a classifier is a matchmaker. A classier has two tasks to perform:

(1) To determine the specific subject of the document to be classified.

(2) To assign appropriate notation from the schedules and tables to the specific subject.

Determination of the Specific Subject of a Document

A document is an embodiment of knowledge and is classified in accordance with its subject contents. It may be clearly noted that the class number is assigned to the subject of the book and not to the book as a physical entity. Determining the subject of a document is an intellectual task. It is an art. Flair in classifying depends upon your knowledge of different subjects. Your efficiency in determining the specific subject of the book increases with experience. That is why it is called an art. However, the specific subject of a book can be determined by the following procedure.

Procedure for Determining the Specific Subject of a Book

First of all, read the title. Most of the titles, if these are plain and straightforward, are indicative of the subject contents of the book. For example, the titles "Human Anatomy", "Cost Accountancy" and "History of Moghul India" clearly indicate the subject of the book.

Some titles are fanciful or symbolic of the subject content of the book. The subject is not clear from such titles: For example, (1) *Asian Drama*, (2) *City of Joy*, (3) *I dare* and (4) *Green Wisdom* by Arthur Galston.

Of these, the first is a book on economics, the second is a book on Calcutta, the third is the biography of an Indian woman police officer Kiran Bedi and the fourth is on plant biology. This can be fairly known by the sub-title. A sub-title always clarifies or delimits the title. Sometimes, a title, though clear of the subject, is vague. For example, *Shakespeare*, *India*, etc.

The first book is a biography of William Shakespeare. The second book is on the culture of India, mostly in photographs. Therefore, it is clear that titles might be deceptive, misleading or inadequate to know the exact subject of the book. Therefore, the advice to the classifier is: Never classify by the title alone.

Other Sources for Determining the Subject of a Book

Blurb: Next to the title, read the blurb of the book, that is, the customary 'About the Book' feature given on the book jacket or outer cover. It provides a brief introduction to the subject, its importance and its treatment in the book. It is indispensable for determining the subject of the book.

Preface: Reading the preface is indispensable for knowing the subject of the book and its scope and limitations in detail. Some authors also give a conspectus of each chapter in the preface. Every classifier must read it between the lines to know the scope and limitations of the book.

Other parts of the book: If the preface does not help fully, then you must glance through the foreword, if any, the table of contents and the text of the book here and there, especially the introductory chapter. Also, look at the index of the book. If there is any published review of the book, that may surely help determine its subject. The last resort is to consult a subject expert. These efforts will yield the subject of the book.

Subject Analysis

Having determined the subject of the book, we are to do a subject analysis in the context of the classification used. In library or book classification, we must analyse the subject properly from its viewpoint of presentation, the form of the internal arrangement of contents or its outer physical format. Take, for example, the subject 'Economics'. The book could be a history of economics or a dictionary of economics. It could be a journal of economics or a lecture on economics, numerical tables on economics or a video cassette on economics. A complex title must be split into its Main Class, sub-topics, form of presentation, etc. The title thus analysed is assigned the notation. Many a time, the full number may be found enumerated. In other cases, the number might have to be built with 'add-to' instructions.

Knowledge of the DDC

To assign a notation to the above-analysed title, we also need to have knowledge of the structure of the DDC schedules and tables, the division of classes and their hierarchical or sequential arrangement in chains and arrays. You must also know the rules for number-building, that is, the grammar of the Dewey Decimal Classification (DDC). As already stated, as a classifier, you are a matchmaker—matching the specific subject of the book with the appropriate number from the schedules. For this purpose, you need to have a broader view of knowledge and its various classes and the trends of the media on current knowledge being published. This kind of knowledge is never perfect but goes on increasing with experience, age and reading.

Steps in Practical Classification

Classification is an intellectual task that is not bound by any mechanical principles. However, Ranganathan formulated certain steps for classification in his CC to convert or translate the specific subject of the book into a class number. Though fully applicable to a faceted classification, these steps are also helpful in a scheme like DDC. The steps are as follows:

Step 0: Raw Title

It is the title given as such on the document. For example, 'Atomic Weight of Gold' or 'Shakespeare'.

Step 1: Expressive Title

Here, add any word or phrase in the title, if needed, to make it fully expressive of the subject. In other words, make clear or explicit what is latent or hidden. If the title is fanciful and an expressive title is not given, then you must spell out the complete subject of the book in your own language. For example, if the title is "Bard of Stratford upon Avon", the expressive title will be "William Shakespeare—An Elizabethan English Dramatist: Biography". In our other example mentioned above, you may add the word "Chemistry" to make the title expressive, that is, "Atomic Weight of Gold in Chemistry".

Step 2: Kernel Title

Remove ancillary or superfluous words from the expressive title. For example, Atomic, Weight, Gold, Chemistry or English, Literature, Drama, Elizabethan, Shakespeare, Life.

Step 3: Analysed Title

The kernel words are analysed in terms of facets or categories, Main Class, standard subdivisions, etc. For example, Chemistry (Division), Gold (Inorganic Chemistry), Atomic weight (Physical Chemistry), English Literature (Basic Class), Plays (Form), Elizabethan (Period), Shakespeare (Author) and Life (Standard Subdivision).

Step 4: Transformed Title

The analysed title is rearranged in terms of the citation order.

For example, Chemistry. Inorganic Chemistry. Gold. Atomic Weight or English Literature. Plays. Elizabethan period. Shakespeare. Life.

Step 5: Title in Standard Terms

In the transformed title, if there is any difference in the terminology of the title and the schedules, then the terminology of the author(s) in the title may be replaced by the terminology of the schedules. That is, we are to use the standardised terminology of the schedules. In the above cases, the term 'play' will be replaced by 'drama' as in Table 3 of the DDC Volume 1.

Step 6: Title in Facet Numbers

In the standardised title, the terms might be replaced by numbers. For example:

Chemistry	54
Inorganic Chemistry	6
Gold	656
Theoretical (Physical Chemistry)	4
Atomic Weight	42

Thus, the number after putting the customary dot after the first three digits is: 546.656 442 Similarly:

English Literature	82
Drama	2
Elizabethan period	3

Shakespeare	3
Biography	B

Step 7: Class Number

Put a dot after the third digit, that is, 822.33B. We have already arrived at a class number. So, in DDC, this step is rather unnecessary.

Step 8: Verification

If possible, the title maybe verified through the Relative Index. The above procedure, though slow, will make you a systematic and accurate classifier.

EXERCISE UNIT 15 – UNIT 17

1. Define notations in the nineteenth edition of DDC.
2. Discuss the properties of decimal fractions in DDC.
3. How would you depict hierarchy in DDC notation?
4. In DDC, 500 stands for which subject?
5. In DDC, 900 stands for which subject?
6. Name seven auxiliary tables in DDC.
7. Discuss the role of the index in DDC.
8. What is the significance of dot (.), space and bracket in a DDC number? Illustrate each with suitable examples.
9. What do you mean by class in DDC?
10. Discuss different types of notes in DDC with examples.
11. Highlight the importance of notes in DDC.
12. How would you classify a title 'central banks' using DDC? Mention the steps.
13. Write down ten Main Classes in DDC.
14. Classify 'Drugs affecting nervous system' using DDC.
15. What are the various steps involved in classifying a document?
16. Define subject analysis.
17. Discuss step-by-step practical classification with DDC. Use a suitable example.

Unit 18

Relative Index and Its Use

Introduction

In Unit 17 of this book block, we explained how to do subject analysis and ascertain the specific subject of a document. You were also instructed about how to assign a class number to the specific subject with the help of the Schedules (Volume 2) and Tables (Volume 1) of DDC. In the process of ascertaining a class number, the Relative Index (Volume 3) also plays a vital role in guiding you to get the appropriate class number from the schedules and tables.

The Relative Index of DDC has always been a part of the system since the very first edition (1876). It is not merely an adjunct or aid to the use of the schedules but an entity, in itself, is of value not less or equal to the schedules. It is considered to be the paramount and enduring contribution of Melvil Dewey to library classification.

Need and Importance

DDC is a classification by discipline. It means that subjects are classified on the context of a discipline. In the schedules and various auxiliary tables, all the concepts and subjects have been arranged logically in their whole-part relationship. That is also known as a systematic arrangement proceeding from the general to the specific. To locate a desired subject and its class number in the schedules, at least a preliminary knowledge of its position in the universe of knowledge is necessary. In other words, we should know the discipline. It is very difficult for any person to have even a preliminary knowledge of all the subjects in the universe of knowledge. Therefore, all persons, whatever their knowledge, have to use a key to the schedules at one time or another. This key is the index called the Relative Index in DDC. A classifier may use the Index for reasons that have been explained below:

1. The Place of Some Subjects in DDC is Illogical

In DDC, the position of some subjects is not very logical or as per universal consensus among scholars. Some misplacements in the original plan of 1873–76 continue to be so. At later stages, some new subjects were adjusted here and there were no vacant numbers were available at their appropriate places. Now, nobody defends the system for its logical structure. As a result, the scheme now has a distorted structure. The number of illogically placed subjects increases with new editions. Therefore, sometimes, even a systematic approach to the schedules might fail to locate a class number.

2. *Limited Knowledge of Classifiers*

Besides the illogical structure of DDC, a classifier, at times, might not understand the subject of the book to be classified. The term may be new to them or the classifier might understand the subject but might not know its location in the overall system. Take the example of the subject of 'Birthday Cards'. At first, one may not even understand to which Main Class it may belong. Some classes, such as engineering, are too crammed with topics to locate the desired subject easily. For these reasons, at times, the DDC Schedules (Volume 2) look like an impregnable fort. In some cases, the hierarchical ladder leads to false ends or blind alleys. There seems to be no way to break open the schedules to reach the desired subject. In such a frustrating situation, the Relative Index provides a royal road to the desired subject in the schedules.

Nomenclature: Relative Index

The index is called the Relative Index. The approach of the Relative Index is entirely opposite to the approach of the schedules. In the Relative Index, all the entries are arranged in an alphabetical sequence. But more importantly, the disciplines are scattered by subjects, whereas in the schedules, the subjects are scattered by the discipline. Thus, the Relative Index brings at one place all the related aspects of a subject scattered in the schedules (Volume 2). Its approach is, thus, complementary to that of the schedules. This index is called relative because it shows a term and its various aspects with respect to one another. Take, for example, the subject 'Birth'. It may have various aspects scattered in the schedules. Some of its aspects, such as birth control, customs, etc., are shown in the following simplified entry from the Relative Index (p. 117).

Birth

Control

Customs

Defects

Literature and teachings of Jesus

So, all the aspects of this subject, otherwise scattered in the schedules, have been collected at one point. This will enable the classifier to study a given topic from different angles and see its ramifications.

Scope of the Index

The Index consists of the following terms in a single alphabetical sequence:

(1) All the key terms/concepts in the schedules
(2) All the examples and illustrations given under entries
(3) Some of the compound concepts that can be obtained by number-building notes
(4) All the concepts/entries given in all the seven auxiliary Tables 1–7 (in Volume 1)
(5) Cross-reference entries for synonymous terms and cross-reference to the related concepts, that is, 'see' and 'see also' entries.

Thus, the total number of more than 80,000 entries in the Relative Index is far more than the total of 29,528 entries in the schedules and tables of DDC.

The Index cannot be expected to contain the names of all persons, cities, organisations, minerals, plants, animals, chemical compounds, drugs, manufactured articles and similar entities. Therefore, for specific names, we should not consult the Index. For example, if our title is *A Biography of Pandit Ravi Shankar*, it will not be fruitful to look into the Index for Ravi Shankar. Instead, we should look at the subject of the biography, namely, the musician's biography. Similarly, if our titles for classification are the Indian Library Association or Jawaharlal Nehru University, we should not try to look up these names in the Index. We should rather look under 'library associations' and 'universities', respectively.

Organisation of the Index

Each page of the Relative Index is divided into two columns divided by a vertical line. Each column consists of entries. The entries are arranged alphabetically. Any entry in the Relative Index is defined as: "A term or phrase followed by information in the form either of a number or of a reference to another term or phrase". For example (p. 203):

Cities local govt.	352.007 24
Sociology	307.76
s. a. City	

Class numbers in the schedules are given against each entry. Another kind of index entry, instead of giving the class number, refers to the other term. For example (p. 124), Boars see Suiformes.

It means that of the two synonymous terms 'Boars' and 'Suiformes', the latter has been preferred in the Index. Therefore, all the entries of this concept have been gathered under Suiformes (p. 1065, Volume 3). And the users who happen to look into this concept under 'Boars' are redirected to Suiformes by a see cross-reference. Another form of entry might refer to related entries in the form of see also (s. a.) entry. For example (p. 687):

Monism philosophy	147.3
indiv phil.	180–190

s. a. spec. branches of phil.

e.g. Metaphysics

The last line in this entry means 'see also' specific branches of philosophy for their monism viewpoint. Let us see another relatively simple entry (p.): Umpiring

American football	796.332 3
Baseball	796.357 3
Canadian football	796.335 3
Cricket	796.358 3
Rugby	796.333 3
Soccer	796.334 3

s. a. other spec. games

In the above entry, after talking about umpiring in some of the games (listed alphabetically), we may, if desired, refer to other specific games, such as hockey, for their umpiring aspect.

Looking Under Key Terms

For lengthy compound titles, we should look into the Index under the key terms. To locate a number for such a title, we might have to look under more than one key term. The choice of the first key term to be looked at is very important and requires insight and experience. The simple rule is as follows.

If, in the title, one term refers to an object/substance and the other is a technique/process/action, then it is better to look under object/substance, that is, the concrete term. For example, if we have to locate the number for 'Lunar Eclipse' in the Index, we should first look under 'Lunar'. Let us take another title, 'Manufacture of Jute Pulp'. Here, we should look under 'Jute Pulp' (Adj + Noun form) instead of 'Manufacture'. Moreover, 'Manufacture' seems too vague a term for immediate location.

But if there is a specific process or technique, then that process may be safely looked under. For example, for 'Bergius Process of Manufacturing Synthetic Petroleum', look under Bergius.

Locating Class Numbers in the Index

In the previous section, you were asked to look under key terms, but the term you are looking for may not have been indexed at all. In the Indian context, there are several terms used differently, for example, a subject like 'Primary Education'. In this case, you will find that there are two key terms, 'primary' and 'education'. If you check in the Index, you will not find any number for primary education. Under 'Education', there is no 'Primary' term listed. This is because in Western countries, it is called 'Elementary Education', and hence it is also essential to know the preferred terms. You are also likely to waste time locating numbers through the index if you do not understand the subject itself or the correct connection of the terms. Let us look at a simple example:

Economic geology of copper

There are three key terms: (1) economics, (2) geology and (3) copper. Under which term will you search in the Index? If you check under 'Economics', you will not find any number. So will be the case if we look under 'Geology'. In this case, there is a possibility of a combination of the two terms 'Economic' and 'Geology'. A number is listed under 'Economic Geology', but it does not help us further in finding the specific number for the whole subject. But if you check under 'Copper', you will come across Copper, Mineral Aspects—Economic Geology (p. 250), and the number is 553.43.

Hence, it is essential to check under appropriate terms. Otherwise, you will be wasting time in searching. It is always advisable to recheck the numbers in the schedules. It helps you understand the hierarchy of numbers, and in a few cases, you will also come to know how the numbers have been allotted/coined.

Abbreviations Used in the Sub-Entries

In every entry, you will find abbreviations throughout the Index. This has been done to save pace. The list of all abbreviations used has been given at the beginning of the Relative Index (pp. xi–xiii). Once you go through this list, then it might be easy to comprehend their full forms. If, in the beginning, you are not able to understand the full meaning of an abbreviated term, you may consult the list of abbreviations. With experience, you will learn to read the abbreviations easily. Some of the abbreviations are as follows:

gen. wks.	=	general works
s. a.	=	see also
soc.	=	social
spec.	=	specific spec.
jur.	=	specific jurisdictions
O.T.	=	Old Testament
St.	=	Saint

All the states of the USA have been given in abbreviated form:

Ia	=	Iowa
Ida	=	Idaho
Wyo	=	Wyoming

All the abbreviations are arranged at their proper places as if they were fully spelt out.

Numbers Given Against Entries

If a concept occurs in the Schedules (Volume 2), the full number is given against it for referring back to the Schedules. For example (p. 125):

Boilers bldg. heating equip. 697.07
s.a. spec. kinds e.g. Steam heating

Let us interpret this partial entry.

(1) The class number for 'Boilers', used as heating equipment for buildings, is 697.07.

(2) The line under 'building heating equipment' means 'see also specific kinds of heating equipment for buildings'. Steam heating has been cited only as an example. It means that in addition to 'Boilers', other heating devices for buildings have been given under their specific names. In fact 'Boilers' entry is a specific

entry for one kind of heating equipment. For example, some other methods of room (building) heating are solar heating, hot water heating and fireplaces. For these types of room heating equipment, we should directly look under these terms. For example, looking under 'Solar' (p. 1023):

Solar

heating

buildings 697.78

In this case, heating is subordinate to solar, and building is subordinate to heating. These subordination aspects have been shown by indenting, that is, by leaving space to the left.

Entries from the Seven Tables

If the entry is from one of the seven auxiliary tables (Volume 1), then the sequence of the number column runs as follows:

First is given the short name of the Table in abbreviated form in italics, followed by a dash and the number proper for the concept. For example (p. 110):

Bhutan area – 549 8

It means that the term 'Bhutan' is from the 'Areas' Table (Table 2), and its number is 549 8. The dash '–' before the number indicates that the number is never used alone but is attached to some number in the schedules. Take another example:

Bhutanese people r.e.n. – 914 18

It means that the term 'Bhutanese People' occurs in the Table of 'Racial, Ethnic, National Groups' (Table 5), where its number is 914 18. Abbreviations for the various Tables as used in the Index are as follows:

Table Number	Full Name of the Table	Abbreviations Used
Table 1	Standard Subdivisions	s.s.
Table 2	Areas	area
Table 3	Subdivisions of Individual Literatures	lit.sub.

Table Number	Full Name of the Table	Abbreviations Used
Table 4	Subdivisions of Individual Languages	lang.sub.
Table 5	Racial, Ethnic, National Groups	r.e.n.
Table 6	Languages	lang.
Table 7	Persons	pers.

Cross-References

Sometimes, we may not find a number against an entry. Instead, we may be directed to some other term by a 'see' or 'see also' note. Understanding these cross-references is vital in using the Index.

Cross-references are of two types:

(a) *'see' Type*

The Index uses standard terminology, wherein only one term for a concept has been used. In the case of synonymous terms, we are referred from the unused term to the used term.

For example:

Linum *see* Flax

Linoleum *see* Floor coverings

Zyriam *see* Permian

Cartesian systems *see* Coordinate systems

Similarly, from abbreviated terms, the reader might be referred to the full form.

For example:

ADP *see* Automatic data processing

However, if a country has two names in English, then an entry is made under both.

For example:

Siam	*area*-593
Thailand	*area*-593
Ceylon	*area*-549 3
Sri Lanka	*area*-549 3

Holland	*area*-492
Netherlands	*area*-492

(b) *'s. a.' Type*

More important are the 'see also' (entered in the index as s. a.) references. Such cross-references direct us to explore related topics entered under different terms in the Index. Consider the following entry (p. 402):

Flags	929.92
mil.sc.	355.15

s. a. spec. mil. Branches

non-verbal commun. See Flag signals

The above entry means that the general number for 'Flags' is 929.92. The class number for 'Flags' in the context of military science (mil. Sc.) is 355.15. Again, as a sub-aspect of military science, there is a s. a. entry directing us to specific military branches, such as the Navy and Air Force, for flags of those branches.

Such a cross-reference is called a scatter reference, as it does not refer to a specific term but suggests other possibilities.

Unit 19
Study of Tables and Schedules in DDC

Introduction

You have already been introduced to the structure, features and characteristics of Dewey Decimal Classification (DDC) (nineteenth edition) in units 15-18 of this book. This unit familiarises you with the seven auxiliary tables, that is, T1 Standard Subdivisions; T2 Areas; T3 Subdivisions of Individual Literatures; T4 Subdivisions of Individual Languages; T5 Racial, Ethnic, National Groups; T6 Languages; and T7 Persons. This unit also brings to your attention important aspects and a summary of schedules representing important divisions of the universe of subjects (000–999) and their use in synthesis or the number-building process.

Tables in DDC

A table has been defined as "a sequence of dependant notation indicating various special concepts used repeatedly with a variety of subjects and disciplines". Seven auxiliary tables are listed in this section, which support the schedules. The use of these seven tables in the number-building process is presented in the following subsections with suitable worked-out examples.

Table 1: Standard Subdivisions

Table 1 is frequently used in DDC. The dash or hyphen (-) preceding each number never stands alone. The hyphen (-) is omitted when you add a specific number from Table 1 to the base number from the schedules. Examples:

Title: Study and Teaching of Library Classification

Class Number: 025.420 7

Analysis:	020	= Library and information science
	025.42	= Library classification
	-07 (Table 1)	= Study and teaching
Synthesis:	025.42 + -07 = 025.420 7	

Table 2: Areas

Table 2 is also one of the important and frequently used tables in DDC for synthesising a class number. Table 2 includes areas, regions and places in general (-1), including physiographical features, population clusters and political and economic groups. It also includes persons in general (-2), ancient world (-3) and modern world (-4 and -9). In the eighteenth edition of DDC (1971), the 'Divide like' instruction was replaced by 'Add to' from Schedule spans and 'Add from' Tables. You will find in the 'Add to' instruction at several places in the Tables and Schedules of the nineteenth edition of DDC for the use of area subdivisions from Table 2 to the base number. For example:

327.3 –.9 = Foreign policies and foreign relations between specific nations

Add 'Areas' notation 3–9 from Table 2 to base number 327, such as Foreign Policy of United Kingdom 327.41 (Table 2). For example:

Title: Buddhist Religious Sects and Reform Movements in Japan.

Class Number: 294.390 952

Analysis:	294.39	= Buddhist sects and reform movements
	-09 (Table 1)	= Historical and geographical treatment
	-52 (Table 2)	= Japan
Synthesis:	294.39 + -09 + -52 = 294.390 952	

Title: Geography of the USA

Class Number: 917.3

Analysis: 910 = General Geography

-73 (Table 2) = USA

Synthesis: 910 + -73 91 + -73 = 917.3

Table 3: Subdivisions of Individual Literatures

The subdivisions under Table 3 consist of specific literary forms -1 to -7, miscellaneous writing -8 and specific periods -81 to -89. The notation from Table 3 is never used alone but might be used as required with the base number for individual literature identified by * under 810 4890 (schedules). Table 3 is followed and supplemented by Table 3-A, which provides additional elements for building numbers with Table 3. Example:

Title: Idealism in English Poetry

Class Number: 821.13

Analysis: 820 = English literature

-1 (Table 3) = Poetry

13 (Table 3-A) = Idealism

Synthesis: 820 + -1 + 13 82 + -1 + 13 = 821.13

Table 4: Subdivisions of Individual Languages

Table 4 Subdivisions of Individual Languages is never used alone but may be used as required with the base numbers for individual languages identified by * under 420–490 in the schedule. Examples:

Title: French Grammar

Class Number: 445

Analysis: 440 = French language

-5 (Table 4) = Grammar

Synthesis: 440 + -5 44 + -5 = 445

Title: English Words in Hindi

Class Number: 491.432 421

Analysis:	491.43	= Hindi language
	-24 (Table 4)	= Foreign elements (Add 'Languages' notation 1–9 from Table 6 to -24)
	-21 (Table 6)	= English

Synthesis: 491.43 + -24 + -21 = 491.432 421

Tables 5: Racial, Ethnic, National Groups

The notation in this table is never used alone, but it may be used as required either directly or with 'Add to' instruction or through the interposition of notation -089 from Table 1, with any number from schedules.

Example:

Title: Religion of Bantus

Class Number: 299.683

Analysis:	299.6	= Religion of Black African and Negro Origin
	299.68	= Of specific groups and tribes (Add to base number 299.68 the numbers following 96 in Racial, Ethnic, National Groups' notation 961–969 from Table 5)
	-963 (Table 5)	= Bantus

Synthesis: 299.68 + -963 299.68 + 3 = 299.683

Table 6: Languages

Languages are never used alone but may be used with those numbers from the schedules and other tables to which the classifier is instructed to add notation from Table 6. The use of this table is mostly confined to the Main Classes, 400 Language and 800 Literature. Example:

Title: Bengali Language Encyclopaedias

Class Number: 039.914 4

Analysis: 039 = Encyclopedias in other languages

(Add 'Languages' notation 2–9 from Table 6 to base number 039)

-9144 (Table 6) = Bengali language

Synthesis: 039 + -9144 = 039.914 4

Table 7: Persons

The notation from Table 7 Persons is never used alone but may be used as required with any appropriate number from the schedules with 'Add to' instruction or through the interposition of notation -024 from Table 1. Example:

Title: Custom of Doctors

Class Number: 390.461

Analysis: 390.4 = Customs of people of various specific occupations (Add 'Persons' notation 09–99 from Table 7 to the base number 390.4)

-61 (Table 7) = Doctors

Synthesis: 390.4 + -61 = 390.461

Schedules in DDC

In the preceding sections and subsections, you have been introduced to the seven auxiliary tables (1–7) and the number-building process with suitable worked-out examples. In the following sections and subsections, you will be introduced to schedules, that is, the Main Classes and their divisions. The worked-out examples under each Main Class will give an idea as to the nature of the titles and the need for following 'Add to' instructions to be found at various points in the schedules to build appropriate class numbers.

1. *Generalities 000*

The schedule of this Main Class deals with not only general aspects of knowledge but also some specific disciplines/subject fields, such as Bibliography 010, Library and Information Sciences 020, Museology 060, Journalism, Publishing, Newspapers 070 and Book Rarities 090. This class is also known as the hold-all class. The second and third summaries in DDC Volume 1 will provide you an idea of the divisions and sections of this Main Class. The following worked-out example covers an important division of this Main Class. Example:

Title: British National Bibliography

Class Number: 015.41

Analysis:	015	=	Bibliographies from specific places (Add 'Areas' notation 1–9 from Table 2 to base number 015)
	-41 (Table 2)	=	Britain

Synthesis: 015 + -41 = 015.41

2. *Philosophy and Related Disciplines 100*

This Main Class includes two important branches of the universe of knowledge, which are philosophy and psychology. The important branches are metaphysics, epistemology, logic, ethics, ancient, medieval and oriental philosophies and modern Western philosophies. The second and third summaries in DDC Volume 1 provide you an idea of the divisions and sections of this Main Class. The following worked-out example covers an important division of this Main Class. Example:

Title: A Survey of Research in Child Psychology

Class Number: 155.407 23

Analysis:	155.4	=	Child psychology
	-0723 (Table 1)	=	Research survey

Synthesis: 155.4 + -0723 = 155.407 23

3. *Religion 200*

This Main Class is mostly devoted to the various aspects of Christianity. Most parts of the notation 210–89 are devoted to Christianity. Other major religions of the world are listed at 292–99. The divisions and sections of this Main Class are listed under the second and third summaries (Volume 1). The following worked-out example covers an important division of this Main Class. Example:

Title: Bible in German language

Class Number: 220.531

Analysis:	220.5	=	Modern versions and translations of Bible
	220.53–.59	=	In other Languages (Add 'Languages' notation 3–9 from Table 6 to the base number 220.5)
	-31 (Table 6)	=	German

Synthesis: 220.5 + -31 = 220.531

4. *Social Sciences 300*

All the important disciplines in social science are listed in this Main Class. Some of the disciplines, such as psychology, history and geography, are listed under 150 and 900, separating from the Main Class 300. At several places in the schedules for social sciences, you will find special tables. The notation from these tables must be applied to the divisions identified by an asterisk. The divisions and sections falling under social sciences are found in Volume 1, p. 476, under the second and third summaries. The following worked-out example covers an important division of this Main Class. Example:

Title: Election Law of India

Class Number: 342.540 7

Analysis:	342	=	Constitutional and administrative law
	342.3–.9	=	Specific jurisdictions and areas (Add 'Areas' notation 3–9 from Table 2 to base number 342)
	-54 (Table 2)	=	India 342.07 = Election law

Synthesis: 342 + -54 + 07 = 342.540 7

5. *Language 400*

The Main Class Language 400 includes important languages of the world. The other major and minor languages of the world are listed under Table 6 Languages. Various aspects of languages, such as etymology, dictionaries, structural systems, etc., are listed under Table 4 Subdivisions of Individual Languages. Individual languages identified by an * in the schedules listed under 420–490 must be further expanded by taking notation from Table 4. The use of notation from Table 4 has already been explained to you in earlier subsections. Example:

Title: English-Telugu Dictionary

Class Number: 423.948 27

Analysis:	420	= English language
	-32 to -39 (Table 4)	= Bilingual dictionaries (Add 'Languages' notation 2–9 from Table 6 to -3)
	-94827 (Table 6)	= Telugu

Synthesis: 42 + -3 + -94827 = 423.948 27

6. *Pure Sciences 500*

This Main Class covers important branches of pure sciences, such as mathematics, astrology, physics, chemistry, geology, biology, botany and zoology. The branches have been minutely divided. At certain places in the schedules, you will find the use of special tables to achieve synthesis for number building. Example:

Title: Size of Venus

Class Number: 532.421

Analysis:	523.42	= *Venus (Add as instructed under 523.41–523.48) (Add to each subdivision identified by * the numbers following 523.3 in 523.31–523.37)
	523.31	= Size

Synthesis: 523.42 + 523.31 523.42 + 1 = 523.421

7. *Technology (Applied Sciences) 600*

In this Main Class, a detailed and elaborate treatment is given to all branches of technology. At different places in the schedules, you will find special tables to assist in number building. The tables have enhanced the synthetic feature in DDC. This Main Class covers important subject fields, such as medical sciences, engineering, agriculture, home economics, management, chemical engineering, manufacturing and buildings. Example:

Title: Treatment of Gastric Ulcers

Class Number: 616.334 06

Analysis: 616.334 = *Gastric ulcers (Add as instructed under 616.1–616.9)

06 (Volume 2, p. 869) = Therapy (Listed under 616.1–616.9)

Synthesis: 616.334 + 06 = 616.334 06

8. *The Arts 700*

In this Main Class, important branches of fine arts, that is, civic art, architecture, plastic arts, drawing arts, painting, graphic arts, photography, music and recreational arts, have been enumerated. Under each art, aspects like description, critical appraisal, techniques, procedures, apparatus, equipment and materials have been listed. The fine arts have been broadly grouped under fine, decorative, literary, performing and recreational arts. Example:

Title: Remodelling of Industrial Buildings

Class Number: 725.402 86

Analysis: 725.4 = Industrial buildings (*Add as instructed under 721–729)

0286 (Volume 2, p. 1238) = Remodeling (Listed under 721–729)

Synthesis: 725.4 + 0286 = 725.402 86

9. *Literature 800*

This Main Class includes important literature of the world, including literary forms such as poetry, drama, fiction, essays, speeches, letters, etc. The basic arrangement is first by language, followed by forms and periods. This Main Class is supported by Table 3, Table 3-A and Table 6 for specific languages. Indian literatures are listed under 891 and 894. Example:

Title: English Short Stories of early 20th Century

Class Number: 823.019 12

Analysis: 820 = English literature

-301 (Table 3) = Short stories

912 (Volume 2, p. 1404) = Early 20th century (Period)

Synthesis: 820 + -301 + 912; 82 + -301 + 912 = 823.019 12

10. *General Geography and History 900*

This Main Class includes important subjects such as geography, history and biography. At a few places in the schedules, you will find special tables to facilitate number building. For important countries, you will also find historical periods. Example:

Title: Travel in Ancient India

Class Number: 913.404

Analysis: 913 = Travel in ancient world

913.1–.9 = Continents, countries, etc. (Add 'Areas' notation 31–39 from Table 2 to base number 91, then add as further...)

-34 (Table 2) = Ancient India

04 (Volume 2, p. 1442) = Travel (Listed under 913.1–.9)

Synthesis: 913 + -34 + 04; 91 + -34 + 04 = 913.404

Unit 20

Auxiliary Tables and Devices

Introduction

Auxiliary Tables and Devices

The DDC started as a purely enumerative classification scheme listing all known basic and compound subjects. Gradually, provisions for the synthesis of class numbers were introduced to cope with the turbulently expanding universe of knowledge throwing forth extremely complex and compound subjects. One provision is to extend any number from any whole or part number from the schedules by the add-to device. The other provision is to extend a number from the schedules to form a number from separate tables now given in Volume 1. Table 1 was introduced in the second edition (1885). Table 2 Areas was separately listed in the seventeenth edition (1965), and the last five tables were introduced for the first time in the eighteenth edition (1971). These are auxiliary tables. It means that these are peripheral or non-essential tables required only for depth classification. In other words, these are supplementary to the schedules. These numbers are never used alone. For small libraries desiring broader class numbers, these may not be used. Their use is optional. The seven tables given in Volume 1 are as follows:

Number	Name	Abbreviation	Pages in Volume 1
Table 1	Standard Subdivisions	s.s.	1–13
Table 2	Areas	area	14–386
Table 3	Subdivisions of Individual Literatures	lit. sub.	387–403

Number	Name	Abbreviation	Pages in Volume 1
Table 4	Subdivisions of Individual Languages	lang. sub.	404–407
Table 5	Racial, Ethnic, National Groups	r.e.n.	408–417
Table 6	Languages	lan.	418–431
Table 7	Persons	pers.	432–452

Number-Building with Tables

It might be noted that these numbers in the tables are never used alone. These are only attachable to a number in the schedule. As already stated, a number in the schedules can be further extended on specific instructions as to what to add, and from where, to a given class number as the base. But the addition of a number from Table 1 Standard Subdivisions can be done without any instruction to do so. Table 2 Areas can be added on your own through the ss-09, Table 5 through the w-089 and Table 7 through the .M-088 whenever needed by a classifier. Otherwise, all the tables from 2 to 7 can be added directly only on instructions given under an entry in the schedules. The use of Tables has made the DDC more synthetic and has also made number-building easier.

Use of Table 1: Standard Subdivisions

A standard subdivision usually represents the viewpoint of presentation of the subject or the medium and form of the document. For example, philosophy, history and research are viewpoints. Serials, conference proceedings, dictionaries and anthologies are forms. All these non-subject recurring concepts are known as standard subdivisions as their name/term and the notation remain the same. For example, the standard subdivision for an encyclopaedia of any subject will always be -03, whether it be an encyclopaedia of philosophy, mathematics or algebra.

Characteristics of Standard Subdivisions

(a) These are non-subject recurring aspects of a subject.

(b) They always begin with a zero, for example, -01 Philosophy and Theory; -05 Serial Publications; -09 History.

(c) By themselves, these do not form a class number but are only attached to a class number.

Use of Standard Subdivisions

To classify a title, first of all, identify the standard subdivision, if any, from the subject proper. The subject proper is given the class numbers from the schedules as usual. Then, to the result, the ss from Table 1 is added at the end. Example:

Title: A Dictionary of Algebra

Class Number: 512.003

Analysis: 512 = Algebra

-003 (Table 1) = Dictionary

Synthesis: 512 + -003 = 512.003

Adding a Standard Subdivision with Varying Numbers of Zeroes

At places, as per instructions or examples in the Schedules, a Standard Subdivision requires more than one zero for attachment to a given Class Number; and in some cases of Main Classes and divisions, these are seemingly attached without a zero. When we add a Standard Subdivision to a Main Class (with two zeros), or to a division (with one zero) the superfluous (or filler) zeroes are removed, for example:

Title: Dictionary of Science

Class Number: 503

Analysis: 500 = Science

-03 (Table 1) = Dictionary

Synthesis: 500 + -03 5 + -03 = 503

However, there are many exceptions to this rule. For example:

200.7 Study and teaching of religion

300.3 Encyclopaedia of social sciences

Whenever such variations occur, clear examples or instructions are given in the schedules.

Using Two Zeroes

Under some class numbers, you will get instructions or examples indicating the use of standard subdivisions with two or three zeroes. For example:

Title: Encyclopaedia of Constitutional Law

The class number for Constitutional Law is 342. Here, we find the instructions/pattern: use 342.001 – .009 for standard subdivisions (Volume 2, p. 333).

Hence, our number will be:

Class Number: 342.003

Analysis: 342 = Constitutional law (Use 342.001–342.009 for standard subdivisions) (Use 342.001–342.009 for standard subdivisions)

-003 (Table 1) = Encyclopaedia (Instead of 03, we are using 003 as instructed) (Instead of 03, we are using 003 as instructed)

Synthesis: 342 + 003 = 342.003

Using Three Zeroes

There are cases when a standard subdivision is attachable even with three zeroes as per instructions. For example, class 351 Central Governments: 351.0001 Philosophy and Theory of Central Governments (351.0002–.0003 standard subdivisions). Therefore:

Title: A Journal on Central Governments

Class Number: 351.000 5

Analysis: 351 = Central governments

-0005 (Table 1) = Journal (Zeros are added as instructed)

Synthesis: 351 + -0005 = 351.000 5

There are no fixed rules regarding the number of zeroes in a standard subdivision. You are simply to look for any special instruction or the pattern for adding standard subdivisions. These instructions/patterns are given under the entry.

Use of Table 2: Areas

It is a systematic list of areas, population clusters and political, natural, physical and geophysical divisions of the world. The major divisions of Table 2 are as follows:

1. Areas and places in general
2. Persons/population clusters
3. Ancient world
4. Europe
5. Asia
6. Africa
7. North America
8. South America
9. Other parts of the world

Adding an Area Number

An area number is added to the ultimate class number. A class number may have an area number in three ways:

(1) It is already a part of the enumerated class number.

315 General statistics of Asia

915 General geography of Asia

950 General history of Asia

(2) Area can be added to any class number through the ss-09.

(3) Area may be added directly on instructions.

Adding Area Number Through Standard Subdivision 09

Some topics warrant the addition of an area number, but there are no instructions to do so under that entry in the schedules. In such cases, it is added through ss-09. You may recall that in the ss-09, we have:

-091 Treatment by area, regions, places in general

-093-099 Treatment by specific continents, countries, localities, extraterrestrial worlds

Under these entries, there appear instructions that read:

"Add 'Areas' notation 1 from Table 2 to base number -09."

It means that the area numbers covered by the span 1 or 3–9 may be added. Since ss-09 can be added to any number in the schedules, so, through this, any area number may be added to any class number without any difficulty. Example:

Title: Commercial Banks in India

Class Number: 332.120 954

Here, the core subject is 'Commercial Banks'. Its class number is 332.12. Under this entry, there is no provision for its geographical treatment. Hence, we will add area notation through ss-091 or -093-099.

Analysis:	332.12	= Commercial banks
	-09 (Table 1)	= Historical and geographical treatment
	-54 (Table 2)	= India

Synthesis: 332.12 + -09 + -54 = 332.120 954

Adding Area Number on Add-to Instructions

DDC, while enumerating some of the subjects, has anticipated the use of area notation and, accordingly, made provision at several places to add geographical place names. Under several entries, an 'Add-to from Table 2 Areas' instruction is given. Usually, such an instruction is extended at subdivision marked for the geographical treatment of the subject. In such cases, adding an area number from the schedules is as simple and easy as adding an ss from Table 1. Example:

Title: Elementary Education in India

Class Number: 372.954

Here, the core subject is Elementary Education. Its class number is 372. Scanning its special summary (p. 529), we find that:

372.9 Historical and geographical treatment of elementary education

This is our appropriate base number. Looking at its subdivisions (Volume 2, page 534), we find:

372.91–.99 Geographical treatments.

Here, we find an 'Add-to' instruction that reads: Add 'Areas' notation 1–9 from Table 2 to base number 372.9.

The number for India in Table 2 is -54. Adding this to the base number, we get: 372.9 + -54 = 372.954.

This is the required number.

Title: Elementary Education in Assam

Class Number: 372.954 162

Analysis:	372	=	Elementary education
	372.9	=	Historical and geographical treatment
	372.91 -.99	=	Geographical treatment (Add 'Areas' notation 1–9 from Table 2 to base number 372.9)
	-54162 (Table 2)	=	Assam

Synthesis: 372.9 + -54162 = 372.954 162

Adding Two Area Numbers

Examples:

Title: Foreign Relations between India and Russia

Class Number: 327.540 47

Analysis:	327	=	International relations
	327.3 -.9	=	Foreign policies of and foreign relations between specific nations (Add 'Areas' notation 3–9 from Table 2 to base number 327... then for foreign relations between that nation and another nation, region, area or place, add 0, and to

the result, add 'Areas' notation 1–9 from Table 2...)

-54 (Table 2) = India 0 = Facet Indicator

-47 (Table 2) = Russia

Synthesis: 327 + -54 + 0 + -47 = 327.540 47

Table 3: Subdivisions of Individual Literatures

Rarely is a class number found readymade in the schedule of 800 Literature. Class numbers for literary work must be constructed with the help of Table 3 or 3-A or both as per Instructions in the Main Class 800 and its subdivisions. Table 3 lists notation for regularly recurring topics applicable to any language literature 810–890. Table 3 lists various forms of literature, such as -1 Poetry, -2 Drama, -3 Fiction and so on. Table 3-A lists various themes in literature. Table 3-A usually supplements Table 3.

Classifying Literary Works of Individual Authors

For works of an individual author, the formula is Base (Language) Number (Volume 2) + Form (Table 3) + Period (Special chronological tables are given under each language literature in Volume 2).

Title: Paradise Lost by John Milton (1608–1674) It is a post-Elizabethan English poetry.

Class Number: 821.4

Analysis: 82 = English literature

-1 (Table 3) = Poetry

4 = Period (1608–1674) (Volume 2, p. 1403)

Synthesis: 82 + -1 4 – 4 = 821.4

Anthologies and Literary Criticism of Literature in Specific Languages

Examples Title: History of English Literature

Class Number: 820.9

Analysis: 82 = English literature
-09 (Table 3) = History

Synthesis: 82 + -09 = 820.9

Use of Table 4: Subdivisions of Individual Languages

It is a table of notation designating regularly recurring topics applicable to any language in the Main Class 400. It is used on instructions. Any asterisked (*) number in the 400 class, via the footnote, leads us to the instructions under 420–490 specific languages. The relevant instruction (on page 600, Volume 2) reads: "Under each language identified by *, add 'Subdivisions of Individual Languages' notation 01–86 from Table 4 to designated base number". Example:

Title: German Grammar

It is a subject of the German language. Its base number is 43, which is an asterisked number. 'Grammar' is a linguistic aspect whose number in Table 4 is -5. Hence, the complete class number is:

Class Number: 435

Analysis: 43 = *German language
-5 (Table 4) = Grammar

Synthesis: 43 + -5 = 435

It may be reminded here that a number in 420–490 without an asterisk cannot be extended by Table 4. For example:

Grammar of Pali Language 491.37

Grammar of Nepali Language 491.49

Use of Table 5: Racial, Ethnic, National Groups

It is a table listing groups of people by their national, racial and ethnic origins. This table is applied mostly on invitation. In case of need, it can be applied through w-089.

Using Table 5 on Instructions

Let us take an example to see the use of this table in building class numbers.

Example Title: Ethnopsychology of German People

Class Number: 155.843 1

Analysis:	155.8	= Ethnopsychology
	155.84	= Ethnopsychology of specific and racial groups (Add 'Racial, Ethnic, National Groups' notation 01–99 from Table 5 to base number 155.84)
	-31 (Table 5)	= German

Synthesis: 155.84 + -31 = 155.843 1

Extending Table 5 by Areas Notation From Table 2

As per instructions preceding Table 5 (page 408), each number in this table may further be extended by a notation from Table 2. This addition of Table 2 Areas to Table 5 can be done in two ways:

(1) Through 0 (zero) as a facet indicator. Any number in Table 5 may be extended by area notation through 0 as a facet indicator. To do this, there is no need for any specific instruction.

(2) Sometimes, instructions exist to directly divide a number in Table 5 by a number in the Areas Table. In such cases, there is no need for a zero to work as a facet indicator.

Extending Table 5 Using Zero as a Facet Indicator

The requisite instruction reads: "Except where the schedules instruct otherwise, and unless it is redundant, add 0 to the number from this table and to the result add 'Areas' notation 1–9 from Table 2". For example:

Germans in Brazil

-31 (Table 5) + 0 + -81 (Table 2) = -31081

Analysis:	305.8	= Social stratification of racial, ethnic, national groups (Add 'Racial, Ethnic, National Groups' notation 01–99 from

Table 5 to base number 305.8... add 0, and to the result, add 'Areas' notation 1–9 from Table 2)

-924 (Table 5) = Jews

0 = Facet Indicator

-43 (Table 2) = Germany

Synthesis: 305.8 + -924 + 0 + -43 = 305.892 404 3

Using Table 5 Through Standard Subdivision 089

In the nineteenth edition of DDC, the use of Table 5 has been universalised. Now, it can be freely added to any class number in the schedules through a standard subdivision, namely:

-089 Treatment among specific, racial, ethnic, national groups.

Here, we are instructed to add 01–99 from Table 5 to base number -089. Example:

Title: Development of Hockey among Punjabi People

Class Number: 796.355 089 914 2

Analysis: 796.355 = Field hockey

-089 (Table 1) = Treatment among specific racial, ethnic, national groups (Add 'Racial, Ethnic, National Groups' notation 01–99 from Table 5 to base number -089)

-9142 (Table 5) = Punjabis

Synthesis: 796.355 + -089 + -9142 = 796.355 089 914 2

Use of Table 6: Languages

This table systematically lists almost all the known languages. It is added to the instructions. Unlike Tables 3 and 4, Table 6 is applicable in many places in the schedules and auxiliary tables. However, sufficient and clear add-to-notes exist under the entries requiring the addition of notation from Table 6. Example:

Title: Bible in Hindi

Class Number: 220.591 43

Analysis:	220.5	=	Bible, Modern versions and translations
	220.53 -.59	=	In other languages (Add 'Languages' notation 3–9 from Table 6 to base number 220.5)
	-9143 (Table 6)	=	Hindi

Synthesis: 220.5 + -9143 = 220.591 43

Classifying Bilingual Dictionaries

As already said, Table 6 can also be used on instructions with other tables. Its important use is with Table 4, which it supplements for many linguistic subjects, especially in bilingual dictionaries. In bilingual dictionaries, the words are given in one language and their meanings in another. The formula for number-building of such dictionaries is:

Base number + -3 (Table 4) + Table 6

There is a clear-cut rule in Table 4 for building the number for bilingual (two languages) dictionaries. You are directed to classify under the language that is more useful in the library concerned. A Russian-English Dictionary in our country will be more useful if it is first classified in Russian. Example:

Title: Russian-English Dictionary

Class Number: 491.732 1

Analysis:	491.7	=	Russian language
	-3 (Table 4)	=	Dictionary
	-21 (Table 6)	=	English

Synthesis: 491.7 + -3 + -21 = 491.7321

Hence, you will note here that the class number for a bilingual dictionary will vary according to the library where it is classified. Here, a question might arise: Under which language is it to be classified first when two languages are equally useful? Table 4 prescribes another rule for such contingencies. A Spanish

Greek Dictionary in our country can be classified under anyone. But the rule says such dictionaries be first classified under the language coming later in the sequence. The number for

Spanish = 451

Greek = 480

In these numbers, 480 comes later in the sequence, and as such, it is taken as the base number. Hence, the class number will be:

Title: Greek Spanish Dictionary

Class Number: 483.61

Analysis:	480	= Greek language
	-3 (Table 4)	= Dictionary
	-61 (Table 6)	= Spanish

Synthesis: 480 + -3 + -61 48 + -3 + -61 = 483.61

Use of Table 7: Persons

It is a table of notation designating persons by their specific occupations and other characteristics, such as their social, economic and marital status. Table 7 is used in two ways: on instructions in the schedules and on your own through the standard subdivision 088.

Using Table 7 on Instructions

390.4 Customs of people of various specific occupations

As per instructions here, to 390.4, we need to add the appropriate notation from Table 7.

Title: Customs of Lawyers

Class Number: 390.434 4

Analysis:	390.4	= Customs of people of various specific occupations (Add 'Persons' notation 09–99 from Table 7 to base number 390.4)
	-344 (Table 7)	= Lawyers

Synthesis: 390.4 + -344 = 390.434 4

Using Table 7 Through Standard Subdivision 088

Under ss-088 (Table 1), there is an instruction to extend it by Table 7, if needed. Example:

Title: Cartoons Drawn by School Children

Class Number: 741.508 805 4

Analysis:	741.5		Cartoons
	-088 (Table 1)	=	Treatment among groups of specific kinds of persons (Add 'Persons' notation 04–99 from Table 7 to base number -088)
	-054 (Table 7)	=	Children

Synthesis: 741.5 + -088 + -054 = 741.508 805 4

Unit 21

Practical Classification

Introduction

You have been introduced to the process of synthesis of numbers in Unit 19 and the use of seven tables in Unit 20 of this book block. This unit is devoted to the process of multiple synthesis required for the advanced/depth classification of highly complex subjects. Multiple synthesis might be defined as the process of number building carried out with more than one 'add-to' instructions. The provisions for multiple synthesis are increasing with each edition of the DDC, though the term 'multiple synthesis' as such has not been used in the DDC.

As in the case of simple synthesis, the basic issue is the identification of the correct base number. The choice of the right base number will depend upon your knowledge of the structure of the DDC and on your perception of those aspects in a subject that are of primary importance. It will also require some experience to become proficient in identifying a base number in a complex subject. Ranganathan's facet formula PMEST might also be of great help. In a basic class, if one of the two aspects is concrete and the other is abstract, the concrete facet will usually form the base number for further synthesis. The core number is the base. There is ample guidance in the schedules to identify the base number. A base is invariably appended with 'add-to' instructions in the schedules. In the process of multiple syntheses, we have to move backward and forward in the schedule to pick up components of some numbers to add them to the chosen base.

Simple Synthesis

To a base number, a full or part number from the schedules is only added on instructions. When you are given such an 'add to' instruction, it is essentially accompanied by an example. On the basis of that readymade number, given as an example, you can allot the number for the document you are classifying. There is ample step-by-step guidance in the schedules to build on the base number. Let us take the title whose worked-out number has been given in the schedules.

Now, we will analyse the different steps given in the schedules for this worked-out example. Example:

Title: Administration of Secondary School Libraries

Class Number: 025.197 822 3

Analysis:	025.19	= Administration of specific types of libraries (Add to base number 025.19 the numbers following 02 in 026–027)
	027.8223	= Secondary school libraries
Synthesis:	025.19 + 027.822 3 025.19 + 7.822 3 = 025.197 822 3	

Multiple Synthesis

The above was an example of simple synthesis. Let us now take an example involving double synthesis:

Title: Administration of Law Libraries

Class Number: 025.196 34

Analysis:	025.19	= Administration of specific types of libraries (Add to base number 025.19 the numbers following 02 in 026–027)
	026	= Special library (Add 001–999 to base number 026)
	340	= Law

026 + 340 026.34 = Law library (Now going back to 025.19, we are to add to this base number the number following 02 in 026.34)

Synthesis: 025.19 + 6.34 = 025.196 34

Example from Social Sciences

Title: International Law for Trade in Tobacco

Class Number: 341.754 713 71

Analysis:	341	= International law
	341.754 7	= International law for trade in specific commodities (Add to base number 341.754 7 the numbers following 380.14 in 380.141; -380.145)
	380.141	= Commerce in products of agriculture. For a specific number of Tobacco, there is an instruction under 380.141 that says: (Add to base number 380.141 the number following 63 in 633–638)
	633.71	= Tobacco; We will add the number following 63 in 633.71, that is, 371, to the base number 380.141

Synthesis: 380.141 + 633.71; 380.141 + 3.71 = 380.141371

This is the number for Tobacco Trade.

Now, again going back to the original base, 341.7547, where we are to add to this number the number following 380.14 in 380.141 371.

Now, adding this number to 341.754 7, we get: 341.754 7 + 380.141 371341.754 7 + 1371 = 341.754 713 71

Repeating the process: 341.754 7 (Base Number) + 1 (From 380.141) + 371 (From 633.71) The number for International Law for Trade in Tobacco is 341.754 713 71.

Example from Science and Technology

Title: Atomic Structure of Uranium

Class Number: 546.431 44

Analysis:	546.431	= *Uranium (Add as instructed under 546)
	4	= Theoretical chemistry (listed under 546). The digit 4 is further amplified. (Add to 4 the numbers following 541.2 in 541.22–541.28)
	541.24	= Atomic structure
	4 + 541.24	
	4 + 4 = 44	

Synthesis: 546.431 + 4 + 541.24; 546.431 + 4 + 4 = 546.431 44

Example from Humanities

Title: Photography of Hindu Religious Festivals

Class Number: 778.9894536

Analysis:	770	= Photography
	778.9	= Photography of specific subjects (Add to the base number 778.9 the numbers following 704.94 in 704.942–704.949)
	704.948	= Religion and religious symbols
	704.9489	= Other religions (Add to the base number 704.9489 the numbers following 29 in 292–299)
	294.5	= Hindu religion

But in this example, we need a number for Hindu Religious Festivals.

294.51–53	=	Relationships, doctrines, public worship (Add to the base number 294.5 the numbers following 291 in 291.1–291.3)
291.36	=	Religious festivals

So, we will add 36 to the following number

291 294.5 + 291.36

294.5 + 36 = 294.536

294.536	=	Hindu religious festivals

Now, we will again go back to 704.9489 to add the number following 29, that is, 294.536.

704.9489 + 294.536

704.9489 + 4.536	=	704.948 945 36
704.948 945 36	=	Art Hindu religions festivals

Now, we will again go back to 778.9.

Here, we are told to add the number following 704.94, that is, 704.948 945 36.

Synthesis: 778.9 + 704.948 945 36; 778.9 + 8 945 36 = 778.989 4536

To sum up, multiple syntheses is simply repeated synthesis wherein we carry out the 'add to' instructions more than once. If you choose the correct base and then follow the 'add to' instructions carefully, there is nothing to be afraid of in the slightly circuitous process. In fact, building the correct class number by repeated synthesis gives joy and confidence.

Order of Precedence

Notwithstanding synthesis, multiple synthesis and in-depth enumeration of multitopical subjects, it is not always possible to provide a co-extensive (covering all facets of the subject) class number for a given subject. For example, let us take a simple title, 'Classification in Public Libraries'. In the DDC, the class number for Library Classification is 025.42, and for Public Libraries, it is 027.4. Separate numbers exist for both, but nothing can be done to combine them. One reason for such problems is that the DDC is still an enumerative classification, intending to broadly group documents (and to be a shelf classification). It is not a device for complete subject analysis of the documents.

Anyhow, as a practical classifier in libraries, you will often find yourself face-to-face with such situations and problems. Inevitably in such situations, we will have to take one facet/ aspect and ignore the other. The problem here is which to ignore and which to consider.

Decision-making in such situations depends upon many factors. Firstly, the aspect emphasised by the author must be considered foremost. It might also depend upon the library policy. If this situation does not apply, then the general (and common sense) rule is that the more specific of the two aspects is to be chosen, though knowing which is more specific of the two is not as easy. To help resolve such situations, some guidance has been provided officially in the Editor's Introduction to the DDC. These include providing Tables of Precedence or Precedence Notes under various entries and some other general rules for comparing the specificity of two or more aspects.

Table of Precedence

A Table of Precedence is a tabulated list of aspects of a subject, fixing the priority of one aspect over the other. The priority may also be fixed in a note form. A Table of Precedence is officially defined as a "note stating the correct citation order under a subject that the Schedules subdivide according to more than one aspect". For example, under 155.42–155.45 Child Psychology by specific groupings (Volume 2, p. 175) is given a table of precedence with a note. Observe the following table of precedence, for example, preschool boys 155 423 (not 155.432).

Exceptional children	155.45
By class, type, relationships	155.44
By age groups	155.42
By sex	155.43

Let us take an example:

Title: Psychology of Exceptional Sibling Children

Class Number: 155.45

This complex subject can be broken into the following viable components:

155.43	=	Psychology of sibling children
155.45	=	Psychology of exceptional children

The preferred class number will be 155.45.

Since, as per the above Table of Precedence, 155.45 Exceptional Children is to be preferred over 155.44 or its derivatives, our preferred class number will be 155.45.

Order of Precedence Note

Instead of giving the order of precedence of topics in a tabulated form, we are given a blanket instruction to use either an earlier or a later number coming in the schedules. These are called precedence notes and have the same purpose and effect as those of Precedence Order Tables. Let us take some examples of both cases.

Using Last Number

For example, under 365 Penal Institutions, the instruction reads: "Unless other instructions are given, class complex subjects with aspects in two or more subdivisions of this schedule in the number coming last in the schedule." Examples:

Maximum security military prisons (camp) 365.48 (not 365.33)

Prison discipline for political prisoners 365.643 (not 365.45)

Similarly, 395 Etiquette (manners)

A similar note instructs us to use the class number coming later in the schedules.

Using an Earlier Number

On the other hand, there are occasions in the DDC when we are asked to use the earlier number in such situations. Examples:

Under 331.3–.6 Labour Force by Personal Characteristics, the instruction reads: "Unless other instructions are given, class complex subjects with aspects in two or more subdivisions of this schedule in the number coming first in the schedules."

Immigrant women labour 331.4 (not 331.62 or its subdivisions)

Middle-aged casual labour force 331.394 (not 331.544).

Other Means for Fixing the Priority of Numbers

When no obvious instructions are provided under that class, then there are some general or commonsense rules for determining the specificity of a subject. Here are some tips as given by the editors in Section 8.55 of the Editor's Introduction (Volume 1, pp. xlvii–xlix).

By the Number of Zeros in a Class Number

There is one very interesting tip to prefer one number over the other. As per this tip, a class number without a zero is to be preferred over a class number with a zero. Similarly, a class number with one zero is to be preferred over a class number with two zeros. Examples:

Social aspects of direct relief to young people 362.71 (not 362.704)

Manufacture of metallic outdoor furniture 684.18 (not 684.105)

Architecture of wooden ceilings 721.7 (not 721.044 8)

Planning and policy making in home affairs department 351.03 (not 351.007 2)

Preferring the Concrete Over the Abstract

Examples:

Curriculum for kindergarten 372.218 (not 372.19) (Preferring concrete over the abstract)

Harvesting of China jute 633.56 (not 631.5)

Grammar of Oriya language 491.45 (not 415)

In the last two examples, we have preferred material (concrete) entities over the process/operation. Besides this, the citation order is also the one used in these two respective classes of agriculture and language.

Table of Precedence for Standard Subdivisions (Table 1)

Usually, two standard subdivisions are not applied in succession to a class number. If a subject poses two standard subdivisions, then only one is applied on a preferential basis, and the other is ignored. The table of precedence is prefixed to Table 1. A brief extract is reproduced below:

Study and teaching	-07
Management	-068
Miscellany	-02
Organisations	-06
Terminology	-014
Dictionaries, etc.	-03
Serial publications	-05

If we examine the preferential order, it becomes obvious that the facet indicator 'general special' is followed by 'viewpoints', and the real form divisions come in the end. It means internal forms are to be preferred over external forms.

Let us take the example Encyclopaedia of Organisations on Applied Psychology. Here, 'Encyclopaedia' and 'Organisations' are standard subdivisions with notation -03 and -06, respectively. Therefore, only one of them is added. As per the preferential table, '-.06' is given preference over '-03'. Therefore, the correct class number is 158.06 and not 158.03 or any number combining the two ss, that is, 158.0306.

Similarly, Directory of Library Schools in India will get the class number 020.711 54 instead of 020.255 4.

Journal of terminology of science 501.4 (not 505)

Therefore, whenever two standard subdivisions come together of a subject, this table must be consulted to know which is to be applied and which is to be ignored.

If, however, a class number is susceptible to two standard subdivisions, such cases in the schedule have been spelt out. Such cases admitting two ss are few but clearly indicated. However, any standard subdivision from 01 to 09 may be added to ss 04. The reason is obvious—04 is not an ss in the real sense.

EXERCISE UNIT 18 – UNIT 21

1. What do you mean by Relative Index?
2. What is the role of Relative Index? Discuss its need and importance.
3. Discuss the scope of an index.
4. What are different abbreviations used in the sub-entries of an index?
5. What do you mean by a cross-reference? Discuss its types.
6. Table 1 and Table 2 in DDC stand for?
7. Discuss the use of seven tables in DDC, with examples.
8. Discuss the role of schedules in DDC.
9. What is the role, use and characteristics of 'standard subdivision'? Give examples.
10. What is the role, use and characteristics of 'individual languages subdivision'? Give examples.
11. Illustrate simple synthesis in DDC using examples.
12. Illustrate multiple synthesis in DDC using examples.
13. Classify using DDC 'Administration of secondary school libraries'.
14. Classify using DDC 'Administration of law libraries'.
15. What do you understand by order of precedence in DDC?

Unit 22

AACR-2R: Preliminaries

Introduction

Anglo-American Cataloguing Rules (AACR) is a content standard for resource description and access. The internationally accepted rules of AACR-2R guide us about the bibliographic information that we need to provide for any type of document.

The history of AACR-2R could be traced to the Anglo-American Cataloguing Code of 1908. Subsequently, the 1908 Code was revised and published as ALA Cataloguing Rules in 1949. After the International Conference on Cataloguing Principles (ICCP) in 1961, the new code was published in 1967, known as AACR. The same was revised in 1978 and published as the second edition of AACR.

AACR2 has been updated by occasional amendments and was significantly revised in 1988 (second edition, 1988 revision) and 2002 (second edition, 2002 revision). The 2002 revision of AACR2 brought in a major revision of the rules dealing with serial publications and sections for non-book materials. A schedule of annual updates began in 2003 that ceased with 2005 publication and has been succeeded by Resource Description and Access (RDA). RDA was released in June 2010. The primary distinction between RDA and AACR is structural. The structure of RDA is based on the FRBR. The Library of Congress (LC), National Library of Medicine (NLM), National Agricultural Library (NAL) and several other institutions and national libraries of other English-speaking countries started a formal test of RDA in 2010, the result of which was published in 2011. RDA is still in a testing phase and will take some time to be internally acceptable. Hence, for our cataloguing practice, we will work on AACR-2R (2002), which is still prevalent throughout the world.

In this unit, we will discuss the basic structure of AACR-2R, types of entries, style of writing and the items to be provided in the catalogue entry. The cataloguing practice will be done on standard-size cards of 12.5 cm × 7.5 cm (5″ × 3″) as is done in the case of manual process of cataloguing.

Structure of AACR-2R

AACR, edition 2, 2002 revision, consists of two parts. Part 1 covers rules for standard descriptions of all kinds of materials. Part 2 deals with determining and establishing headings or access points in the catalogue, uniform titles and references. The rules in these parts proceed from general to specific. Part 2 is followed by appendices.

In part 1, the basic rules for the description of all library materials are included in Unit 1. They are of general applicability. The rules for specific types of materials are given in Units 2–12 and Unit 13 deals with analytical entries. The areas/items to be included in the description are:

- Title and statement of responsibility
- Edition
- Material or type of publication-specific details
- Publication, distribution, etc.
- Physical description
- Series
- Note
- Standard number and terms of availability.

In part 2, the rules for the determination of choice of access points and form of headings are provided. These rules apply to all library materials irrespective of the medium. Unit 21 deals with the choice of access points, and Units 22 to 26 deal with the construction of access points. There are no units between

13 and 21. Appendices A–E provide rules for capitalisation, abbreviations, numerals, glossary and initial articles.

Let us discuss the types of entries, sequence and punctuation used between the descriptive elements in the next section. Before we go into the details of the entries and punctuation marks used, we must know the extent of the description to be included in the catalogue.

Levels of Description

First, you must determine whether all the elements of the description must be included in the catalogue or not. The catalogue entries vary from library to library on the basis of the description of the items. The descriptions are categorised into levels on the basis of the amount of information to be included. The code has recommended that all descriptive elements might not be useful to all types of libraries. The inclusion of these descriptive elements is categorised according to three levels. The library can choose any level of description for all the materials. The library also has a choice to use all the levels in one catalogue, depending on the type of materials described.

The first level provides the minimum information necessary to identify a given document. This level is used in small libraries. The second level can be called a standard description. It provides all the data that might be considered necessary for the description of documents. This level is used for medium to large-sized libraries. This is normally used by the majority of libraries, as it serves the requirements of most users. The third level describes the documents covering every possible element of description included in the code. This level is used in large and special libraries.

In these units, we will be following the second level for the description of materials. Your library, however, may choose any level of description, but the heading and access points will be the same. Now, let us look into the elements included at different levels.

First Level of Description

The first level of description includes at least the elements set out in this schematic illustration:

Title proper/first statement of responsibility, if different from main entry heading in form or number or if there is no main entry heading. Edition statement. Materials (or type of publication) specific details. First publisher, etc., date of publication, etc. Extent of item. Note(s). Standard number.

Second Level of Description

The second level of description includes at least the elements set out in the schematic illustration below:

Title proper [general material designation] = parallel title: other title information/first statement of responsibility relative to the edition. Material (or type of publication) specific details. First place of publication, etc.: first publisher, etc., date of publication, etc. Extent of item: other physical details; dimensions. (Title proper of series/statement of responsibility relating to series, ISSN of series: numbering within the series. Title of subseries, ISSN of subseries; numbering within subseries). Note(s). Standard number.

Note the difference between the first and second levels of description of a title illustrated below:

The first level of description

Class No. Book No.	*Ball,*	*Avis Jane*
    Acc No.	 *Buffalo,*	*Caring for an aging parent:* *NY: Prometheus Books, 1986* *134p.; 24 cm.* ○

The same book under the second level of description will be:

	Ball,	*Avis Jane*
		Caring for an aging parent: have I done all I
	can't	*Avis Jane Ball.-Buffalo: NY: Prometheus Books,*
	1986.	
		134p.; 24 cm.-(Golden Age Books).
		Previous ed. Published as. What shall I do with a
	100	*Years? 1982*
		○

Third Level of Description

The third level of description includes all the elements set in the rules applicable to the item being described. This level applies in very rare cases.

Style of Writing

Let us discuss the card catalogue and types of entries before we study the description and other details of an entry.

In the Cataloguing Theory Course, you have learnt about the various physical forms of catalogues. You have also learnt the advantages of the card catalogue. It is the most popular tool used in libraries. The entry is made on standard-size cards of 12.5 cm × 7.5 cm (5″ × 3″). Certain vertical and horizontal lines are drawn on the card. The vertical lines are known as indentions. There are two vertical lines and one horizontal line in red. The first vertical line is known as the first indention, and the second vertical line is known as the second indention. There is one more indention, known as the third indention, but this is an imaginary line on the card. The horizontal line is used for writing the heading of this entry. The vertical lines (indentions) and the horizontal line are shown in the illustration shown in the previous section.

The card, which is illustrated above, was used for making an entry earlier when libraries were following the manual system for catalogues. Normally, a card used to contain a hole at the middle bottom to facilitate the holding of cards through a rod attached under the catalogue tray. The entries might be of different types. Now, let us see the different types of entries made according to AACR-2R.

Types of Entries

You might be aware that when a reader wants a book, they approach the catalogue to look under the name of the author, joint author, title, subject, series, etc. They are called access points. A number of entries are prepared to satisfy different approaches. The number of access points (approach points) depends upon the nature of the document or item to be catalogued or the approach of the users. Two or more entries might be prepared for each item. The catalogue entries can be categorised into two types:

(1) Main entry

(2) Added entry

Every document will have a main entry. The number of added entries will vary from document to document, depending on the nature of the document, as mentioned above.

Main Entry

The AACR2 defines the main entry as "the complete catalogue record of an item, presented in the form by which the entity is to be uniformly identified and cited. The main entry may include the tracings of all other headings under which the record is to be represented in the catalogue". Generally, the main entry is the author entry in AACR-2R. In some cases, a title entry might also become the main entry, depending on the nature of the document.

Added Entry

Added entries provide access to other headings in addition to that of the main entry heading. It is a secondary entry under which a bibliographical entity is represented in the catalogue. The AACR-2R defines an added entry as "An entry, additional to the main entry, by which an item is represented in a catalogue:

a secondary entry". The added entries are prepared under the headings of any one of the following:

Joint author, title, series, collaborators, subject, etc.

The descriptions in the main entry and the added entry depend upon the system followed by the library. We will follow the unit card system for the inclusion of descriptions in the entries. A unit card is a "basic catalogue card in the form of a main entry which when duplicated may be used as a unit for all other entries for that work in the catalogue by the addition of the appropriate heading" (ALA rules 1949 and AACR-1).

In the unit card, the contents in the main and added entries are the same. However, an additional heading is added in case of an added entry. This heading of the added entry is the access point. The tracing in the main entry will help us know the number of added entries prepared. Until now, you have learnt about the two types of entries: The main entry and one or more added entries for every item catalogued.

Items in the Catalogue Entry

You have learnt about the types and number of entries to be prepared for each item to be catalogued. You have to learn, in detail, each element of information to be included in every entry. The total information to be included is taken from one or more sources of information. However, if the information is not supplied on the title page, the information might be taken from any other bibliographical sources. The information taken from outside the title page should be enclosed in square brackets. Let us discuss the details of the information to be written in a catalogue entry. Broadly, the details are as follows:

- Heading
- Descriptive elements
- Punctuation marks
- Call number
- Tracing

Heading

The heading is the word or group of words under which the entry is made. This might be the name of a person, a corporate body, a pseudonym or the title of the book. In the case of the name of a person, the heading comprises of the last name (family name) followed by the forename (personal name) of the person. For example, 'Ball, Avis Jane' mentioned in the example above represents its heading.

In case the name of the author cannot be accommodated on the first line, then it continues from the third imaginary indention. It applies to corporate authors too. But when the book is entered under the title, it begins from the first indention and continues from the second indention. This type of transcribing the entry is known as hanging indention. In case of hanging indention, all the information about the collaborators, editions, imprint, etc., continues from the second indention only. The same has been illustrated in the example card above.

Different Areas and Descriptive Elements

The description of every document is categorised into areas. Each area consists of elements. Every area of description is connected with punctuation, such as a full stop, space, dash and space (. –). The elements are connected with different punctuation marks. Let us discuss the areas of description in detail.

'Title and Statement of Responsibility' Area

This area consists of the following elements:

(i) **Title Proper**

Rule 1.1B 1 states how to record the title in an entry. It directs the transcription of the title proper exactly as per the wording, order and spelling, but not necessarily as to punctuation and capitalisation. The title proper is written from the second indention and continued from the first indention.

If there is any alternative title, it should be treated as part of the title proper. If the work contains an alternative title, the first part of the title is given with a comma and the word or its equivalent with commas, and the first word of the alternative title should start with a capital letter as illustrated below:

A book of bits, or A bit of a book!, by Mike Milligan.

(ii) General Material Designation (GMD)

This indicates the class of material to which it belongs and is an optional addition. The AACR-2R gives two types of GMD: (i) British use and (ii) North American use. The following is the list of GMD:

> **British agencies:** Braille, cartographic material, computer file, graphics, manuscript, microform, motion picture, multimedia, music, object, sound recording, text and video recording.
>
> **North American agencies:** Art original, art reproduction, Braille, chart, computer file, diploma, filmstrip, flash card, game, picture, globe, kit, manuscript, map, microform, microscopic slides, model, motion picture, music, picture, realia, slide, sound recording, technical drawing, text, toy, transparency and video recording.

The terms from the above list are used in all descriptions for which general material designations are given. The punctuation for the GMD is a square bracket. That is, it must be transcribed immediately following the title proper. An example is given below:

> Roads of New Delhi [cartographic material]

This is the British way of transcribing. The North American system is as follows:

> Roads of New Delhi [map].
>
> AACR-2R further states that this type of giving information is only optional.

(iii) Parallel Title

A parallel title is a title in another language or script. It must be recorded in the order found in the item to be catalogued as per rule 1.1D1, which states that it should be in the order indicated by their sequence on the chief source of information. The parallel title must be preceded by an 'equal to' sign (=). For example:

> *On world government = World politics*

(iv) **Other Title Information**

Other title information, such as subtitle, is given following the title proper or parallel title to which it pertains. The punctuation for other title information is ':' (colon). If the other title information is lengthy, it can be given either in a note or abridged. When other title information is being abridged, see that there is no loss of essential information. Never omit the first five words of the other title information. Indicate omission by the mark of omission.

(v) **Statement of Responsibility**

It identifies the persons responsible for the intellectual or artistic content of the item or corporate bodies from which the content emanates. In other words, it is the author's statement relating to the work. The punctuation used for the statement of responsibility is a diagonal slash "/". If there is more than one statement of responsibility, each must be preceded by a semicolon (other than the first).

'Edition' Area

The AACR-2R rule number 1.2B1 states that the edition statement must be transcribed as found on the item. Standard abbreviations and numerals have to be used in place of words. The edition area is preceded by a full stop, space, dash and space (. –). It is transcribed after the statement of responsibility.

'Material (or Type of Publication)-Specific Details' Area

This area is not used for printed monographs but is used in the description of cartographic materials, music, computer files, serial publication, microforms and in some other circumstances.

'Publication, Distribution, etc.' Area

This area is used to record information about the place, name and date of all types of publishing, distributing, releasing and issuing activities (Rule 1.4B1).

'Physical Description' Area

The physical description of an item includes the number of volumes, pages, illustrative matter and size. This is also known as collation. This is recorded in a separate para (Rule 4.5A.1). In case, it is continued along with earlier areas, it should be separated by a full stop, space, dash and space. However, it can also be continued along with the earlier areas of description with the punctuations assigned for the area. However, we are treating this area as a new paragraph.

The description of the physical aspect of the book is written in a separate paragraph. The elements are page numbers (p.). The preliminary pages are in Roman number and others in Arabic. A full stop and a colon follow the page number. The mark 'ill.' Is for illustration, and lastly, the dimension of the book (generally the height of the book) is in centimetre. A fraction of a meter is to be converted to the next higher number. The size of the book is preceded by a colon. In case, there are no illustrations, the physical description for the above book will be written as:

xvii, 510p.; 2Scm.

'Series' Area

Sometimes books are published under series. This information is provided after the physical description, and the series statement is enclosed in parentheses. Before transcribing the series statement, it is to be preceded by the punctuation '. –'. Some of the series might have other elements, like:

(i) Statement of responsibility, which is an editor of the series usually
(ii) Subseries
(iii) International Standard Serial Number
(iv) The number of the series and also, maybe, for the subseries

In case, the series has a statement of responsibility, the series information will be immediately followed by 'I' and statement of responsibility, followed by a comma and ISSN, if any.

'Note' Area

There are cases where all the information about a document cannot be given in the areas so far stated. In such cases, when further description of a document is necessary, it is given as notes, usually in a separate paragraph. Some of the items in the note area are as follows:

(i) Nature, scope or artistic form
(ii) Language
(iii) Source of title proper
(iv) Variations in title
(v) Parallel title
(vi) Statement of responsibility
(vii) Edition or printing history of the index
(viii) Material specific details
(ix) Publication and distribution
(x) Physical description
(xi) Accompanying material
(xii) Series
(xiii) Dissertation
(xiv) Contents

We can give any information if it is helpful to the readers for identification of the document.

Standard Number

The standard number of the book—International Standard Book Number (ISBN) or International Standard Serial Number (ISSN)—may be written either in continuation or in a separate paragraph. If it is written in continuation, the area should be preceded by full stops, space, dash and space (. –). Give such a number with the agreed abbreviation and standard spacing or hyphenation, that is, ISBN -0-04-418007-1.

Call Number

The call number consists of the class number and the book number. The call number is provided by the classifier and usually recorded on the verso of the title page. Location on the card class number is transcribed one line above the first horizontal line after leaving one space from the left edge of the card. The book number is transcribed on the first horizontal line after leaving one space from the left edge of the card. This has been illustrated in the example shown at the beginning of the unit.

Accession Number

The accession number is the serial number of the item acquired in the library and is transcribed in the catalogue entry. This is for the use of library staff. Libraries might not transcribe the accession number in added entries. This is usually recorded on the verso of the title page. There is no rule prescribed for this purpose. For the sake of uniformity, we will transcribe the accession number on the fifth line from the red horizontal line of the card, as is done in the example card at the beginning of this unit.

We have completed the items to be included in the catalogue entry. There are many areas/elements, and it might be difficult for a beginner to remember them in a sequence. It might also be difficult to remember the punctuation marks to be preceded by each element. It is necessary to remember the location of each area/element in the catalogue entry. Now, let us consolidate all the items and prepare a skeleton card for ready reference.

Punctuations

While describing all the areas and the elements, we have also been discussing the use of punctuation. Punctuations prescribed in the code should be followed as it is. The style and type of punctuation so far described above are again explained in the skeleton card below. This will help you remember when, where and what type of punctuation is used.

Skeleton Card

The skeleton card with punctuation marks and descriptive areas/elements is given to create the confidence to write the description. The sequence of description and punctuation marks are common to all the items to be catalogued. The remembrance of the skeleton card will help in cataloguing practice. You must follow the cataloguing practice as given in the skeleton card, especially with reference to paragraphing. The entries in bibliographies and in a few published documents you come across might contain all the elements written in a single paragraph. Some of the computerised catalogues also do not follow paragraphing.

The skeleton card gives the general descriptive elements applicable to most of the items. The additional description is given whenever the item has additional information. Note the type of punctuation used for each element. Once you remember the skeleton card, your job becomes easy. In the case of the unit card system, the added entry for the above skeleton card is prepared by adding the added entry heading above the name of the author from the second indention. We will discuss this in the next section. A skeleton card was given at the start of this unit.

Added Entries and Tracing Section

So far, we have been discussing the format of the main entry in a unit card system. Added entries are prepared to provide access to the document through other headings, such as the title of the document, subject heading, joint author, other collaborators, etc. The added entries are secondary cards prepared to help in searching a document through other access points. Added entries are mentioned in the main entry card in the tracing section. The tracing section directs you to what additional entries have been prepared for the document. The body of contents of the main entry card and the added entries remain the same in the unit card system. In the added entries, additional heading is added on the top of the card to indicate the access point. This is illustrated with the following example:

Title: THE DEVIANT PUPIL – SOCIOLOGICAL PERSPECTIVES
Author: V. J. Furlong
Pub: Open University Press
POP: Milton Keynes
Call no: 371.93 FUR
Accession no: 7862
Pages: xx, 226
Date of Publication: 1985
Size of the book: 24 cm.
ISBN: 0-335-15225-2, 0-335-15126-4 (pbk.)

You are provided with a faithful reproduction of the title page of a book. It is a simple book written by a single personal author. There is a title and name of the publisher. 'Other information' is provided to you to complete the cataloguing process. You now have all the information required to catalogue the book. The different entries are explained in the following cards:

1. Main entry (Author entry; as mentioned in the previous section)
2. Subject added entry (Subject in title area)
3. Title added entry (Based on the title of the book)

The main entry for the book is complete. The heading for the author has been given on the title page. The title of the book also is reproduced without any change. The name of the author is transcribed in the statement of responsibility area. Next comes the place of publication, name of the publisher and date of publication. Appropriate punctuation marks are given, as already discussed. The next two paragraphs contain the physical description of the book and ISBN number. Now you might have a doubt about the ISBN number because, in the other information area, two ISBN numbers are given. The first ISBN number is applicable to the hardbound book, and the second number is given for the paperback edition of the book. The abbreviation 'pbk.' Refers to 'paperback book'. Hence, you must give only one number, whichever book you are cataloguing. In case you have both editions, you should give both the ISBN and accession number.

The last part, 'Emotionally disturbed children', is tracing, and it refers to the subject heading (as per the Sears List of Subject Headings (SLSH)) and the other title of the book. We will discuss subject headings in the next section. The tracing section directs you to what additional entries are to be prepared for the book. In this case, two additional entries are to be made, which are shown in the added entry cards. The subject headings in the tracing section are mentioned by Arabic numerals, and the other added entries are to be mentioned by Roman numbers. As only one title added to entry is to be prepared for this book, these have been mentioned above.

Under the unit card system, we have to prepare as many cards as are required and only then add the added entry information on the top line. That is why you see that the subject entry card is a duplication of the main entry. The only additional information transcribed is the subject heading taken from SLSH. Subject heading is always written in capital letters. The added entry for the title card is also a duplication of the main entry. The information given is only the short title of the book. Sub-titles need not be given in the added entries. The complete card is not repeated here, but in the library, you have to write the full card. This completes the cataloguing of this book. The subject added entry is shown below for proper understanding.

371.93 *FUR*	*Furlong,*	EMOTIONALLY DISTURBED CHILDREN Vj
Acc No		*The deviant pupil: Sociological perspectives.* *REST IS SAME AS IN MAIN ENTRY*

Subject Headings

Subject headings are commonly known as subject cataloguing. The cataloguer tries to bring out the subjects treated in the books to the notice of the readers by assigning appropriate headings. It is the name of the subject that is used as a heading, and thus, it is an entry element or an access point in the catalogue. Unit 26 of this book, SLSH (eighteenth edition) along with its features and principles are discussed. In addition, the process of deriving subject headings is also mentioned in detail. Please refer to the unit to learn the process of deriving subject headings.

Need for Subject Headings

In any library, the inquiry for a book may be made by author, editor, title, series or by subject. Entry under author, title, series or any other collaborator can be easily made, as they are the entities known to the cataloguer. The information about them is usually provided on the title page or in some other place. Hence, they are the known elements, and accordingly, the cataloguer provides appropriate entries as laid down in the code that the library is using. But, in the majority of cases, especially in academic and special libraries, the approach to the catalogue is by subject. Researchers usually require documents for their subject contents. It is found from experience that most library users are interested in the subjects of their interest rather than an author or title of a book.

Here, we can compare classification and subject cataloguing. A classifier tries to give the most specific class number, which is almost co-extensive with the thought content of the book and tries to bring together like subjects in one place. Subject cataloguing also does the same function through verbal heading(s) instead of notation. The purpose is the same, but assigning subjects in the verbal plane is more difficult than assigning class numbers.

For this purpose, C.A. Cutter brought a uniform catalogue code titled *Rules for a Dictionary Catalogue* (1904) in which he gives a few guidelines for the choice of subject headings. The List of Subject Headings of the American Library Association (ALA) also tried to formulate some basic principles to provide subject headings. The most comprehensive work is that of the Library of Congress Subject Headings (LCSH). In 1923, Minnie Earl Sears compiled a list of subject headings meant for small libraries. It is now in its eighteenth edition and fairly useful in small and medium size libraries. For your cataloguing practice, you will use Sears's list.

Basic Principles

You should know some of the basic principles for determining subject headings. Then only, you will be in a position to formulate the correct type of subject headings. Some of the principles involved are:

(a) *Common Usage*

The words or phrases that are used to express a subject must be in common usage. Obsolete words or words with dual meanings should not be used. Prefer British spelling instead of American spelling to keep consistency. Words in contemporary use are preferred. However, there are instances when several words may be in currency, but you need to prefer only one. For instance, 'Home Economics' is also called 'Domestic Economy', 'Home Making' or 'Household Management'. In such cases, you must choose only one term consistently. The term Negroes was once in common use for African natives. It is now considered an objectionable word and has been replaced with Blacks. When in doubt, check the words used in the list of subject headings and adapt accordingly.

Another general rule is to use a popular or common name rather than a scientific or technical name. Even in the LCSH, popular terms are used instead of technical names. For example, it prefers 'cockroaches' instead of 'blattariae'. It is prudent to use the terms familiar to the majority of the readers who use the library. Technical libraries, for example, might use 'toxicology', for which a public library might prefer the term 'poisons'.

(b) *Uniformity in headings*

Sometimes, we come across synonyms (that is, words with the same meanings). When a subject can be represented by more than one term, choose the one more common in usage. For example, the term 'Porcelain' is also represented by the words 'China clay' or 'Chinaware'. We uniformly choose only one term, preferably 'porcelain', and give cross-references to other terms. Uniformity in subject headings is very important. The terms, once selected, should be used consistently, unless they have become obsolete and are now represented by new terms.

(c) *Direct and specific entry*

In subject cataloguing, the most important aspect is to use specific terms that are co-extensive with the thought content of the book. You must enter the work directly under the most specific term, which precisely represents the content of the book. This can be made clear by an example. If our book is about 'British Labour Party', the entry should be directly under 'Labour Party' (UK) and not under 'Political Science' or even under 'Political Parties'. If a reader wants information on computer programming languages, the direct entry should be under 'Programming Languages' and not under 'Computers'. Again, under programming languages, if the book deals with Fortran as the language discussed in the book, the direct or specific entry should be under 'FORTRAN (Computer Programming Language)' and not under 'Computers' or not even under 'Programming Languages'. You can now visualise the need for such entries. If a reader asks what books on Fortran language are available, you need not search all the entries on 'Computers' or 'Programming Languages'. Directly check under the specific topic you are looking for. No doubt there are ways and means of connecting such correlated topics by cross-reference, which is discussed below.

(d) *Gross references*

In case of subject headings, cross-references play a significant role. Without them, subject indexing will be incomplete. Cross references are of two types, 'see' and 'see also' references. The function of 'see' references is to direct the reader from terms or phrases not used as subject headings to the terms and phrases used as subject headings.

'See' references are used in the following situations: Synonyms or near synonymous terms, inverted headings, variant spellings, etc.

'See also' references are made from the general to the specific and not usually, vice-versa.

Unit 23

Choice and Rendering of Headings and Statement of Responsibility

Introduction

In the previous unit, you learnt the basics of cataloguing practice. You know now how to write the different elements of a catalogue. The elements included in the description might vary from book to book. Once a document is in your hands, you must study the title page, which is the main source of information for cataloguing purposes. The title page provides you with the name of the author, other collaborators if there are any, the title of the book, the place of publication, the name of the publisher, ISBN number, etc. In a few cases, you might have to go beyond the title page to look for other information. For example, series are usually given on other pages.

The author who is responsible for the thought content of the document is important for cataloguing purposes. Books are written by one author or more than one author or by corporate bodies. In this unit, we are going to discuss books written by a single personal author. The author's name becomes the heading of a main entry, or it is an access point for search in the catalogue. In this unit, we are going to discuss how to render the names of personal authors and corporate bodies as a heading and also the other headings in added entries.

Personal Author

Books are identified with their authors or titles. The author is mainly responsible for the thought content of the book. The author may be personal or corporate. In this unit, we will be discussing personal authors. The AACR-2R defines a personal author as the one who is "chiefly responsible for the creation of the intellectual or artistic content of a work". For example, "writers of books and composers of music are the authors of the works they create; cartographers are the authors of their maps; and artists and photographers are the authors of the works they create".

The main entry in the catalogue is made under the name of the personal author when it is so established. The source to find the name of the personal authors is the title page, which is called the chief source of information. In a dictionary catalogue, the main entry is made in the name of the personal author or corporate author or by the title, depending on the nature of the publication. The first part of the catalogue is the heading. A heading can be the name of a person or a single word or a phrase placed at the head of a catalogue entry to provide an access point in the catalogue. As we will discuss about personal author in this unit, our task is to establish under which part of the name of the author the entry is to be made. Let us see how different names are established.

The general rule for AACR-2R (Rule 21.1A2) states that "enter a work by one or more persons under the heading for the personal author, the principal personal author or the probable personal author". Rule 21.1A1, which concerns the works of single personal authorship, states that "enter a work, a collection of work or selections from a work or works under the heading for that person".

Heading for Personal Author

Unit 22 of AACR-2R deals with the choice of names of persons. The rule states to choose the name "by which he or she is commonly known. This may be the person's real name, pseudonym, title of nobility, nickname, initials or other appellation". This is a general rule. A problem arises when we want to find the commonly-known name. Names vary from country to country. Cultural background, language, tradition, etc., govern the patterns of names. The origins and history of names are monumental, and it is not possible to discuss them here. Only a few basics that Indian libraries commonly confront will be discussed in this unit.

Western Names

Western names usually have two or three parts. The last part is called the family name or surname. In cataloguing, the surname is made the heading. It is called the entry element. Below are given a few names, and the part of the name that is underlined, is the entry element.

George Bernard Shaw

Bertrand Russell

Ralph W. A. Eliot

The style or format of writing the heading in a catalogue is:

Shaw, George Bernard

Russel, Bertrand

Eliot, W. A. Ralph

Indian Names

The entry element for Indian authors is not uniform. It varies from region to region. The AACR-2R prescribes some broad rules (rule number 22.25). The rules direct us to enter under the first word of the personal name in cases of authors born before the middle of the 19th century, like Panini, Aryabhatta, Asvaghosa, Bhattoji Diksita, etc., and for the later Northern Indian authors under the surnames, say, Kapoor, Raj; Khurana, Rakesh; etc. Southern Indian authors are usually entered under their forenames, such as Jagannathan, V. R.; Rama Rao, C.; etc. However, there are many exceptions in both cases. There is one full chapter in Ranganathan's book *Classified Catalogue Code* on Indie names. You are advised to study that chapter to learn more about Indian names.

Cataloguing Practice

In Unit 22, we discussed the style of writing cataloguing entries and what its format should be. Let us put that knowledge into practice. In practice, the actual title page of a book will be given with as many details as are required to catalogue the book. In rendering several elements, we also come across a few problems. We will discuss those problems and the solutions provided by AACR-2R.

Single Personal Author

When a book is written by a single author, the heading is made under the name of the author in an inverted form. In Unit 22, the example of the book titled *The Deviant Pupil* showed you how to prepare the main entry and the added entries in the case of a book written by a single author. Let us take another example where a few other elements are present. Whenever we are going to discuss an example, the title page of the book will be reproduced, and other information will be provided to complete the cataloguing.

Example 1

In this case, two added entries are made under one subject, that is, COMPUTER, and the Title—Introduction to Digital Technology. There are two extra elements in this example compared to the example given in Unit 22. There is an edition statement. Editions are written in figures though it is in words on the title page. In the 'notes' area, its previous publication history has been given. The designation of the author is given on the title page but not in the entry. The name of the publishers given in the entry is enough to identify the publisher (we have removed 'and Sons' from the publisher's name).

Example 2

INTRODUCTION TO
INTERNATIONAL RELATIONS

PIERRE - MARIE MARTIN

Translated from the French
By ARTI SHARMA

Edited by
J.C. JOHARI

STERLING PUBLISHERS PRIVATE LTD.
New Delhi-110016, Bangalore-560001

Other Information

Call No.	327 MAR
Accession No.	11200
Date of Publication	1986
Pages	183
Size	21½ cm.

Before you start cataloguing, the first job is to understand how the main entry is to be prepared. In this example, apart from the author, two more persons are responsible for the publication of the book. They are called collaborators. There is no doubt about the heading. It should be under the author. Let us first prepare the main entry and then discuss the other problems involved.

Cataloguing – AACR II and MARC 21 **Main Entry**

327 MAR	Martin, Pierre-Marie
	Introduction to international Relations/Pierre-Marie Martin, translated from the French by Arti Sharma, edited by J.C. Johari - New Delhi, Sterling Publishers, 1986.
11200	183p.; 22 cm.
	1. International Relations I. Johari, J.C. II. Title

There is no problem as far as the heading is concerned. In the statement of responsibility, the names of the translator and editor, who are called collaborators, are given. This type of collaboration is also called 'mixed responsibility'. Each collaborator is preceded by a semicolon.

The size of the book is given in the main entry as 22 cm. Though in the information, it is stated as 21.82 cm. Whenever there is a fraction of a centimetre, it is given in the higher whole number. We would like to take this opportunity to discuss some more details about the sizes of the documents:

(i) If the volume measures less than 10 centimetres, record the height in millimetres.

(ii) If the width of the volume is either less than half the height or greater than the height, give the width following the height preceded by a multiplication sign, like 18 × 6 cm, 18 × 30 cm, etc.

(iii) In a multivolume set, if the sizes of volumes differ, give the largest size.

Further, read rule number 2.5 D in AACR-2R. The added entries are given in the tracing section. They are:

(i) Subject,

(ii) Collaborator or editor and

(iii) Title.

Please note that added entries are not given in the case of all translators. The rule (21.30KI) in this regard states, make added entry for a translator if:

1. The main entry is under the heading of a corporate body;
2. The main entry is under the title;
3. The translation is in verse;
4. The translation is important in its own right;
5. The work has been translated into the same language more than once;
6. The wording of the chief source of information of the item implies that the translator is the author;
7. The main entry heading may be difficult for catalogue users to find.

In our example, the translator does not fall under any of these categories, and hence, no added entry is to be prepared. We will need to prepare an added entry for the editor as indicated below:

Added Entry – Editor

327		Johari, J. C.; ed.
MAR	Martin, Pierre Marie.	
		Introduction to international
	relations ..	
		(Rest as in the main entry)

Shared Responsibility

It is a common practice for two or more authors to get together and write books. The AACR calls such works a shared responsibility. The heading in the main entry in such cases depends upon the number of authors and their share of contribution to the work. On the title page of the book, the names of the authors are normally printed alike, but in some rare cases, any one of the authors might be given prominence either by wording or by layout. The AACR calls such cases a shared responsibility not indicated or shared responsibility indicated as the case may be and provides different entry elements for them.

The AACR-2R has defined shared responsibility as "Collaboration between two or more persons or bodies performing the same kind of activity in the creation of the content of an item. The contribution of each may form a separate and distinct part of the item, or the contribution of each may not be separable from that of the others".

There are specific rules applicable to shared responsibility. The AACR-2R has elaborated the scope of shared responsibility to which the rules can be applied. Rule 21.6A gives the scope of the rules as:

(i) Works produced by collaboration with two or more persons

(ii) Works for which different persons have prepared separate contributions

(iii) Works consisting of an exchange between two or more persons (like correspondence, debates, etc.)

(iv) Collaboration can also be between two or more corporate bodies or between a corporate body and a person

Principal Responsibility Indicated

In a work of shared responsibility, a particular author might have undertaken more responsibility for the creation of the work. The AACR-2R makes a distinction under two categories:

(i) Principal responsibility indicated and

(ii) Principal responsibility not indicated.

Let us first discuss the meaning of the principal responsibility indicated. In cases of books where there are two or more authors and if one of the authors is attributed with principal responsibility by giving prominence, such as by wording or layout, etc., the rule (rule number 21.6B 1) prescribes to make the main entry under the author who has been given prominence. For instance, if there are three authors and they are printed on the title page as shown below:

Loyd Enrick
SHEPHERD B. CLOUGH
Theodore F. Marburg

then the indication is that the main entry heading should be made under the author Shepherd B. Clough because his name is given prominence by typography. Let us take another example of three authors:

Connie Haynes
With
Eve Kraft and John Conroy

In this case, the main entry heading should be under Connie Haynes because she has been given prominence by wording.

This is called 'Principal Responsibility Indicated', where the author can be the first, second, or third author, but if the name is shown as distinct from other authors by wording or layout, the main entry heading is made under that author. In case two authors are shown as principal authors, then the entry is made under the first named principal author.

Principal Responsibility not Indicated

Usually, when there are two or more authors, and they are printed alike on the title page, it means they are given equal status. AACR-2R calls such situations 'Principal Responsibility not Indicated'. Under this category, it further distinguishes shared responsibility as follows:

(i) Books written by two or three authors

(ii) Books written by more than three authors

The entry element in case of books written by two or three authors should be under the first named author, and if the principal responsibility is not attributed to any one of them, either by wording or layout, added entries are made for the other two authors.

When books are written by more than three authors, and principal responsibility is not indicated, the main entry is made under the title of the book and added entry for the first named author only. In the statement of responsibility, too, only the first named author is transcribed, and leaving three dots, 'et al.' is in square brackets. It is a Latin abbreviation for 'and others'.

Books Written by Three Authors

The general rule in the case of three authors is to make the main entry under the name of the first author if anyone. The other two authors are not shown as principal authors by wording or typography. In such cases, the second and third authors are given added entries. Based on this explanation, the following example is given:

DEVELOPMENTAL PSYCHOLOGY

Robert M. Liebert
State University of New York at Stony Brook

Rita Wicks-Nelson
West Virginia Institute of Technology

Robert V. Kail
Purdue University

Prentice- Hall, Englewood, Cliffs, New Jersey

Other details can be given with it as per convenience

There are three authors, and all three are given equal status. No author has been shown either by wording or layout as the principal author. In such cases, the rule is to make the heading in the main entry under the first named author and to give added entries to the other two authors. The main entry for this example is shown below:

Main Entry

155

LIE Liebert, Robert M.

Developmental psychology/ Robert M. Liebert, Ritta Wicks- Nelson, Robert V. Kail _ 4th ed. - Englewood cliffs, New Jersey : Prentice- Hall, 1986.

6130 viii, 548.;24 cm.

ISBN 0-13-208109-1

Continued on next card.

Main Entry (continued)

155 Continued 1.

LIE Liebert, Robert M.

1.Psychology, Developmental .I. Wicks- Nelson, Ritta. II. Kail, Robert V. III.. Title.

Books Written by More Than Three Authors

In cases of books written by more than three authors, the AACR-2R gives the following rules: "If responsibility is shared between more than three persons or corporate bodies and principal responsibility is not attributed to anyone, two, or three, enter under title and make an added entry under the heading for the first person or corporate body named".

Based on this rule, we have worked out an example of a work written by more than three authors.

PRINCIPLES
OF PSYCHOLOGY

Richard H Price
Mitchell Glickstein
David L. Horton
Ronald H. Bailey

Holt, Rinehart and Winston
New York, Chicago, Sand Francisco

Other Information	
Call No.	150 PRI
Accession No.	64244
Date of Publication	1982
Pages	xvii, 650
Size	26 cm.
ISBN	0-03-048411-1

In this example, there are four authors, and none are attributed principal responsibility. Hence, the main entry is prepared under the title of the book. Added entry is provided only to the first mentioned author. Accordingly, the main entry for the book is shown below:

Main Entry

150		
PRI	Principles of psychology / Richard H.	
		Price (et al.). _ New York: Holt,
		Rinehart and Winston, 1982.
		xvii, 650.; 26 cm.
5819		ISBN 0-03-048411-1
		1. Psychology. I Price, Richard H.

In the statement of responsibility, we have shown only the first named author on the title page of the book. The name of the author is followed by three dots, which indicates that we have omitted some more names of authors. An indication to the extent that other authors are also associated is shown by 'et al.', which means 'and others'. You will notice the continuation of the title and responsibility area from the second indention. This type of entry is known as hanging indention. Further, only the first named author is provided with an added entry as indicated in the tracing section.

Books Under Editorial Direction

Let us now take up books published under the names of editors. Many people write short articles, and someone takes the responsibility of collecting, editing and publishing those articles in a book form, giving a title for the book. AACR-2R calls this a collective title.

"A collective title is one in-which three or more works or parts of works by one author are published together or it may be two or more works or part of works by more than one author published together."

For books published under the editors (also sometimes called compilers), the main entry heading will be the title. Added entry is made for the principal editor (or the compiler, as the case may be) or the first named editor on the title page. Based on the above explanation, an example has been worked out below:

ARTIFICIAL
INTELLIGENCE

The Case Against

Edited by
Rainer Born

Croom Helm
London & Sydney

Other Information

Call No.	001.535 ART
Accession No.	86765
Date of Publication	1987
Pages	xxv, 220
Size	23 cm.
ISBN	0-7099-3293-6

From the title page, you can note that the book is edited by one person. In fact, in the book, there are eight contributions by different authors with different titles to their individual contributions. It is not likely that anyone would ask for the book by the name of a contributor. In this case, the thought content is not of the editor, and hence the main entry is made under the title of the book with an added entry for the editor. Accordingly, the main has been worked out as shown below:

Main Entry

001.535

ART Artificial intelligence: the Case

against / edited by Rainer Born. –

London: Croom Helm, 1987.

xxxv, 220p.; 23cm.

8245 ISBN 0-7099-3293-6

1. Artificial intelligence. I Born,

Rainer, ed.

The entry has been written in hanging indention. Two added entries are made for this example—one for the subject and the other for the editor—as indicated in the tracing section. If there is more than one editor, a similar principle is followed, as is done in the case of shared responsibility. For up to three editors, all names are provided in the responsibility section. In case, there are more than three editors, then indicate the name of the first editor followed by three dots and [et al.].

Pseudonymous Authors

Sometimes authors hide their real names intentionally and write under an assumed name. This is called a 'pseudonym'. A pseudonymous author is one who writes under a fictitious name. In some instances, two or more authors join together and write under one pseudonym.

The interesting part is that sometimes an author writes under their real name as well as an assumed name. These problems are solved by cataloguing so that the books of one author are placed together. The AACR-2R recommends the following solutions:

Rule number 22.2B1: If all the works by a person appear under one pseudonym or if the person is predominantly identified in reference sources by one pseudonym, choose the entry element under that pseudonym. Further, rule number 22.2B2 states that for a person who uses several pseudonyms and also writes under their own name, the entry must be made under the predominant name. In case, the predominant name cannot be determined, the entry must be made as it appears in the later editions of their works.

If two or more persons collaborate and use a single pseudonym, use the pseudonym as the heading for the works produced by their collaboration.

In all the above cases, the reference must be provided from the pseudonym to the real name or vice versa. The example given below will further clarify the rules stated above.

THE GIFT OF MAGI

By
O. Henry

Illustrated by
Erik Blegvad

Hawthorn Books
New York

Other Information

Call No.	813.52/OHE
Accession No.	3011
Date of Publication	1972
Pages	29
Size	17 cm.

There are few illustrations

The title page is simple. There is a simple personal author, but the author's name is fictitious. It is the pseudonym, and the actual name of the author is William Sydney Porter. However, the author is predominantly known by their pseudonym, so the heading will be under the pseudonym. Accordingly, the main entry card has been worked out.

Main Entry

813.53		
OHE	Henry, O	
		The gift of magi / by O. Henry;
	illustrated by Erik Blegvad. _ New York :	
	Howthorn Books, 1972.	
		29p.: ill. ; 17 cm.
3011		O. Henry is the pseudonym of
	William Sydney Porter.	
		1. American fiction. I. Title.

In this example, other than the added entries for subject and title, we also need a reference entry for the real name of the author. Also, notice that the pseudonymous name of William Sydney Porter is O. Henry, and not Henry, O. Hence, the name is not inverted. There are several works under O. Henry specially written for children. The 'See' reference entry for this example is illustrated below:

	Porter, William Sydney	
		See
		Henry, O.

Corporate Bodies

As per AACR-2R, a corporate body is "an organisation or group of persons that is identified by a particular name and that acts, or may act, as an entity". Some of the best-known examples of corporate bodies are governments, different agencies of the governments, religious bodies, associations, institutions, conferences, fairs and festivals and so on.

We will try to give some illustrative examples to help you make entries for corporate bodies. We will take up some simple examples of corporate bodies under (i) Government; (ii) Committees and commissions; (iii) Institutions, associations and societies; and (iv) Conferences, seminars and symposia. All the basic rules you have studied so far are also applicable to corporate bodies. There is no difference in making different entries. The only change is in the heading. You must establish the correct heading for corporate bodies as you do in the case of personal authors. The basic rule is to enter a corporate body directly under the name by which it is predominantly identified.

Government as Corporate Body

Government is one of the biggest publishers in many countries. The word 'government' means the totality of corporate bodies (executive, legislative and judicial) exercising powers of jurisdiction. The heading for the government is the geographic name of the area (country, province, state, municipality, etc.). For instance, if we are treating the Government of India as an author, the entry heading should be the geographical name, that is, India. If there is any conflict in the name of a country, state or province, it is distinguished by an individualising element, such as Germany (Democratic Republic), Germany (Federal Republic), Korea (North), Korea (South), etc.

Government Officials

Government dignitaries acting in their official capacity are entered as such and not by their names. Sovereigns, Presidents, Governors, Prime Ministers and others are entered by designation, not by their names. Examples: United Kingdom – Sovereign (1952: Elizabeth IT); India – President (1962–67: Radhakrishnan); India – Prime Minister.

Note: In the case of the head of State (President, Governor, etc.), add the period of incumbency and name as terms of addition. If the name varies according to sex (king, queen, etc.), use a generic term suitable to both sexes, such as Sovereign, instead of king, queen, etc. In the case of a head of government who is not a head of state, add only the official designation. Do not add the period and name.

Government Agencies

There are several government bodies that usually fall under the executive, legislative or judicial jurisdiction. The rules prescribed for government bodies or government agencies should be clearly understood. Some of the agencies are entered directly under their names. However, there are several cases where subordinate bodies also can be entered directly under their names. In this section, some examples of such agencies are enumerated. They are only illustrative, and from experience, you will be in a position to pick up the correct entry elements for such bodies. For example, India: Ministry of Defence; India: Ministry of Information and Broadcasting; India: Supreme Court, etc.

The purpose of inserting Parliament is to bring together the publications of Lok Sabha and Rajya Sabha in one place.

Given below are some examples of subordinate bodies entered directly, though they have a parent organisation:

(1) India – Central Statistical Organisation

Hierarchy is: India

Ministry of Planning

Central Statistical Organisation

(2) India – Director General of Employment and Training

Hierarchy is: India

Ministry of Labour

Director General of Employment and Training

In the examples shown above, the middle body is not taken into consideration for the entry element, and the heading is made under the lower body because there is no ambiguity.

Committees and Commissions

The Government frequently appoints several committees and commissions to deliberate on several aspects. These committees and commissions submit their reports to the government. Committee reports are vital from different angles.

They are constantly sought in libraries for reference or research work. Some libraries make separate sections in their libraries for government reports because of their importance. Committee and commission reports might become popular either by the name of the committee and commission or by the names of the chairpersons of these committees and commissions. The names of some committees and commissions are as follows:

(i) Education and National Development: Report of the Education Commission, 1964–66. Chairman of the Commission: D.S. Kothari

(ii) Committee on the Status of Women in India, 1971. Report

(iii) Committee on Taxation of Agricultural Wealth and Income, 1972. Chairman: K.N. Raj

(iv) Finance Commission, 1972. Report

Chairman: K. Brahmananda Reddy

These are either directly entered under the name of the committee or commission or the subordinate bodies of the government. Additional entries are provided for the chairman. Based on the above discussion, let us work out an example under committees and commissions.

The committee here is a subordinate body appointed by the Ministry of Shipping and Transport of the Government of India. However, it can be subordinately entered directly under the heading for the whole government, omitting the name of the intermediate body in the hierarchy, that is, the Ministry of Shipping and Transport. Nevertheless, a cross-reference might be given from an indirect heading, including the name of the ministry. The date given, along with the name of the committee, is the year of its appointment. This serves as a term of addition in case another such committee is constituted at a later date. Sometimes, the reports of many such committees become popular by the names of the chairman of such committees. Hence, additional entries are provided for the chairman. In this example, two special added entries are made—one under the name of the Chairman and the other the second title entry referring to the Chairman as Lokur Committee Report (as the committee is popularly known by the name of the chairman).

Report of the Wage Revision Committee for Port and Dock Workers for Major Ports, 1974

Ministry of Shipping and Transport
1977

Other Information:

Call No.	33L28 IND
Acc. No.	3098
Pages	vi, 354
Size	20cm
Note	Chairman of the Committee: B .N. Lokur.

Main Entry

331.28

IND — India. Wage Revision committee for
Port and Dock Workers for Major
Ports. 1974.
Report. [New Delhi]: Ministry of Shipping
and Transport, 1977.
3098 — vi, 354p.; 20cm.
B.N. Lokur, Chairman.
Also known as Lokur Committee Report.
1. Wages port Workers. I. Lokur, B.N.
II. Title. III. Title: Lokur Committee report.

Institutions, Associations and Societies

In this section, we will discuss institutions, associations and societies. These can be termed organisations. Organisations can be at the international, national or local level. Some of the examples of the above-stated organisations are given below:

> International bodies, like United Nations, UNESCO, WHO, FAO, ILO, etc.

In every discipline, there are one or more international organisations, like International Federation of Library

Associations and Institutions, International Academy of Political Science and Constitutions Studies, Commonwealth of Nations, North Atlantic Treaty Organisations (NATO) and so on.

In the same way, every country has their national organisations, like the Indian Library Association, National Academy of Art, Indian Institute of Architects, Institute of Chartered Accountants of India, Geographical Society of India, etc.

The publications of these bodies are usually directly entered under their names. We have worked out an example covering the topics discussed above.

AMA

Management Handbook

Edited by the Russell F. Moore

American Management Association Inc.

New York

Other Information:

Call No.	658.02/AME
Acc. No.	3094
Date	1970
Pages	xx,48
Size	24 cm.
Note	On the back of the title page it is stated that the copyright is with the American Management Association, Inc.

The main entry heading is under the name of the association. Usually, when a book is edited by someone, the entry is made under the title. However, notes are different. Here, the works emanate from a corporate body of an administrative nature, dealing with the procedures and operations of the body itself.

As per rule number 21: 1, .. B2, the entry is made under the body. Added entries, as shown in the tracing, must be made.

Main Entry

658.02		
AME	American Management Association.	
		AMA management handbook/
	edited by Russell F. Moore. New York.	
	The Association, 1970.	
		Xx, 48p.; 24 cm.
3094		
		ISBN 0-8144-5212-4
		1. Management Handbooks,
	Manual etc. I. Moore Russell F.	
	II.	Title

Institutional publications are quite common, and such publications are constantly added to the collection of academic and research libraries. Cataloguing these publications as per AACR-2R usually does not pose much difficulty. Institutional publications are entered directly under the name of the institution unless the rule provides for entering subordinates under the name of a larger body. In the next section, we will now discuss the proceedings of conferences, seminars and symposia.

Conferences, Seminars, Symposia

Another type of common publication is the proceedings of conferences, seminars, workshops, symposia, etc. Many conferences are held annually or at different intervals. The papers presented at these conferences, their deliberations and the recommendations are published in the form of proceedings. Many of these proceedings contain research findings that are constantly in demand in academic and special libraries. They require special treatment, and AACR-2R has provided guidelines to catalogue them.

Some of the rules to remember in case of conferences are as follows:

(i) The indications of the number, frequency or years are omitted at the beginning of the name of the conference, such as All India Library Conference.

(ii) The number, year and place of the conference are given as terms of addition in parentheses after the name of the conference, such as All India Labour Conference (twenty-sixth, 1980, Delhi).

Proceedings of the Ninth Lunar and Planetary
Science Conference, Houston, TEXAS
March 13 17, 1978

Compiled by
The Lunar and Planetary Institute
Houston, Texas

Pergamon Press
Oxford

Other details may be added as per convenience

Main Entry

523.3

LUN Lunar and Planetary Science
Conference (9th :1978: Houston).
Proceedings of the Ninth Lunar
and Planetary Science Conference,
Houston, Texas, March 13-17, 1978/
4038-40 compiled by the Lunar and Planetary
Institute .- Oxford: Pergamon Press
1978.
3v.; 26 cm.
Continued on next card.

Main Entry (Continued)

523.3		Continued 1
LUN	Lunar and Planetary Science	
		Conference (9th :1978 : Houston).
		1.Moon Congress, Conferences,
	etc.	I. Lunar and Planetary
	Institute (Houston Texas). II. Title	

In accordance with the rules, the word 'Ninth' at the beginning of the title has been omitted. It is shown in parentheses, along with the year of the conference and the place where it was held.

Unit 24

Cataloguing Multivolumes, Serial Publications and Non-Print Media

Introduction

In this unit, we will be covering some important aspects of cataloguing, that is, the entries for books published in multi-volume books, serial publications and non-print media. Generally, books are published in a single volume. When thought content cannot be accommodated in a single volume of reasonable size, it is published as a multi-volumed or multipart publication. Multi-volumed books are published in various ways. We will study these aspects and also offer suitable methods to catalogue them.

Serials are the backbone of special libraries. No worthwhile research on a subject can be undertaken without a representative collection of serials pertaining to the specialisation. For their effective use, the serials are properly organised. This Unit tries to explain, with proper examples, the rules of AACR-2R concerning serial publications.

The bibliographic description of printed material might be confined to the description of the physical nature of the material. But in the case of non-print material, it is essential to describe the content in full and with specific details. This is necessary because mostly non-print materials are generally equipment dependent and cannot be browsed directly. In such cases, most of the required information must be obtained by seeing the inside material. The cataloguer should be familiar with the General Material Designation (GMD), the physical characteristics of individual materials and the software and hardware required for the purpose.

AACR-2R provides specific rules for cataloguing different types of non-print material. The General Rules for Description are given in Chapter 1 of AACR-2R, which describes different types of library material, both print and non-print. The procedure to be followed for describing non-print material is to first identify the type of format and the material it belongs to and then refer to the rules given in the specific chapter for that type of material. Individual chapters for the description of non-print material direct the cataloguer to the General Rules in Part 1, Chapter 1.

Multi-Volume Books

Let us now take up another type of publication, called multi-volume books. Generally, books are published in a single volume, but when thought content cannot be accommodated in one volume of reasonable size, it is published in more than one volume. The AACR-2R calls multi-volumes multi-parts and defines it as "a monograph complete, or intended to be completed in a finite number of separate parts". Multi-volume books might be published in various ways, such as those listed below:

(i) The title page is common to all publications;

(ii) Each volume has its own title besides the common title of all the volumes;

(iii) All volumes may have continuous pagination or separate pagination for each volume;

(iv) All volumes may or may not have the same publication date.

There are several other peculiarities in the publication of multi-volume sets. The authors or editors of each volume need not be the same. The sequence of publication also need not be in serial order. For example, volume two can be published before volume one.

Descriptive Element in Multi-Volumes

The rules regarding the choice of heading in case of multi-volumes are the same as applicable to all other publications we have discussed so far. The differences come in the case of descriptive elements. The variations occur in the following three areas:

(i) Title

(ii) Pagination

(iii) Date of Publication

Let us discuss the above elements in brief. Title in multi-volume publications, usually, there are two types of titles:

(i) Common title or common title pages for all the volumes;

(ii) Separate title for each volume in addition to a common title.

The descriptions for these two types vary, as the first category consists of only one title for all the volumes, and the second category consists of a generic title and a specific title for each volume.

When a set of volumes has different titles, the information about each title is given in the note area as the content of the volumes. Let us make this clear with examples of above-stated types of multi-volume publications.

Example of a Common Title

Hanumanth Rao; *Indian History and Culture*/Hanumanth Rao and K. Basavesvara Rao. Guntur: Sri Vigjnana Manjusha, 1970, 3v.

In this set of three volumes, the title pages of three volumes are identical. The only exception was that in each volume, the number of volumes has been written as Volume 1, Volume 2 and Volume 3.

Example of Different Title in Addition to a Common Title

The second type of example is given below, also with three volumes, but each volume has its own title in addition to the common title:

Naqvi, Shariful Hasan

Readings in Indian History, 3v.

V1. *Ancient India*; V2. *Medieval India*; V3. *Modern India*

Pagination

In the physical description area, when a printed monograph is in more than one volume, the number of the volumes must be recorded as 3v, 4v, etc.

There are also cases where the number of bibliographical volumes varies with the actual physical volumes, in which case it is written as 6v. in 4, 8v. in 5, etc.

In the multiple sets of volumes, there are several variations in pagination. Some volumes may have continuous numbering of pages, and in many cases, individual volumes get their own pagination. The AACR-2R has suggested the following method to show the pagination in the physical description area.

If a set of volumes is continuously paged, the pagination must be given in parentheses after the number of volumes, like 2v. (xviii, 826p.); 3v. (xxxi, 1017p.); etc.

Preliminary pages that figure in the subsequent volumes are ignored. If there is a separate pagination for each volume, it can be given in two ways—either 3 v. or 3 v.; (xii, 428; xix, 536; ix, 620p.).

In this case, we have shown only the number of volumes first. Alternatively, the number of pages of the three volumes has been given.

Date of Publication

When several volumes of a set of monographs are released, they need not to be published in a single year. They may be published during a specified period. In such cases, we must take the first publication of the volume published first and the last date if the publication is complete, like 1968–1976, which means the volumes were issued between 1968 and 1976. In case, the publications of all the volumes are not yet completed, the date should be kept open. For example, 1968, which means that some more volumes are likely to be published. The date should be closed when it is known that the series has been completed.

Sizes of Volumes

In the physical description area, the recording of sizes must be done as follows: If the volumes in a multi-volume set differ in height and the difference is two centimetres or less, give the largest size. If the difference is more than two centimetres, give both the smallest size and the largest size, separated by a hyphen, like -21-25 cm.

Examples of Multi-Volumes

MODERN ELECTROCHEMISTRY
AN INTRODUCTION TO AN
INTERDISCIPLINARY AREA

John O'M Bockris
and
Amulya K.N. Reddy

A Plenum / Rosetta Edition

There is no problem in the case of transcribing authors, and you have already worked out such examples. There is an edition statement on the title page. It is not clear what type of edition the publishers are referring to. In such cases, rule number 1.2B3 states that "in case of doubt whether a statement is an edition statement, take the presence of such words as edition, issue, version...as evidence that such a statement is an edition statement, and transcribe it as such".

The book is in two volumes and has continuous pagination. However, there are some other peculiarities in pagination. Both the volumes have preliminary pages numbered in Roman numerals and the index in both volumes has been separately numbered, again in Roman numerals. Incidentally, the AACR-

2R has not envisaged such a problem. Rule number 2.SB20, at best, states: "If a set of volumes is continuously paged, give the pagination in parentheses after the number of volumes. Ignore separately paged sequences of preliminary matter in volumes other than the first."

Other Information	
Call No.	541.37 BOC
Accession No.	18156-18157
Date of Publication	1973
Size	22cm.

Published by Plenum Publishing Corporation, New York. The book is in two volumes
The Pages are : VI -xxxii, 622, lx

V2-xxvii, 623-1432 Jvi

The example has been worked out below:

Main Entry

541.37 BOC	Boclris, John O M
18156 - 18157	Modern electrochemistry : an Introduction to an interdisciplinary area/ John O M. Bockris and Amulya K.N.Reddy. _ A Plenum / Rosetta ed. _ New York: Plenum Publishing , 1973. 2v. (xxxii, 1432, I vi p.) : 22 cm. 1. Electrochemistry. I Reddy, Amulya , K. N. II. Title.

We have accordingly given the volume number and the preliminary pages of the first volume, followed by the total number of pages. There is no direction as to what action is to be taken for the end pages. We have only given the end pages of the second volume and ignored the end pages of the first volume. The alternative is to transcribe it as 2v. only and ignore the pagination completely, as stated in rule number 2.5B17.

An Outline of

STATISTICAL Theory

Volume One
(Probability and Probably Distribution)

A.M. GOON
M.R. GUPTA
B. DASGUPTA

Calcutta
The World Press Private Limited
1985

Other Information	
Call. No.	310/GOO
Accession No:	15492-93
Pages	xiv, 516, xv, 551
Size	22 cm.

The book is in two volumes with the common title *An Outline of Statistical Theory*. The title of Volume 2 is *Statistical Inference*.

Volume 2 has its own title, that is, 'Statistical Inference', and was published in 1987. What is new in this example? The book is in two volumes with a common running title and its own title. In such cases, rule number 1.7B18 helps determine how the content of the volumes is to be recorded. The two volumes were published in different years, and we must resort to rule number 1AF8 for its rendering. The volumes have separate pagination and must be recorded as described in rule number 2.5B17 or 2.SB21.

The book is written by three authors, but none of them is indicated as the principal author, either by wording or layout; hence, entry is made under the first named author. We are sure that you remember this rule. The volumes were published in different years, and hence the years are shown as described in rule number 1AF8, which states that "If two or more dates are found on the various parts of a multi-part item...give the earliest and latest dates."

Main Entry

310
GOO Goon, A. M.
An outline of statistical theory / A.M. Goon, M.K. Gupta, and B. Dasgupta. _ Calcutta: World press, 1985 _ 1987.
2 v.(xiv, 516 ;. xv, 551p.); 22 cm.
15492 _ 15493
Contents. 1 Probability and Probability distribution- v.2 statistical inference .
1.Statistical . I Gupta, M.K. II. Dasgupta, B. III. Title.

The pagination in the two volumes are independent of each other, and rule number 2.5B21 states that "lithe volumes, in a multi-volumes set are individually paged, give the pagination of each volume in parentheses after the number of volumes". This is an optional rule. You can simply state '2v' without showing pages too. Other entries that are made are shown in the tracing section.

Serial Publications

Cataloguing serial publications is problematic because of the peculiar nature of publications. We will discuss some of the problems in section 10.4.2. However, here, we only provide you with some examples. Cataloguing of serials in both the codes, AACR2 and CCC, has several elements in common, and hence, in this unit, we will restrict to only those governed by AACR-2R rules.

Definition of Serial Publication

The definition of serials as per AACR-2R is a publication in any medium issued in successive parts bearing numerical or chronological designations and intended to be continued indefinitely. You come across them daily and probably read some popular magazines. Some of these serials are called periodicals, journals and magazines without much distinction. Periodicals and journals are synonymous, but a magazine refers to a popular journal that does not have a lasting value. The AACR-2R includes several other publications under serials, such as newspapers, annuals (reports, yearbooks, etc.), journals, memoirs, proceedings, transactions, etc., of societies. Reports, proceedings and transactions emanate from corporate bodies but can be catalogued as serials.

Problems in Cataloguing

Cataloguing of serial publications poses several problems. The physical characteristics associated with its bibliographic description, such as the title of the serial, its frequency, sponsors, etc., change very often. Additionally, sometimes a single periodical might split into two or more with different titles or two or more distinct periodicals might merge to constitute a single periodical with a different name. This necessitated that serial should be treated as a special class of material in so far as their cataloguing is concerned. This situation calls for special rules in catalogue entries that will stand the test of time and allow necessary changes as and when called for. Normally, a bibliographical description for a main entry of a serial publication includes the following information:

1. Title and statement of responsibility area
2. Edition area
3. Numeric and alphabetic or chronological or other designation areas
4. Publication/distribution area
5. Physical description area
6. Series area
7. Note area
8. Standard number
9. Terms of availability area

The chief source of information is the title page of the first issue. Some serial publications issue separate title pages, which can be used for cataloguing purposes. In case the first issue is not available, the issue that you are cataloguing might be utilised for the purposes.

The rules pertaining to the cataloguing of serial publications are given in Chapter 12 of the AACR-2R.

In case some of the rules are not stated, a direction is given as to which rules are applicable.

In the following pages, four examples are worked out, which will enable you to understand the cataloguing of serial publications.

Worked-Out Examples of Serials

American
Journal of Mathematics
Founded by the Johns Hopkins University

Edited by
J.H.Sampson
(and several others)

Published under the Auspices of the Johns Hopkins University
with the Editorial Cooperation of American Mathematical Society

Volume 110, November 5
October 1988

The Johns Hopkins University Press
Baltimore, Maryland
U.S.A.

Other Information:

Call No.	510.5
Size	26 cm
Date of 1 st issue	1879
Periodicity	Six issues a year
Library lacks	Vols. 1-68

The rules governing the cataloguing of serial publications are given in Chapter 12 of AACR-2R. Some explanations are given in the above worked-out example. The main heading is made under the title, though the periodicals are a publication of a corporate body. When the publication is of an administrative nature dealing with the corporate body itself, the heading should be the name of the corporate body as per rule number 21.1B2.

Main Entry

510.5

American journal of mathematics.-
Vol. 1, no. 1 (1879) - . Baltimore.
Johns Hopkins University Press,
1879
v.; 26 cm.
Six issues a year
Library has v.69 (1947)
1.Mathematics periodicals. I.
Johns Hopkins University. II.
American Mathematical Society.

Rule number 21.3B1 directs us to give the numeric or alphabetical designation of the first issue of the serial we are cataloguing. Accordingly, we have given Volume 1, No. 1 (1879). The rule also states transcribing the year of publication in parentheses. The parentheses are followed by a hyphen, four spaces and a full stop, space and hyphen before giving the place and name of the publisher.

The year of publication is repeated as stated under rule number 12.4F1. The specific material designation for a serial still in progress is 'v'. Another physical description is usually the height of the serial. You must indicate the periodicity of the periodical, as done in the example above. Some of the usual periodicities are as follows: Weekly, Issued twice a month, Monthly, Quarterly, Annual, Irregular, Frequency varies, etc.

The above-shown periodicities are only illustrative. There are a few other types that can be recorded as given in the concerned periodical. However, periodicity needs not be mentioned if it is already part of the title of the serial.

Library holdings are shown as directed under rule numbers 12.7B20 and 1.7B20. Three added entries are made, two covering the corporate bodies associated with the publication.

Example

Keesing's
Record of World Events

Edited by Roger East

Volume 57 (1987)

57th Year of publication
(formerly Keesing's Contemporary Archives)

Longman

Other Information:	
Call No.	050/
Periodicity	Monthly
Size	26 cm.
Date of first issue	1931
Library holdings	From Vol. 8 1938

Main Entry

050

Keesing's record of world events. - Vol. 57 (1987-). [London]: Longman, 1987
v.; 26 cm.
Monthly.
Library has v. 8 (1938)-
Continues: Keesings contemporary archives.
1. History Periodicals.

Additional Main Entry

050

KEE Keesings contemporary archives. Vol.

1 (1931) Vol. 56 (1986).-

[London]: Longman, 1931 1986.

56v.; 26 cm.

Library Lacks v. 1-7 (1931-1937).

Continued by Keesing s record of

World events

1.History Periodicals

In the example above, the periodical, which was published in 1931 as *Keesing's Contemporary Archives*, has changed its name in the year 1987. Rule number 21.2C states that "if the title proper of serial changes make a separate main entry for each title". Hence, you find an additional main entry under the original name of the periodical. In the additional main entry, the volume numbers have been shown as closed, and as per rule number 12.3F, the periodical is treated as a completed serial. You must have noticed that the title *Keesing's Record of World Events* is a continuation of *Keesing's Contemporary Archives*. This information is given in the note section as per rule number 12.7B7.

Cataloguing of Non-Print Media

Chapter 1 of Part 1 in AACR-2R provides general rules for describing all types of material. We will look into some specific rules relevant to cataloguing non-print materials.

Sources of Information

Non-print materials do not have a title page, as in the case of books and other printed documents, giving complete and concise bibliographic information. Information needs to be assembled from various sources, such as the parts of the material itself, containers, labels, accompanying materials, etc. Problems may arise due to incomplete, inaccurate and conflicting information found in different sources. The problem gets compounded when the material is in multiple parts. The specific chapters for each type of material provide details on the chief sources of information and the prescribed sources of information for different data elements. However, for some of the non-print materials, the chief sources of information to be followed in general are mentioned below:

Type of Material	Chief Source of Information
Computer files	Titles Screen The item itself
Graphic materials (pictures, posters, wall charts, etc.)	The item itself Title frame
Maps and other cartographic materials	The item itself Title page
Microforms	The label (if two, both taken together)
Motion pictures and video-recordings	The item itself and its label(s)
Printed music	The object itself
Sound recording:	
Doscs-	
Tapes	
Three dimensional objects (models, dioramas, games, etc.	

If necessary information cannot be found in the sources mentioned above, the information is taken in the following order of preference:

(a) Any other source that forms part of the item

(b) Accompanying item

(c) Any available source

(d) Compose yourself

As you already know, if any information is taken from outside the item, it is enclosed in square brackets.

Organisation and the Levels of Description

The bibliographic description of non-print media follows similar norms as for books and other print materials. The main structure of the bibliographic entry comprises the heading, the description area and the subject description. The description is divided into the following areas:

- Title and statement of responsibility
- Edition
- Material (or type of publication)
- Publication, distribution, etc.
- Physical distribution
- Series
- Note
- Standard number and terms of availability

Each of these areas is further divided into several elements. The structure of the bibliographic description as per the AACR-2R rules is described below:

First Level of Description

Title proper/First statement of responsibility. – Edition Statement. – Material or type of publication-specific details. – First publisher, distributor, etc., date of publication, etc.

Extent of item

Note

Standard number

Example

The Confederacy/produced
by Multi-Media Productions
Multi-Media, c 1972.
4 film strips (ea, 37 fr. Each)

Second Level of Description

Title proper [general material designation] = parallel title: other title information/first statement of responsibility; each subsequent statement of responsibility. – Edition statement/First statement of responsibility. – Material or type of publication-specific details. – First place of publication, distribution, etc.; first publisher, distributor, etc., date of publication, etc.

Extent of item: other physical details; dimensions. – (Title proper of series/statement of responsibility relating to series, ISSN of series; numbering within the series. Title of subseries, ISSN of subseries; numbering within subseries).

Notes Standard Number

Example

The Confederacy [filmstrip): the lost cause revisited/ produced by Multi-Media Productions. – Stanford, CA: Multi-Media, c 1972.

4 film strips (ea. 37 fr. Each): col.; 35 mm. - (The Basis of our beliefs).

Third Level of Description

All elements that are required by the rule are to be included. Apart from that, the optional elements might also be included for the purpose. The third level of description is generally required by National Libraries and Research libraries. The National Bibliographies usually follow the third level of description.

Example

The Confederacy [films trip]: the lost cause revisited/ produced by Multi-Media Productions. – Stanford, CA: Multi-Media, c 1972.

4 film strips (ea. 37 fr. Each): col.; 35 mm. + 2 sound cassettes (37 min. 40 sec.) + teacher's manual (6p.; 22 cm.). – (The Basis of our beliefs).

Sound accompaniment is compatible with manual and automatic operation.

The difference between level one and level two for non-print material is the expanded physical description in level two. The GMD and artistic content of the material are included in the body of the entry rather than in the note section in the second level. The only drawback in the second level is that it does not provide for the accompanying materials statement.

The problems peculiar to non-print materials are the physical structures and access modes. The filing of the material will depend on the access mode. The following access modes are possible:

- Author/title
- Form
- Subject

The structure of the catalogue card for non-print material depends on the access modes of the users. Therefore, all these three access points should be included in the card.

From the point of view of cataloguing non-print media, the most important feature of AACR-2R is the expansion of treatment given to notes for the different media formats. Other areas accommodating special requirements for the treatment of non-print media in AACR-2R are:

- Material (or type of publication)-specific details—used for cartographic material.
- Physical description—physical characteristics of the material, type of equipment required, etc.
- Recording of numbers other than ISBN and ISSN in the notes area rather than in the standard number and terms of availability area (Rule 1.7BI9).

GMD

GMD refers to the designation of the broad class of publication to which the material belongs. This is an optional addition in AACR-2R, which is quite useful for describing non-print media. AACR-2R provides two such lists: List 1 for British agencies and List 2 for agencies in Australia, Canada and the United States (Rule 1.1Cl).

List 1	List 2
braille	art original
cartographic material	art production
computer file	braille
graphic	chart
manuscript	computer file
microform	diorama
motion picture	filmstrip
multimedia	flash card
music	game
object	globe
sound recording	kit
text	manuscript
videorecording	map
	microform
	microscope slide
	model
	motion picture
	music
	picture
	realia
	slide
	sound recording
	technical drawing
	text
	toy
	transparency
	videorecording

Example

30 Power hits Mega mix

Compact disc digital audio

World Digital Sound Limited Bombay, 1995

Other Information:

Call No. : 784.5

Acc. No. : 3487

Contains : 30 songs

1. La Cucamacha/Carriga: 2. Swamp things/ Norris; 3. Move it up/ Bortolotti ,....;30. Light my fire/Bortolotti.

Main Entry

784.5 POW	Power hits mega mix [sound	
3487	recording]. Bombay: World Digital Sound, 1995. 1 compact disc (60 min.): digital, Stereo; 5 in. Contents. 1. La Cucamacha/ Carriga 2. Swamp thing/ Norris .. 30, Light my fire/ Bortolloti. 1.Popular music	

Here, we will give some explanation for your understanding. In the physical description area, the term 'sound' has been dropped for 'sound CD' since the GMD already uses the term 'sound recordings'. The playing time is given as per rule 6.5B2. Other physical details include the type of recording (stereo), etc. The dimension has not been given as it is of standard dimension. This is according to rule 6.5D6. Here, in the entry, the diameter has been provided as per rule 6.5D2.

The added entries for this product will include:

(i) Added entry for subject: POPULAR MUSIC

(ii) Access to each of the 30 songs listed on the cover

Unit 25
Machine-Readable Cataloguing (MARC) 21 Cataloguing

Introduction

The bibliographic description of a document includes all the data elements necessary to uniquely identify it along with its access points. The bibliographic description is based on an internationally agreed standard (ISBD). While practising cataloguing with AACR-2R through Units 22–24 in this book you learnt that the basic elements of a card catalogue are:

(1) Main entry (heading section, either author or title),
(2) Title and statement of responsibility (author and other collaborators),
(3) Imprint (publication details),
(4) Physical description,
(5) Note,
(6) Resource identifiers (class number, book number and accession),
(7) Subjects, and
(8) Access points (name, title or other elements as added entries).

AACR2 and MARC are two different entities. AACR2 provides rules for describing items in a catalogue record, whereas MARC is a communication standard and provides a framework for catalogue records.

MARC is the basic format for representing library resources in the catalogue. The MARC format is generally used for records entered into an online catalogue. MARC is a generic term loosely used to refer to all standard, machine-readable formats developed by international agencies, such as UNIMARC, LCMARC, USMARC, MARC 21 and all national-level MARC standards. In this unit, we will discuss the MARC 21 format and learn the process of cataloguing with it.

MARC Standards

MARC is a standard for the description of items catalogued by libraries and used for the exchange of bibliographic information among automated library systems.

During 1966–68, it was developed by Henriette Avram at the LC as a pilot project to create records that could be read and interpreted by computers and also shared among libraries. It was used for automating the process-to-print cards or catalogues (book catalogues, microfiche catalogues, etc.).

By 1971, MARC formats evolved as a national standard for disseminating bibliographic data in the United States and gradually became an international standard by 1973. Several versions of MARC have been developed around the world at national and international levels (LC MARC in the 1960s, US MARC in the 1980s, MARC 21 in the late 1990s, etc.). MARC 21 is a result of the harmonisation of the US and Canadian MARC formats, and UNIMARC (widely used in Europe) is the current and most predominant standard now. The MARC 21 standards include formats for authority records, holdings records, classification schedules and community information, in addition to the format for bibliographic records.

MARC is the basic format for representing the library's resources in the catalogue. However, not everything in MARC is captured on the Online Public Access Catalogue (OPAC) display of a record. MARC allows the information contained in a catalogue record (or bibliographic record) to be exchanged between systems. This has facilitated copy cataloguing, which enables you to import records from LOC or OCLC.

There are five widely used MARC 21 communication formats for representing and exchanging bibliographic, authority, holdings, classification and community information data in machine-readable form.

MARC 21 Structure

The structure of a MARC record is divided into three elements:

1. *Record Structure*

It is the overall framework for the record based on the international standard Format for Information Exchange (ISO 2709) and its American counterpart, Bibliographic Information Interchange (ANSII NISO Z39.2).

2. *Content Designation*

It is a set of symbols by which data in the record are identified and manipulated. Codes and conventions are established explicitly to identify and further characterise the data elements within a record and to support the manipulation of that data.

3. *Data Content of the Record*

In this element, record-specific information is given field-by-field. This is based on external standards, such as the ISBD, AACR2 or other cataloguing rules, LCSH, any subject thesauri and classification schedules used by the organisation that creates a record (DDC, UDC, etc.).

The record structure of a MARC record includes the leader, which identifies the beginning of a new record. The record structure also includes the record directory. The content designation has both fixed fields and variable fields. Data content comprises a description, subject headings, classification numbers and main and added entries. A MARC 21 record in its communication format, therefore, comprises three basic sections of data:

1. Leader
2. Directory
3. Data content

We will elaborate each of these sections in the following paragraphs:

(1) *Leader:* First 24 characters (character positions 00–23 of each bibliographic record) of a record contain data related to the record length, type of record, bibliographic level, encoding level, descriptive cataloguing form, etc. It consists of data elements that contain numbers or coded values that define the parameters for the processing of the record. This is something that cataloguers do not have much control on. Only a few coded data are needed to be determined by the cataloguer, such as the type of record and bibliographic level.

(2) *Directory/Record Directory:* The directory begins immediately after the leader. The directory consists of several 12-character entries. It is generated by the computer for locating data fields with the help of their address. The addressing mechanism comprises three components—field tag, field length and starting position, which are placed consecutively without any space in between. The first three digits of each entry contain a tag. Following each tag, the next four positions show the length of the field, and the next five positions tell the starting point for this field. It also contains 12 characters. Field terminators mark the end of the directory.

(3) *Data Content:* This section has the related bibliographic data as data fields. The data in a MARC record is organised into variable fields, each identified by a 3-digit tag stored in the Directory entry for the field. Each field ends with a field terminator character. The last variable field in a record ends with a field terminator and with a record terminator. Two types of variable fields are found: Variable control fields and variable data fields. The variable control fields might contain either a single data element or a series of fixed-length data elements identified by relative character position. These fields are identified

by field tags but do not contain indicator or subfield codes. Variable data fields are also identified by a field tag. Two kinds of content designation are used within variable data fields: Indicators and subfield codes. The indicators are two one-character positions that contain values that interpret the data found in the field. Every field does not have an indicator. Each subfield code is preceded by a character called delimiter and is followed by an alphabetic or numeric character.

The following table illustrates some sample MARC tags with the indicators and subfields.

Main Entry	Ist Indicator	Ist Indicator	Subfields
Personal name 100 (NR)	0 Forename 1 Surname 3 Family	Blank	a Name (NR) q Qualification (NR) c Title [e.g. King] (R) d Dates (NR)
Corporate name 100 (NR)	0 Inverted name 1 Jurisdiction name 2 Name in direct order	Blank	a Name (NR) b Subordinate unit (R) n Number (R) d Date (R) c Location (NR)
Meeting name 111 (NR)	0 Inverted name 1 Jurisdiction name 2 Name in direct order	Blank	a Name (NR) n Number (R) d Date (R) c Location (NR) e Subordinate unit (R)
Conference name 111 (NR)	0 Inverted name 1 Jurisdiction name 2 Name in direct order	Blank	a Name (NR) n Number (R) d Date (R) c Location (NR) e Subordinate unit (R)
Uniform title 130 (NR)	0-9 Nonfiling characters	Blank	a Title (NR) n Number of part of work (R) p Name of part of work (R) l Language (NR) s Version (NR) k Form subheading (R) c Date of work (NR)

Sample catalogue entry from the LC is reproduced below both in a general format and the MARC format to illustrate the representation of a MARC bibliographic record.

Fig. shows the LC online catalogue entry for a book.

MARC 21 Tags and Subfields

The MARC 21 tags are grouped by hundreds according to what type of fields they are. If you want to refer to a group of tags in the same, say, 100, the shorthand for this will be '1XX'. The major tag groups are listed below:

0XX Control info, classification, codes, etc.
1XX Main entries
2XX Titles, edition, imprint
3XX Physical description, etc.
4XX Series statements
5XX Notes
6XX Subject access fields
7XX Added entries
8XX Series added entries, holdings, location, etc.
9XX Locally-defined uses

In subsequent sections, we will discuss different tag groups with relevant examples. The 001 field is generated by OCLC, LC, or your local library management system, wherever the record is created.

0XX Control Fields—General Information

These are control numbers and other kinds of control and coded information used in the processing of machine-readable bibliographic records. These fields have no indicators or subcodes.

001 Control Number
003 Control Number Identifier
005 Date and Time of Latest Transaction
006 Fixed-Length Data Elements—Additional Material Characteristics
007 Physical Description Fixed Field
008 Fixed Length Data Elements

The leader (000), control number (001), MARC code for the organisation (003) and date and time of the last transaction (005) are computer-generated fixed fields, and the cataloguer has no control over them. The coded general information (008) is partially computer-generated fixed fields.

The 006 and 007 fields are used to describe physical characteristics that cannot be coded in the fixed fields. The 006 field is used for additional material information that is not included in the fixed field. For instance, if you have a serial that is issued on CD, then this field might be used. The 007 field is used to describe additional physical characteristics that cannot be covered in the fixed field, such as electronic resources.

Example

000 1327cam a22003375i 4500
001 17375048
005 20141003092408.0
008 I20706s2011 ce s 000 0 eng

01X–09X Control Information, Number and Codes—General Information

Fields 01X–09X contain standard numbers, classification numbers, codes and other data elements relating to the record. Some commonly used ones are listed below:

020 International Standard Book Number
022 International Standard Serial Number
080 Universal Decimal Classification Number
082 Dewey Decimal Classification Number
083 Additional Dewey Decimal Classification Number

In the case of tag 020 (ISBN), the field might include terms of availability and cancelled or invalid ISBNs, such as ISBNs with invalid check digits or that are not applicable to the item being catalogued. The indicators and subfields for this tag are listed below:

Main Entry Fields

100 Main Entry - Personal Name (NR)
110 Main Entry - Corporate Name (NR)
111 Main Entry - Meeting Name (NR)
130 Main Entry - Uniform Title (NR)

The main entry fields are not repeatable. As an illustration, the indicators and subfield codes for the personal name as the main entry field are given below. For each of the above fields, you might refer to the LC website at: http://www.loc.gov/marc.

100 - Main Entry - Personal Name (NR)

First Indicator	Second Indicator
0 - Forename	# Undefined
1 - Surname	
3 - Family name	
Subfield Codes	
$a - Personal name (NR)	$1 - Language of a work (NR)
$b - Numeration (NR)	$n - Number of part/section of a work (R)
$c - Titles and words associated with a name (R)	#p - Name of part/section of a work (R)
$d - Dates associated with a name (NR)	$q - Fuller form of name (NR)
$e - Relator term (R)	$t - Title of a work (NR)
$f - Date of a work (NR)	$u - Affiliation (NR)
$g - Miscellaneous information (NR)	$0 - Authority record control number (R)
&j - Attribution qualifier (R)	$4 - Relator code (R)
$k - Form subheading (R)	$6 - Linkage (NR)
	&8 - Field link and sequence number (R)

Example: 100 1_ $a Herath, R. M., $e author.

In the above example, the first indicator is 1, which indicates the entry is under the last name as indicated in the table above, and the second indicator is left blank. The subfield code $a indicates the personal name of the author and the $e indicates the relator term, which, in this case, is the author.

Title and Title-Related Fields

210 Abbreviated Title (R)

222 Key Title (R)

240 Uniform Title (NR)

242 Translation of Title by Cataloguing Agency (R)

243 Collective Uniform Title (NR)

245 Title Statement (NR)

246 Varying Form of Title (R)

217 Former Title (R) The commonly used tag in this group is FR.

Let us look into the indicators and the subfields in this case:

245 - Title Statement (NR)

First Indicator	Second Indicator
0 - No added entry	0 - No non-filing character
1 - Added entry	0-9 - No. of non-filing character
Subfield Codes	
$a - Title (NR)	$n - Number of part/section of a work (R)
$b - Remainder of title (NR)	$p - Name of part/section of a work (R)
$c - Statement of responsibility, etc. (NR)	$s - Version (NR)
$f - Inclusive dates (NR)	$6 - Linkage (NR)
$g - Bulk dates (NR)	$8 - Field link and sequence number (R)
$h - Medium (NR)	
$k - Form (R)	

By now, you must have got a fair idea of preparing MARC 21 entry for any record. For your reference, the following figure compares the fields in the second level of description in AACR-2R with the MARC format to help you create MARC records.

Second level description AACR-2R	MARC format
Title Proper = Parallel title: other title information/first statement of responsibility: each subsequent statement of responsibility. — Edition statement/first statement of responsibility relating to the edition. — First place of publication, etc.: First publisher, etc. date of publication, etc. — Extent of item: other physical details; dimensions. — (Title proper of series) — Note(s). — Standard number	020##$a 13-digit ISBN 345 XX $a Title = $b Parallel title: other title information/ #c first statement of responsibility; each subsequent statement of responsibility. 250 ## $a Edition statement/ #b first statement of responsibility relating to the edition. 260 ## $a First place of publication, etc.: $b First publisher, etc. $c date of publication, etc. 300 ## $a Extent of item: $b other physical details; $c dimension 490 0 $a Title proper of series/statement of responsibility relating to series; 4v series vol. no. 500 $$ $a Note(s)

Some worked-out examples of different types of publications are given below to further familiarise yourself with the MARC 21 format:

Example 1

Main title	An evaluation study of Lahul & Spiti District/Government of Himachal Pradesh, Department of Economics & Statistics.
Published/Created	Simla: Directorate of Economics & Statistics, Himachal Pradesh. (1977)
Description	ii, 56 p. ; 27 cm.
Subjects	Lahul and Spiti (India)—Statistics. Lahul and Spiti (India)—Rural conditions—Statistics.
Dewey class no.	330.954/52
Type of material	Book

MARC 21 Format

043 —	$saa-ii—
082 00	$a 330.954/52
245 03	$a An evaluation study of Lahul & Spiti District/ $c Government of Himachal Pradesh, Department of Economics & Statistics.
260 —	$a Simla: $b Directorate of Economics & Statistics, Himachal Pradesh, $c [1977]
300 —	$a ii, p.; $c 27 cm.
651 –0	$a Lahul and Spiti (India) $x Statistics.
651 –0	$a Lahul and Spiti (India) $x Rural conditions $x Statistics.
710 1–	$a Himachal Pradesh (India). $b Directorate of Economics and Statistics.

Example 2

Main title	Event volunteering: international perspectives on the volunteering experience at events/edited by Karen Smith and others.
Published/Created	New York: Routledge, 2014.
Description	xviii, 211 pages: 24 cm.
ISBN	9780415821032 (hardback)
Subjects	Voluntarism—International cooperation. Special events—International cooperation. Business & Economics/Industries/ Hospitality, Travel & Tourism, Travel/ General.
Notes	Includes bibliographical references and index.
Series	Routledge advances in event research series.
Dewey class no.	301/.14

MARC 21 Format

020 —	$a 9780415821032 (hardback)
082 00	$a 302/.14 $2 23
245 00	$a Event volunteering: $b international perspectives on the volunteering experience at events/ $c edited by Karen Smith and others.
264 –1	$a New York: $b Routledge, $c 2014
300 —	$a xviii, 211 pages; $c 24 cm
504 —	$a Includes bibliographical references and index.
650 –0	$a Voluntarism $x International cooperation.
650 –0	$a Special events $x International cooperation.
651 –0	$a BUSINESS & ECONOMICS/ Industries/ Hospitality, Travel & Tourism. $2 bisacsh
650 –7	$a TRAVEL/ General. $2 bisacsh

EXERCISE UNIT 22 – UNIT 25

1. What do you mean by AACR-2R? Discuss its genesis.
2. Define RDA.
3. Discuss the structure of AACR-2R.
4. What are the levels of description in a catalogue?
5. Write a note on the style of writing in cataloguing.
6. What are the different types of entries in cataloguing?
7. Discuss the different items in a catalogue entry with examples.
8. What do you mean by GMD in cataloguing?
9. Give the physical description of a catalogue card with proper marking.
10. Discuss the need for a subject heading in a catalogue card.
11. Discuss, in detail, the basic principles of cataloguing.
12. Define gross-reference in the context of cataloguing.
13. Discuss the process of writing an author's name in a catalogue. Give examples.
14. Discuss the AACR-2R cataloguing of a document with shared responsibility with some suitable examples.
15. How is principal responsibility identified in a document with shared responsibility?
16. Draw AACR-2R–based catalogue for a document with serial publication.
17. Draw AACR-2R–based catalogue for a document with multiple volumes.
18. How would you catalogue non-print media? Give examples.
19. Discuss MARC 21 structure in detail.
20. Illustrate MARC 21 tags and subfields using suitable examples.
21. Differentiate between AACR-2R and MARC 21.

Unit 26

Structure of Sears List of Subject Headings (Eighteenth Edition)

Introduction

The language, as such, is both affluent and poor in its vocabulary. The flexibility in our day-to-day language allows conveying ideas in different ways. But to convey ideas in science, academics and serious business, we need to convey them in a straightforward language devoid of all such luxuries. And so is the requirement of our information retrieval languages. An uncontrolled language affects the precision of information retrieval due to the retrieval of irrelevant material. Vocabulary control is a process to minimise the retrieval of irrelevant literature. For example, putting a query 'bridge' to a library catalogue or a search engine retrieves a lot of information that includes information on flyovers and the game bridge. Anyone interested in finding information on the game 'bridge' would have to further specify their query as 'bridge (game)', resulting in a more meaningful recall. Vocabulary control involves using standardised names of subjects in databases/catalogues, etc.

The SLSH (popularly called Sears List) is an example of a vocabulary control tool. It is used for assigning standardised subject headings to documents. LCSH is another example of a vocabulary control tool. The difference between the two is that SLSH is used in public and small libraries with a collection of up to 20,000 books, whereas LCSH is useful for large libraries.

History of the Sears List

It was first designed in 1923 by Minnie Earl Sears (1873–1933) to fulfil the demands of small American libraries for broader subject headings for use in their dictionary catalogues. These libraries found LCSH too big and specialised. Since then, the Sears List has always been published by the H. W. Wilson Company, New York (Now the company has been taken over by Ebsco), its proprietors and copyright holders. Its editor is an employee of the company. Its new editions are produced regularly to:

- Incorporate new subjects,
- Restructure the form of old headings based on the changing information needs and information-seeking behaviour of the users,
- Give new terms to old subject headings based on current usage,
- Delete the obsolete subjects, and
- Discover new relations between subjects.

Orientation to the online electronic environment started with the thirteenth edition (1986). It was the first edition to be created as an online database for editorial use. It started changes in the form of de-inverting the inverted headings to suit searching OPACs and online databases. It was believed that most library users search for subjects in an electronic database under the natural form of their names. For example, 'Library, Public' was changed to 'Public library'. Similarly, 'Chemistry, organic' was changed to 'Organic chemistry'. In the fifteenth edition (1994), edited by Dr. Joseph Miller, the de-inversion process was completed.

Another important change introduced since its fifteenth edition is its thesaurus format of listing subject headings using standard thesaural abbreviations, that is, NT, BT, RT, USE and SA, instead of the earlier x, xx and SA codes. The thesaurus format conforms to the ANSI/NISO (American Standards Institution) (1993). Nevertheless, Sears still remains a list of subject headings. It is not a thesaurus. The eighteenth edition

(2004) has been edited by Joseph Miller in association with Ms. Joan Goodsell. Dr. Miller retired in December 2012 after successfully editing six editions from the fifteenth (1994) to the twentieth (2010). Its current editor is Ms. Eve Miller, who brought out the twenty-first edition in May 2014.

Features of the Eighteenth Edition

Its philosophy is to accommodate change while maintaining continuity. There are about 500 new subject headings in the eighteenth edition. The total number of preferred headings is likely to the tune of 8000, yet the number of headings that can be coined or subdivided is, as usual, much larger. Many of the new headings are suggested by the working librarians, bibliographic product vendors and specialists with the H.W. Wilson Company. It simply means the new terms are from the recently published literature. This is how its currency is maintained.

Principles of Vocabulary Control

Every system of controlled vocabulary is based on some principles regarding:

1. Choice of preferred headings (that is, the vocabulary used),
2. Levels of specificity of terms (depth of subject analysis allowed), and
3. Form and structure of preferred headings (grammar of headings).

These issues make principles of the system and grammar of the headings (indexing language). The choice and structure of the headings are determined by user studies, information-seeking behaviour and the literary warrant. The level is determined by the strength of the collection, the level of users and, above all, the library policy.

Principles of the Sears List

From the very beginning, as a matter of policy, the Sears List has always been based on the principles of LCSH, with certain modifications needed for simplification to suit small libraries. The principles of the Sears List are:

1. Direct and specific entry,
2. Common (popular) usage, and
3. Uniformity and consistency.

It may be noted these are the same principles that C.A. Cutter (1837–1903) gave in his famous *Rules for a Dictionary Catalog* (1873). These principles have been explained on pages xvi–xx of Sears (eighteenth edition; 2004).

1. Specific Entry

It means a subject should be entered under its most specific heading, not under the class to which it belongs. For example, Lily should be entered under 'Lilies', not under 'Flowers'. Duck is entered under 'Ducks', not under 'Birds' or even 'Water Birds'. Similarly, 'Lung Cancer' is entered under 'Lung Cancer', not 'Cancer—Lungs'. But specificity is a matter of relativity depending upon the strength of the collection, the levels of the users and the policy of the library.

2. Direct Entry

It means the specific heading chosen should be entered directly instead of a subdivision. For example, 'Ducks' entered as such instead of 'Water Birds—Ducks'. Similarly, use 'Lung Cancer' instead of 'Cancer—Lungs'.

3. Common Usage

The terms chosen as preferred headings should be from common usage. If a word has more than one spelling, then the popular ones are chosen for this purpose. (It may be noted that Sears uses American spellings, but the Indian libraries should use British spellings.) It uses common and popular terms instead of scientific or technical terms or jargon. Sears uses terms current among lay users. For example, it uses 'Language Disorders' instead of 'Dysphasia', 'Cancer' instead of 'Carcinoma' and 'Renaissance' instead of 'Renascence'.

4. Uniformity

Using a list of subject headings brings uniformity. Once a heading is chosen for use, it should be used consistently and uniformly until a decision is taken to the contrary. It, however, does not mean that old terms cannot be changed or deleted or new terms cannot be added. It is not a frozen system. Controlled vocabulary also changes and grows with time.

Structure of the Sears List

Sears List is an alphabetical [word by word arranged according to ALA Filing Rules (1980)] general list of standard names of subjects in the English language for use in small- and medium-sized libraries. It provides subject headings for the entire range of knowledge. The eighteenth edition (2004) has the following bibliographic details:

Sears, Minnie Earl. *Sears List of Subject Headings*–eighteenth edition/edited by Joseph Miller; associate editor, Joan Goodsell. New York; Dublin: The H.W. Wilson Company, January 2004. li, 804p, ISBN 0-8242-1040-9. www.hwwilson.com

Parts of Sears List

It is in one volume, divided broadly into two parts:

1. Prefatory and introductory part, including the list of about 500 (common) subdivisions and the list of key headings.
2. Alphabetical list of subject headings in word-by-word order (by ALA filing rules, 1980) given in two columns on every page.

The introductory part describes brief history and principles of the Sears List. But essentially, it is a sort of operation manual to use the list to select and use proper subject headings. It also provides instructions to further divide the chosen subject heading, if needed, and to coin new subject headings as per the grammar of the Sears List.

List of Subject Headings

The core of the system is the word-by-word alphabetical list of subject headings. All the headings are of two types:

1. Non-preferred headings,
2. Preferred headings—Subdivisions used to subdivide a preferred heading.

A. *Non-Preferred Headings*

These headings are those that are not to be used. Such headings are given in light-type face print. These are usually variants or less popular synonyms of the preferred heading to which it directs the cataloguer. Against each such non-preferred heading is invariably given the instruction 'USE', directing us to the preferred heading. For example:

Earth Magnetism

USE **Geomagnetism**

Genes

USE **Heredity**

Obviously, the subject heading following the word USE is always printed in boldface, and a full entry exists for such headings at their proper alphabetical place. To explain the above, we are not allowed to use the term 'Cyclopedias'. Instead, we are directed to use the subject heading 'Encyclopedias and Dictionaries'.

B. *Preferred Headings*

These are the headings that can be assigned to a document. These are printed in boldface. Along with it is given the full entry with its DDC class number(s) scope or definitional note, if any, instruction for its further subdivision and all the Narrower (NT), Broader (BT) and Related (RT) terms. For example, take the following simple entry:

Marketing (May subdiv. geog.) **381; 658.8**

Use for materials on the principles and methods involved in the transfer of merchandise from producer to consumer. Materials for food buying are entered under **Grocery Shopping**.

UF Distribution (Economics)
Merchandising

SA Subjects with subdivision Marketing, for example, **Farm Produce-Marketing** (to be added as needed)

BT **Business**

Management

NT **Direct marketing**

Direct selling

Telemarketing

RT **Advertising selling**

It means the following in practical terms:

- The SH Marketing (printed in bold typeface) can be used as a heading. Its synonymous terms Distribution (Economics) and Merchandising are non-preferred terms and hence are not to be used as subject headings.
- 'May subdiv. geog' in the parentheses means this heading may be subdivided geographically (by a place name), such as Marketing - India; Marketing - Uttar Pradesh; Marketing - Lucknow.
- 381 and 658.8 are its DDC numbers from the Abridged DDC-14 (2004).
- The three terms given against the abbreviation UF (Used for) are non-preferred (synonyms) of the heading used. For this, the cataloguers will have to make 'see' references from these terms to the entry terms, for example:

  Distribution (Economics) *See Marketing*

  Merchandising *See Marketing*
- BT means (hierarchically) Broader Term. Its practical implication is to prepare 'See also' entry from broader to the narrower terms above given as the preferred heading:

  Business *See also Marketing*

  Management *See also Marketing*
- NT means Narrower Term. These are subordinate terms to the preferred heading. For this, we must make 'see also' references from broader to narrower terms. That is, make a cross-reference from BT to all its NTs:

Marketing *See also Direct Marketing*

See also Telemarketing

Note: Never make any cross-reference from NT to BT.

RT means Related Terms. These are the terms at equal levels of hierarchy but are related to the entry in some way. Its practical implication is to prepare 'see also' entries on a reciprocal basis. For example, in the entry:

Marine plants (May subdiv. geog.) 579

RT Freshwater plants

So, we will prepare the following two entries for the:

RT: Freshwater plants *See also Marine plants*

Marine plants *See also Freshwater plants*

Note: 'See also' references are only made to the terms on which publications are available in the library. Otherwise, it will be a misleading direction, which is called a blind reference.

Subdivisions

Strictly speaking, preferred headings are of two types. About 500 preferred subject headings are used as direct headings as well as subdivisions to other headings. For example, Marketing is a heading and also used as a subdivision:

Marketing – India

Television – Marketing

Periodicals (May subdiv. geog.) 050

Library Science – Periodicals

Geography – Periodicals

Grammar of the Subject Headings

Grammatically, the subject headings are of four types:

1. Single nouns: Christmas; Computers; Gardening
2. Compound headings: Church and state; Occupational health and safety; National parks and reserves

3. Adjectives + nouns: Christmas trees; Compressed air
4. Phrases: Crimes without victims; Fathers of the church; Radio in education; Hearing in animals; Insects as carriers of disease; September 12 terrorist attacks, 2012

Rules for singular and plural terms are quite clear. Abstract words that cannot be counted are in singular form: Ability, Success, Art. Concrete words are always in plural form: Trees, Museums, Credit cards, Dams.

Key Headings

In the list, all subjects are not listed. For some subjects, models are given to coin subject headings on that pattern. On the basis of these models, analogous headings can be coined. Major key (or model) headings are:

Author:	Shakespeare, William, 1564–1616
Ethnic groups:	Native Americans
Country:	United States
State:	Ohio
City:	Chicago (III)
Language:	English language
Literature:	English literature
Public figures:	Presidents—United States
Wars:	World War, 1939–1945

It means that if we have a subject pertaining to any country, we will look under the United States for a similar SH for that country and then adapt the heading accordingly. Let us say our subject is 'Geography of Japan'.

We will look under the United States, where an analogous heading is

United States – Geography

So, our subject heading will be

Japan – Geography

Similarly, for the Gazetteer of Kerala, we will look under Ohio and adapt the heading:

Kerala – Gazetteers

For historical buildings of Jaipur, we will look under Chicago and form the following headings:

Historic buildings – Jaipur

For a book on 'Biography of Chetan Bhagat', we will look under Shakespeare, William to get the following subject heading:

Chetan Bhagat, 1974 – Biography

A Dictionary of Kannada literature will get the subject heading:

Kannada literature – Dictionaries

Adding Subdivisions

Some of the subject headings are already subdivided, while all the subject headings in the list might be further subdivided by any of the ~500 subdivisions given on pages xlv–l of the Sears List to make a heading more specific:

Science	Philosophy
Science	Periodicals
Girls	Education
Trees	India
Education	Bibliography
Bible	Study and teaching
India	History—1857–1947
Mumbai	Description and travel

These subdivisions are either generally applicable to all the subject headings or somewhat restricted in use suitable for a given category of headings. These subdivisions are like the standard subdivisions of the DDC (given in Table 1), which can be added anywhere without any specific instruction to use them. It may be noted that though the list of subdivisions is given separately, instructions to apply these subdivisions are given for each separately in the main list under that heading. For example, to use 'Indexes' listed as a subdivision, we go to the main list (p. 376, Sears–18). There, we find the instruction to use it as a subdivision under the names of subjects:

English literature	Indexes
India	History – Indexes
Newspapers	Indexes

As stated earlier, some headings are both a subject heading as well as a subdivision. It is due to the growing complexity of subjects and documents. For example, 'Bibliography' is a subject heading as well as a subdivision. There are four types of subdivisions:

1. Topical: Birds—Eggs
2. Bibliographical: Hindi language—Dictionaries
3. Geographical: Trees—India; City planning—Chennai
4. Chronological: India — History—20th Century; Hindi literature—21st century

Categories of Subject Headings Omitted

As stated earlier, Sears List is a list/register of headings and provides patterns and instructions to coin new headings for subjects. Paradoxically, the headings that can be newly formulated from the Sears List are much more than those listed therein. Apart from those implied in the Key Headings, these are unlisted but coinable headings. Omitted headings mostly pertain to specific names of individuals, corporate bodies, associations, institutions, commercial organisations, processes, products, events, historical and mythical figures, natural and geographical entities (mountains, rivers and lakes), vegetables, fruits, animals, chemicals and all creatures (living, extinct or mythical). All these can form subject headings and are supplied by the cataloguers as per the instructions. All specific names are subject headings. We can have the following subject headings though these are not listed in the Sears List:

Kapil Dev	Biography
Kurukshetra University	Administration
Prem Chand	Characters
Taj Mahal	Maintenance and repair
Urdu language	Dictionaries

Haryana	Boundaries
Himalayas	Geography
Ramayana	Quotations
Parrots	Eggs
Maruti Udyog Limited	Accounting
Punjab National Bank	Officials and employees
India	Bibliography
Sikhs	Canada
Beas (River)	Maps

Note: It may be remembered that literary books of fiction, drama, poetry, etc., will have no subject heading as these books have no subject. For example, *Hamlet* by William Shakespeare or *Gitanjali* by Rabindra Nath Tagore will get no subject heading. However, books on literary history and criticism will have subject headings.

Limitations

It may be noted that the Sears List is designed for American, Christian and Western cultures. It also uses American spellings, for example, 'catalog' instead of 'catalogue'. We can adapt it to use Indian/British spellings. For other cultures and countries, it might not be wholly suitable. It has headings that have no relevance in India at the moment. For example, Only child [family], Unmarried fathers, Teenage fathers, etc. It does not have headings for Indic subjects and concepts. There is no specific heading for Caste system, Gurdwara, Sati, Child marriage, Dowry, Bride burning, etc. It has about 60 subject headings on the Bible alone, whereas there is only one entry on Vedas. Sikh scripture Guru Granth Sahib does not have even a single entry. For such subjects, the Indian libraries will have to make their own subject headings or modify and adapt the existing ones. For example, for History of (Sikh) Gurdwaras in Punjab, we must adapt the heading 'Ohio—Church—History' to get Punjab—Gurdwara—History. Indeed, it makes the work on subject headings interesting, challenging and creative.

Unit 27
Keyword Indexing

Introduction

Specialised indexes to technical literature are an accepted means for directing scientists to sources of information pertinent to their interests. Indexes based on the titles of documents or authors of the documents are a poor substitute for a micro-document. Limitations of titles, such as indicators of document content or absence of terminology control, lead to various problems in indexing micro-documents. The establishment of index entries is a matter of judgement and experience and constitutes a considerable part of the intellectual effort involved in the manual compilation of indexes. The accelerated pace of scientific development, along with the demand for speedier communication, has accentuated to establish an alternative method of subject indexing. It is argued that such demand can be satisfied using a machine in the form of a series of extractions, each containing a significant, or key, word as its nucleus.

Keyword Indexing: Concept

Keyword indexing is a system of indexing techniques that uses natural language for indexing keywords or significant terms of a title. Significant words are words that have a relatively high correlation with the actual thought contents of the documents. The concept was first given by Andrea Crestadoro in 1864 in the name of Keyword-in-Title (KWIT). Another term, 'catchword indexing', was used to refer to keyword indexing during 19th century. British books in print used catchword indexing for quite a long time, and the well-recognised journal 'Nature' also used this technique to derive keyword entries for their journal articles. In keyword indexing, the keywords are generated without using any vocabulary control device, like a thesaurus. The word chosen might be a single word, multiple words or even phrases that convey the contents. The significance of such keywords could be determined only by referring to the statement from which the keyword had been chosen. The statement acts as a modifier pointing up the more specific sense in which a keyword has been applied. Several keywords might be selected for a title to provide access from different access points of users. This principle is currently being applied in various indexing systems with a slight variation. There are eight known variants of keyword indexing: keyword in context (KWIC), keyword out of context (KWOC), keyword augmented in context (KWAC), keyword with context (KWWC), key term alphabetical (KEYTALPHA), word and author index (WADEX), double KWIC (DKWIC) and key letter in context (KLIC).

Structure and Format of Keyword Indexing

An entry of a keyword index is in three parts:

(a) **Keywords:** Subject-denoting words or significant words that can be used as approach terms.

(b) **Context:** The remaining part of the title that serves as the context for the keyword.

(c) **Identification or location code:** An identification number (usually the serial numbers of the entries in the main part) to provide the location of the document.

Indexing Process

The overall process of indexing involves the followings steps:

(a) **Choosing keyword:** Keywords are chosen either from the title and/or abstract of the document. An indexer or an editor marks the significant terms and also marks words in the 'stop list'. The stop list is the list of words considered to have no significant value for indexing, and no indexing entries need to be produced through those terms. These insignificant terms include articles (a, an and the), prepositions, conjunctions, pronouns, auxiliary verbs and some general terms (like aspect, viewpoint, reference to, etc.). The larger this list, the fewer expected index entries. The keywords thus selected serve as approach terms. For a document titled 'Treatment of skin diseases by using Homeopathy', the significant terms or keywords will be 'treatment', 'skin', 'disease' and 'Homeopathy', and the stop list will be 'of, by, using'.

(b) **Entry generation:** Index entries in a KWIC index or any of its versions are generated in association with all the words in the batch of titles that are not stored in the stop list. The title is so manipulated that the keyword comes in the beginning (or in the middle), followed by the rest of the title. The word is printed and displayed 'in context', that is, together with the remainder of the title in which it appears. Each significant word is normally written in either boldface or capital letters. In this way, a single line entry, which includes a title and source reference of some type, is produced for a significant/keyword word in the title. In the above example, there will be four index entries for four significant words, each of them coming in the beginning by rotation. The last word and first word of the title are separated by symbols like a stroke (/), an asterisk (*) or an equal sign (=). An identification or reference number is provided at the right end of each entry to link one entry with another.

TREATMENT of skin disease by using Homeopath 133

SKIN disease by using Homeopath/ Treatment of 133

DISEASE by using Homeopath/Treatment of skin 133

HOMEOPATHY/Treatment of skin disease using 133

(c) **Filing:** All the index entries are arranged alphabetically.

DISEASE by using Homeopath/Treatment of skin 133

HOMEOPATHY/Treatment of skin disease using 133

SKIN disease by using Homeopath/ Treatment of 133

TREATMENT of skin disease by using Homeopath 133

In the above example, the first words (disease, homeopathy, skin and treatment) are the 'keywords'. The part of the title followed by each keyword is the 'context'. The number attached to every entry on the extreme right is the 'identification code'.

Variants of Keyword Indexing

1. *KWIC*

KWIC was developed by H.P. Luhn of IBM at the International Conference of Scientific Information held in Washington in 1958. This mechanised system is based on titles of documents indexed on the principle that the title of a scientific document represents its contents. The significant words in the title indicate the subject of the document. The index is produced by rotating each significant term in the title at the beginning. The remaining part of the title also appears with each significant term to keep the context intact (in-context).

KWIC indexing may be carried out on various levels depending on the purpose that the index must serve. The process may be applied to the title of an article, its abstract or its entire text. Keywords can be defined as those that characterise a subject more than others. To derive them, rules must be established to differentiate between significant and non-significant. Since significant terms are difficult to predict, it is more practical to isolate them by rejecting all obviously non-significant or common words. Such words might include terms like 'report', 'analysis', 'theory' and the like, as well as conjunctions, prepositions, auxiliary verbs, etc. The remaining significant or 'key' words would be extracted from the text, together with a certain number of words that precede and follow them. The KWIC index is generated by making the keywords, assuming a fixed position within the extracted portions, and arranging these portions in the alphabetic order of the keywords.

Let us take the title 'Prevention of diseases of wheat caused by insects' to demonstrate the index entries generated through the KWIC principle. In this title, 'of' and 'by' have no significance, and 'prevention', 'disease', 'wheat' and 'insects' are the keywords. While generating entries through KWIC, we must keep in mind that every keyword should come as an approach term. The remaining terms should be written in such a manner that the context of the document must be intact. To maintain the context, stroke (/) should be placed in a proper position so that the searcher of the document can understand what the starting or ending point of the title is. Although capitalisation, or making bold, is the job of the machine, the indexer must identify the significant terms associated with the document. It is the job of the editor to mark the keywords before the title is punched so that the key puncher is able to tag them and instruct the computer.

Diseases of wheat caused by insects/Prevention of	13243
Insects/Prevention of disease of wheat caused by	13243
Prevention of disease of wheat caused by insets/	13243
Wheat caused by insect/Prevention of disease of	13243

In the computer-generated index, the keywords can be positioned at the centre too.

Prevention of	**DISEASE** of wheat caused by insects/	13243
Disease of wheat caused by	**INSECTS**/Prevention of	13243
Wheat caused by insects/	**PREVENTION** of diseases of	13243
Of diseases of	**WHEAT** caused by insect/Prevention	13243

Let us take another example. We have a document entitled 'Monetary Policy of India', with identification number 3642. The entry will be as follows:

INDIA/Monetary Policy of	3642
MONETARY Policy of India/	3642
POLICY of India/Monetary	3642

Or

Policy of	INDIA/Monetary	3642
Of India/	MONETARY Policy	3642
Monetary	POLICY of India/	3642

We have another document entitled 'Indexing of articles in medical library', with identification number 24513. The entry will be as follows:

ARTICLES in medical library/Indexing of	24513
INDEXING of articles in medical library/	24513
LIBRARY/ Indexing of articles in medical	24513
MEDICAL library/Indexing of articles in	24513

Or

Indexing of	ARTICLES in medical library/	24513
Medical library/	INDEXING of articles in	24513
In medical	LIBRARY/Indexing of articles	24513
Articles in	MEDICAL library/Indexing of	24513

In the above examples, the context of the document remains intact despite the fact that four different approach terms appeared one by one at first.

KWOC

KWOC is another version of keyword indexing wherein each keyword is taken out and printed separately in the left-hand margin with the complete title to provide complete context. The identification number of the document is written on the right. For example, entry for the document 'Prevention of diseases of wheat caused by chemicals' under KWOC will be as follows:

DISEASES	Prevention of diseases of wheat caused by chemicals	13243
CHEMICALS	Prevention of diseases of wheat caused by chemicals	13243
PREVENTION	Prevention of diseases of wheat caused by chemicals	13243
WHEAT	Prevention of diseases of wheat caused by chemicals	13243

Sometimes, the keyword is printed as a heading, and the title is printed in the next line instead of the same line as shown below:

DISEASES

Prevention of diseases of wheat caused by chemicals 13243

CHEMICALS

Prevention of diseases of wheat caused by chemicals 13243

PREVENTION

Prevention of diseases of wheat caused by chemicals 13243

WHEAT

Prevention of diseases of wheat caused by chemicals 13243

In the earlier example, 'Indexing of articles in medical library', with identification number 24513, the entry will be as follows:

ARTICLES	Indexing of articles in medical library	24513
INDEXING	Indexing of articles in medical library	24513
LIBRARY	Indexing of articles in medical library	24513
MEDICAL	Indexing of articles in medical library	24513

Or

ARTICLES

Indexing of articles in medical library 24513

INDEXING

Indexing of articles in medical library 24513

LIBRARY

Indexing of articles in medical library 24513

MEDICAL

Indexing of articles in medical library 24513

For the earlier example, 'Online information storage and retrieval', with identification number 66213, the entry will be as follows:

INFORMATION	Online information storage and retrieval	66213
ONLINE	Online information storage and retrieval	66213
RETRIEVAL	Online information storage and retrieval	66213
STORAGE	Online information storage and retrieval	66213

Or

INFORMATION

Online information storage and retrieval 66213

ONLINE

Online information storage and retrieval 66213

RETRIEVAL

Online information storage and retrieval 66213

STORAGE

Online information storage and retrieval 66213

ADULTS A description study of Indian * in the North Indian region

ADVANCED The * evolution of globular cluster stars

The KWOC format preserves the title verbatim. But it fails to provide the convenient adjacent context that the KWIC format provided.

In a true KWOC, an asterisk appears in the printed title in the position of and instead of the keyword that features as a heading. Given below is an example that explains how an asterisk appears in the title while index entries are generated.

KWAC

KWAC is the most improved version of KWIC. In many cases, the title cannot represent the thought content of the document. The keyword of a fancy title (a title that is not self-expressive) can be a problem in retrieving relevant documents. In order to solve the problem of retrieving irrelevant documents, KWAC provides additional keywords, taken either from the abstract or from the original text of the document or its contents and then inserted into the title to give further index entries. Here, the meaning of 'augmented' is 'in addition to'. The Chemical Biological Activities (CBAC) of BIOSIS uses the KWAC index, which is enriched by another title-like phrase formulated by the indexer. Let us understand the KWAC by an example, 'African women in agricultural development'.

Here, the concept 'African women', in reality, does not include all women of Africa but only the women of Sierra Leone. The main focus of the study is the employment conditions of women in agriculture. After a detailed study of the document, it came to light that 'working hours' is the central theme of the document. An indexer should augment these concepts in keywords for effective retrieval.

Sierra Leone	African women in agricultural development	6452
Employment conditions	African women in agricultural development	6452
Working hours	African women in agricultural development	6452

Similarly, a title entitled: The use of peer tutoring and programmed radio instruction cannot be understood unless the term 'peer-tutoring' is explicitly indexed. Terms like educational radio, programmed instruction and non-formal instruction are added to augment the actual concept of the document.

Let us take another example, 'Prevention of disease of wheat caused by insects', with identification number 13243. The entry will be as follows:

Streak mosaic	Prevention of disease of wheat caused by insets	13243
Arthropods	Prevention of disease of wheat caused by insets	13243
Malvika	Prevention of disease of wheat caused by insets	13243

Here, streak mosaic is the name of disease, arthropods are the insects causing the disease and the wheat variety on which this investigation took place is Malvika. So, we need to augment all these concepts into the original title to make it searchable.

In another example, 'Classroom behaviour of urban students in India', with identification code 46135, the entry will be as follows:

Discipline	Classroom behaviour of urban students in India	46135
Boarding school	Classroom behaviour of urban students in India	46135
Hostellers	Classroom behaviour of urban students in India	46135
Metro Cities	Classroom behaviour of urban students in India	46135

Here, the term 'behaviour' means 'discipline', and this study was conducted for boarding school hostellers of metro cities. Unless these concepts are added, the actual content of the document cannot be understood, and its retrieval is also affected.

KWWC

KWWC is another version of KWIC, where only the part of the title (instead of the full title) relevant to the keyword is considered the entry term. Sometimes, for clarity and delimitation of the scope of the subject, a secondary aspect of the scope of the subject is added to the primary aspect, separated by a punctuation mark. The keyword index of Indian Science Abstracts (ISA) used KWWC for its indexing. An example of KWWC for the title 'Bacterial contamination in Indian distilleries using waste molasses' is as follows:

Alcohol Fermentation/Effect of Bacterial contamination	963
Bacterial contamination/Effect on Alcohol Fermentation	963
Fermentation, Alcoholic/Effect of Bacterial contamination	963
Molasses/Alcohol Fermentation; Effect of Bacterial	963

Let us see another example, 'Implacability of distillation theory in radio frequency breakdown in isomeric liquid'.

Distillation theory

Implacability in radio frequency breakdown in isomeric liquid 667

Isometric liquid

Implacability of distillation theory in radio frequency breakdown 667

Radio-frequency breakdown

Implacability of distillation theory breakdown in isomeric liquid 667

KEYTALPHA

It is permuted subject index that lists only keywords assigned to each abstract. In KEYTALPHA, only keywords are taken from the title instead of the full title. Keywords are arranged side by side without forming a sentence. The entry generation of a document entitled 'Acquisition of journals in a university library in Japan' will be as follows:

Acquisition, Journals, Japan, Library, University	335
Journals, Japan, Library, University, Acquisition	335
Japan, Library, University, Acquisition, Journals	335
Library, University, Acquisition, Journals, Japan	335
University, Acquisition, Journals, Japan, Library	335

Considering the earlier example of 'Prevention of diseases of wheat caused by insects', the index entries will be as follows:

DISEASES, Insects, Prevention, Wheat	13243
INSECTS, Prevention, Wheat, Diseases	13243
PREVENTION, Wheat, Diseases, Insects	13243
WHEAT, Diseases, Insects	13243

WADEX

WADEX stands is an improved version of the KWIC index wherein the names of authors are also treated as keywords along with significant subject terms. It helps satisfy the author approach too. WADEX can be used for both retrospective and current searches. Alphabetically sequenced entries are printed out of context. Words are either single words or hyphenated word pairs or 'tagged words'. WADEX is arranged in two columns, both columns printed simultaneously, with dictionary entries at the top and pagination at the bottom, by computer. It is used in 'Applied Mechanics Review'. AKWIC index is another version of WADEX.

For example, a title entitled 'Selected Water Resources Index for Wisconsin' can be indexed through various terms, like 'Wisconsin University', 'Madison Water Resources Center', 'water resources', 'water rights', 'water supplies' and 'water treatment'. Here, 'Wisconsin University, Madison Water

Resources Center' is the corporate author of the title and 'water resources' and 'water rights' are the significant terms of the title. So, the index entry will be as follows:

Wisconsin University Water Resources for Wisconsin	6636
Madison Water Resources Center Water Resources for Wisconsin	6636

DKWIC

It is another improved version of the KWIC index. The keyword is extracted from the title and regarded as the main index term. The remaining words are rotated using a wrap-around format. In the DKWIC index, a specific search for two words in combination is possible. DKWIC indexes have most of the features, facilities and failures of KWIC and KWOC indexes. Entry for the title 'The computer analysis of weather forecast', the entries will be as follows:

COMPUTER

Analysis of weather forecast – The*	36
Forecast – The* analysis of weather	36
Weather forecast – The* analysis	36

ANALYSIS

Computer* of weather forecast – The	36
Weather forecast – The computer* of	36
Forecast – The computer* of weather	36

The entry term is indicated by an asterisk (*) and is not repeated in the rotated titles.

KLIC

KLIC was developed by Kent. This system allows the truncation of words instead of the complete word. The truncation of titles, either at the beginning or at the end, can be specified, and the computer will pick up any term containing that fragment.

The Chemical Society (London) published a KLIC index as a guide to truncation. The KLIC index indicates which terms any particular word fragment will capture.

Advantages and Disadvantages of Keyword Indexing

Like every indexing system, keyword indexing has its own advantages and disadvantages.

Advantages of Keyword Indexing

1. The main merit of keyword indexing is the speed and economy with which an index can be produced, owing to its machine origin. It has, therefore, become feasible to issue keyword indexes at frequent intervals, perhaps monthly.
2. The absence of interpretation of contents leads to perfect consistency and predictability. If a word appears in the title of the document, then it is certain that, unless the word is in the stop-word list, an entry will be generated under that word. There is no possibility of inconsistency in the allocation of terms in such systems as there is with human indexers. No scope for error or dispute exists.
3. In the knowledge-based economy, human intellect has become costlier day by day and difficult to find. It does not require intellectual effort or trained indexing staff as it is produced by a computer. The computer interfiles the entries from a number of batches of input and prints the cumulative index.
4. Today, most users search for documents by their title rather than their author. A keyword index is very useful for such use.
5. KWIC permits the cross-correlation of subjects to an extent not realisable by conventional procedures.
6. Nowadays, authors, especially in the field of science and technology, use representative and meaningful titles that express the contents of documents. So, the use of keyword indexing leads to better results.
7. Keyword indexing satisfies the current approaches of users.
8. There is no need for vocabulary control devices to handle indexing.

Disadvantages of Keyword Indexing

1. It is good for science and technology but not effective in the field of humanities and social sciences, where no controlled vocabulary is used.
2. It depends on the title of the document. If the title is not representative, the system will become ineffective, particularly in humanities and social science subjects. For example, what conclusions about the subject content can you draw from a title like: 'Black money white power?' or 'Integration: For and against'. Some evidence suggests that titles are becoming more informative, but they will always be limited in the amount of information they can convey.
3. KWIC is normally produced by computer, and the format is of fixed field length. Due to this fixed field length, part of the title is truncated when the title is lengthy. This truncation leads to funny results far away from context.
4. Scattering of related terms occurs because of alphabetical arrangement. The search for a topic might have to be done under several keywords. It takes a long high search time. Several pages of entries under one information for some documents need to be rapidly rejected. Sub-arrangement at entry terms can break down long sequences of entries listed under the same keyword.
5. Searchers very often face high recall and low precision.
6. It is ineffective for an exhaustive approach for a large collection.

Unit 28
Chain Indexing (DDC–Nineteenth Edition)

Introduction

Library cataloguing is broadly divided into two categories: Descriptive cataloguing and subject cataloguing. Descriptive cataloguing is now ISBD based for which rules for the description of documents are provided by many international codes, such as the AACR2-1978+. CCC (fifth edition, 1964), developed by S.R. Ranganathan, is not based on ISBDs for descriptive cataloguing. Descriptive cataloguing, which satisfies the author, collaborators, title and series approach to library documents, provides a full bibliographic description of the documents for their identification and choice. The second process of cataloguing is called subject cataloguing. It serves another major and important function of a catalogue—to serve the subject approach to the documents and help determine what a library has on a given subject. It serves the unknown item approach to library documents, whereas descriptive cataloguing helps to retrieve a document of which either author, title, collaborator or series is known. In a dictionary catalogue, this approach is served by subject headings assigned to a given document either as keywords derived from its title/summary or given from a separate tool, such as a standard list of subject headings or a subject thesaurus. Subject headings can also be derived by a procedure, such as PRECIS (by Derek Austin), POPSI (by G. Bhattacharyya), cyclic indexes (such as by T. Craven) or Ranganathan's Chain Procedure. The process of formulating and assigning subject headings and preparing subject-added entries is known as subject cataloguing.

Classified Catalogue

A classified catalogue has two parts: Classified part and alphabetical part. The main part is the classified part in which all (main) entries are arranged by the call numbers of the system used. It means that, here, the main arrangement of entries and subsequent access is by subject. The subject approach is mostly completed in two stages. Since the lay users are not familiar with the nuances of the classification scheme, an alphabetical approach is essential to the main part. Hence, a classified catalogue is always bipartite. It has aptly been said that words are the ultimate key to information retrieval. For the alphabetical subject approach to the main part, Ranganathan has formulated class index entries, which are termed subject-added entries in a dictionary catalogue. Subject headings for the class index entries in the alphabetical part are derived by a procedure now known as chain indexing.

Problems of Subject Cataloguing

C.A. Cutter (1837–1903) first provided systematic guidelines for subject cataloguing in his famous work, *Rules for a Dictionary Catalog* (1876, third edition 1903). Apart from that, pioneers like Julius Otto Kaiser (1868–1927) also formulated basic but simple rules for subject indexing. To bring uniformity and consistency in subject cataloguing, some readymade lists of standardised subject headings were prepared. The pioneers among them are the ALA List of Subject Headings and the voluminous LCSH for big and research libraries. Then came the SLSH in 1923. The latter two lists are still popular.

But it has been observed that no authoritative and consensual rules have been formulated for subject cataloguing to overcome the problems it usually poses. Subject cataloguing, being a highly intellectual work, is a field full of uncertainties. J. Mills (1992, p. 307) aptly writes, "The failure of cataloguers to develop a consistent and coherent theory of alphabetical subject cataloguing is a notable feature in the history of cataloguing…".

Here, there are no concrete and unambiguous rules like the rules given in AACR2. It is a work of flair at best. Indeed, it is a work of skill and intelligence. Many librarians find it difficult to design subject catalogues due to a lack of expertise.

Ranganathan considered the subject headings in dictionary catalogues illogical and quite ineffective and saw no justification in continuing the use of headings that way. The subject headings lists give us only a choice among synonymous terms, and some current concepts are always missing, as if by default. But such lists do not present any uniform rule or help select more specific headings. No help is provided in eliminating the wrong headings. Identical materials may get entered under different headings, and the users/cataloguers are led to different paths. Moreover, all such lists are heavily biased towards the country and culture of their origin. The indexers in other countries have to make many adaptations and additions to use them. Hence, there is widespread dissatisfaction with the subject headings on account of numerous drawbacks.

In many cases, the cataloguers will not be certain as to under which headings the user would approach. 'See' and 'see also' references make the catalogue bulky, thus increasing the cost of cataloguing, especially in manual catalogues.

Advent of Chain Indexing

In his Theory of Library Catalogue (1938), Ranganathan introduced the chain procedure to derive subject headings for the alphabetical part of a classified catalogue. From a hit-or-miss method, the assignment of subject headings became a sure and almost mechanical method. It is an economical, cleverly simple, but ingenious method of mechanically deriving subject headings from the class number of the document itself. It completely eliminates the endless permutation of components of a heading in cyclic methods. Ranganathan claims in his CC (fifth edition, p. 30) that its advantages due to the economy are being appreciated all over the world. British National Bibliography (BNB) and the Indian National Bibliography (INB) have been its major users.

Mechanism of Chain Indexing

A hierarchical class number consists of linked digits that can be unravelled in a chain of verbal terms to show back each link. In this context, a chain may be defined as a hierarchical string of terms obtained by retranslating the meaning of each digit of the class number into a natural language. It is the reverse process of reverting to the verbal plane from the notational plane. In the unravelling of the chain, we proceed from general to specific, that is, in the PMEST order, if using CC. But the corresponding component terms get automatically arranged from specific to general to maintain the context. Each step in the unravelling of the chain is called a link. So, there are as many links in the chain as the number of digits in the class number. A digit is any distinct symbol, whether semantic or indicative of the facet or phrase. For example, 500.2 Physical Science (DDC nineteenth edition) has five digits in all. The first digit makes the first link. The first two digits make the second link. The last link is the closing link of the chain, which emanates from the full class number. Apart from these two links, a few more links in the chain have been identified and formally defined by Ranganathan in his CCC (fifth edition; 1964), Chap. KB, pp. 287–89. These are as follows:

False Link

A link emanating from a non-semantic digit is an indicator digit. This is either a punctuation mark (in the CC) or the digit 0 (zero) or a '.' (dot). Such a link does not represent a subject but is an indicator of the type of facet to follow. Ranganathan also designates the time facet as a false link as it might not correspond to some verbal heading (CCC (fifth edition), Rule KB Number 5, p. 288).

In the context of the DDC, the statutory filler zeroes, to make the number of digits a minimum of three, will also be considered false links. The dot after the third digit and the initial zero in a standard subdivision are false links. For example, take the following chain for class number 500.2:

5	=	Natural Science
50	=	False Link

500	=	False Link
500.	=	False Link
500.2	=	Physical Science

But the two most important links of practical use are unsought and sought links.

Unsought Link

It is a substantive heading on which there is no published material or on which a user is unlikely to ask or look for material on that subject in the library. But it is not anything absolute and might differ from library to library. It might depend upon the factors listed in the CCC itself (KB3, p. 288). To simply summarise, it varies on the local situation depending upon:

Library users' interests and needs and

Level and kind of services provided by the library.

Hence, each library has to make a policy on what and how to define and designate unsought links.

Tips for Students

The sorting out of sought or unsought links requires experience and knowledge of the subject. It needs flair too. However, for students like you, there is a simple mantra to decide the issue: Ask a question to yourself 'Is any library user likely to ask for material on this topic?' If the answer is yes, then treat it as a sought link; if no, it might be an unsought heading. Some cases might be on the fence, seemingly belonging to both sides. In such cases, give the benefit of the doubt and treat that as a sought link. Anyhow, this sort of judgement can only be learned with error and trial, which takes time.

Sought Link

It is a link that is neither false nor unsought. Some library user is most likely to ask for some material on it. The first link is always a sought heading. The last link, too, is a sought heading if it does not end with a time facet. A link from the time facet is a false link. Each sought heading generates one class index entry. Thus, the number of class index entries depends upon the number of sought headings in the chain.

Upper Link

It could be any link other than the last link. It is relative, like the broader/narrower terms. An upper link for one might be a lower link for another. For example:

Class Number		Subject
954	=	History of India
900	=	History
950	=	Asia, History
954	=	India, History

Here, 950 is the lower link for 900, while for 954, it is the upper link.

Lower Link

It is a link that is next to its upper link. In the above example, 950 is the lower link of 900, while 954 is the upper link of 950. The last link has no lower link.

Missing Link

It is a bypassed link that occurs in an un-modulated chain. It is an invisible link without its rightful upper link.

Step-by-Step Method

Chain indexing was devised to prepare class index entries for a classified catalogue. According to Rules KSD (CCC, fifth edition, pp. 327–34), the subject heading for a dictionary catalogue can also be derived by chain indexing. According to Professor G. Bhattacharyya (1936–2006), a close associate of Ranganathan, there are eleven steps in deriving subject headings from a class number and subsequently preparing class index entries. But these eleven steps also include the steps for synthesising the class number from a raw title. Here, we will only learn to derive class index entries from a given class number. The chain indexing was designed for CCC (first published in 1934), and the classification used for this purpose was CC (first published in 1933). Later, in 1950, it was found that chain indexing could also work with any hierarchical classification system. We will make use of DDC (nineteenth edition; 1979) to illustrate the working of chain indexing.

Working with the DDC

It is not easy to work out chain indexing with a system such as the DDC due to its many cognitive and structural defects. The DDC aims at only grouping subjects rather than individualising each document on the shelves as aspired by the CC. However, the DDC, being largely a hierarchical scheme, is amenable to chain indexing with some modifications and concessions.

Core Steps

- Make the first link from the first digit, which is always a Main Class digit and provides the anchoring context to the latter headings.
- Make the second link from the first two digits, the third from the first three digits and so on until the last digit of the whole class number.
- Write the links vertically, one below the other, in two columns—class number digit(s) on the left and corresponding verbal heading, as taken from the schedules, on the right, the latter preceded by an equal to sign.
- Always qualify the terms in the new link by the terms of the upper link to maintain the full context.
- Supply a heading for the missing link, if any.
- Categorise all the headings into sought headings and unsought headings.
- Against any false link, write 'FL' without writing the terms of the upper link.
- After solving all the links of the chain, pick up all the sought links and arrange them in the specific to general order. It simply means starting picking the sought links from the last sought link in the chain and moving upward to the first link, which is listed last in the sorted and arranged sought headings.

- Sought headings might be edited by the indexer to make the terms a bit tidy by removing the intervening terms, which are no more needed to keep the headings in context. Ranganathan allows the use of an axiomatic phrase, if it exists, to replace the whole heading to make it brief and cryptic (CCC fifth edition, Rule KD3, p. 300).

Example

Let us learn the procedure with the help of the examples given below.

Title History of India during the Mogul King Shah Jahan.

Class No. 954.0257

Chain:

954.0257	=	History of India during the Mogul King Shah Jahan
900	=	General Geography and History, etc. (USH)
930/990	=	History (SH)
950	=	Asia, History (SH)
954	=	India, Asia, History (SH)
954.	=	False Link
954.0	=	False Link
954.02	=	Asian Dynasties, India, History (SH)
954.025	=	Mogul Empire, India, History (SH)
954.0257	=	Shah Jahan, Mogul Empire, India, History (SH)

Now, the sought headings are sorted in the following order, along with some editing of the headings.

Shah Jahan, India, History	954.0257
Mogul Empire, India, History	954.025
Muslim period, India, History	954.02
India, History	954
Asia, History	950
History	930/990

You might note the replacement of headings for 954.02 and the insertion of heading 930/990 for History, which is a sort of missing link.

Preparation of Class Index Entries

It may be noted that a class index entry is not a bibliographic entry but a reference. It does not refer to any specific publication. It is about the reading materials or topics enshrined in various documents in the library. It has three parts:

(a) Heading: A sought heading derived from the class number. Ranganathan prescribes it to be written in capital letters or red ink.

(b) Directing elements: It reads, "For documents in the Class and its Subdivisions, see the Classified Part of the catalogue under the Class Number".

(In the case of a library catalogue in book form, if the directional element is long, it might be removed altogether (CCC fifth edition, KF22, p. 306).) In the case of periodical publications, this directional element is also not required. It is omitted except in the case of ordinary class index entries of a periodical publication.

(c) Class number: It is also called class index number.

For the above sorted sought headings, the class index entries are as follows:

SHAH JAHAN, INDIA, HISTORY.

For documents in the Class and its Subdivisions, see the Classified Part of the catalogue under the Class Number 954.0257

MOGULS, INDIA, HISTORY.

For documents in the Class and its Subdivisions, see the Classified Part of the catalogue under the Class Number 954.025

MUSLIM PERIOD, INDIA, HISTORY.

For documents in the Class and its Subdivisions, see the Classified Part of the catalogue under the Class Number 954.02

ASIA, HISTORY.

For documents in the Class and its Subdivisions, see the Classified Part of the catalogue under the Class Number 950

INDIA, HISTORY.

For documents in the Class and its Subdivisions, see the Classified Part of the catalogue under the Class Number 954

HISTORY.

For documents in the Class and its Subdivisions, see the Classified Part of the catalogue under the Class Number 930/990

Since the spellings of the term 'Mogul' vary from book to book, it is essential to use one spelling once and for all and make cross-reference entries from others in popular use.

Mughals *see* Moguls

Also, in the above entry, we have supplied the missing link of 930/990.

An Example with a Standard Subdivision

Title A History of Arya Samaj in 20th Century

Class No. 294.55630904

Chain:

A History of Arya Samaj in 20th Century = 294.55630904

200	=	Religion
290	=	others [than Christian religion]
294	=	Religions of Indic origin
294.	=	FL
294.5	=	Hinduism
294.55	=	Sects and Reform movements, Hinduism
294.556	=	Reformed Hinduism
294.5563	=	Arya Samaj
294.55630	=	FL
294.556309	=	History, Arya Samaj
294.55630904	=	20th Century History, Arya Samaj

The sought headings sorted from the above chain are:

1. History, Arya Samaj 294.556309
2. Arya Samaj 294.5563

3. Reformation movement, Hinduism 294.556
4. Sects, Hinduism 294.55
5. Hinduism 294.5
6. Indic religions 294
7. Religion 200

You may note that the third, fourth and fifth headings have been a bit modified to replace them with popular or standard terms in literature or edited to tidy them.

Following class index entries will be made for this chain:

HISTORY, ARYA SAMAJ.

For documents in the Class and its Subdivisions, see the Classified Part of the catalogue under the Class Number 294.556309

ARYA SAMAJ.

For documents in the Class and its Subdivisions, see the Classified Part of the catalogue under the Class Number 294.5563

REFORMATION MOVEMENT, HINDUISM.

For documents in the Class and its Subdivisions, see the Classified Part of the catalogue under the Class Number 294.556

SECTS, HINDUISM.

For documents in the Class and its Subdivisions, see the Classified Part of the catalogue under the Class Number 294.55

HINDUISM.

For documents in the Class and its Subdivisions, see the Classified Part of the catalogue under the Class Number 294.5

INDIC RELIGIONS.

For documents in the Class and its Subdivisions, see the Classified Part of the catalogue under the Class Number 294

RELIGIONS.

For documents in the Class and its Subdivisions, see the Classified Part of the catalogue under the Class Number 200

Authority Record

If we modify headings as we did above, then a formal subject authority list will have to be maintained to record such decisions for uniformity in their later use. Indeed, it will make the chain indexing less mechanical.

Chain Indexing for a Dictionary Catalogue

A dictionary catalogue is unipartite, and all the entries and references are arranged in a single A/S order. Here, apart from a few 'see' and 'see also' references, all are bibliographic entries that specify a document in the library. The subject headings are also given to a specific book rather than a class of subjects. After a lot of experience and wide discussion, Ranganathan discovered that chain indexing could be applied with certain modifications to derive subject headings for a dictionary catalogue (CCC fifth edition, Rule KSD, 1964). Back in 1953, Ranganathan was told by A.J. Wells and Eric J. Coates (both of the BNB) that those who use the dictionary catalogue would like to have benefits of subject headings derived mechanically and consistently from class numbers and also retains the benefits of a list of subject headings. He found the chain indexing versatile enough to produce subject headings for a dictionary catalogue with some modifications in rules. He produced an alternative set of rules for this purpose (CCC fifth edition, Rule KSD 403–405, pp. 330–331).

Modified Rules

In the case of subject headings obtained by chain procedure for a dictionary catalogue, the chain is conceptually divided into parts: The first part (Main) comprises the links before the common isolate or standard subdivision digit.

Common Isolate Part

It is part of the chain beginning with the common isolate digit till the next common isolate digit, if any.

Subsequent Parts

In this way, every common isolate, including the geographical isolate, is a part of its own. Each phase in a complex class is also regarded as a separate part of the chain.

Example

Title A Dictionary of Hinduism

Class No. 294.503

Chain:

A Dictionary of Hinduism 294.503 by Richard K. Martin

	First Part	
200	=	Religion
290	=	others [Non-Christian religions]
294	=	Indic Religions
294.	=	(FL)
294.5	=	Hinduism
	Second Part	
294.503	=	Hinduism, dictionaries

In the second part, it may be noted that the heading for the common isolate has been used as a subdivision instead of a lead heading. Secondly, the lengthy heading for the standard subdivision 03 Dictionaries and Encyclopaedias has been shortened to Dictionaries only for brevity. The subject headings for the first part will be as usual. The subject headings for the second part, along with the full entry, will be:

HINDUISM— DICTIONARIES

Martin, Richard K.

A Dictionary of Hinduism/by Richard K Martin. – New Delhi: Munshilal Manoharlal, 1979.—xvi, 207p.; 25cm. 294.503 MAR

Rule KSD 499 states that "There is to be a See also Subject Entry corresponding to each of the Sought links of the Chain, upper or lower to the Link contributing the Main Heading of the Specific Subject Entry" (p. 332). This will require the following 'see also' entries:

Hinduism *See also* Hinduism—Dictionaries

Indic Religions *See also* Hinduism—Dictionaries

Religions *See also* Hinduism—Dictionaries

We can also have a 'see' entry:

Dictionaries, Hinduism See HINDUISM—DICTIONARIES

Advantages of Chain Indexing

During the 1950s and 1960s, chain indexing became very popular and was lauded as Ranganathan's ingenious contribution to subject indexing. Its use was popularised in Great Britain by B.I. Palmer, A.J. Wells, Eric J. Coates and D.W. Langridge. It was used by the BNB for about two decades until it was replaced in the early 1970s by PRECIS, designed by Derik Austin (1921–2001), to suit the computerised production of the BNB. Its advantages over other indexing systems prevalent then are as follows:

1. It serves as an alphabetical subject key to the main part of the classified catalogue.
2. No separate list of subject headings, like the SLSH or the LCSH, is required. Lists are costly publications and are too frequently revised to incorporate new subjects. The subject headings are derived from the class number of the document already assigned by the classifier.
3. It mechanises, to a large extent, the choice and rendering of subject headings.
4. It is thus simple and speedy.
5. It helps avoid arbitrary decisions.
6. Its terminology, being drawn from a classification schedule, ensures coordination and correspondence

between the class number and the subject headings. This coordination is not possible by using a separate list of subject headings.

7. It brings out symbiosis between classification and cataloguing, hitherto considered two parallel techniques.
8. A single subject heading is rarely co-extensive with the subject of the book in the case of the use of lists of subject headings. Usually, a large number of subject-added entries are prepared for a single book.
9. It brings economy in the number of subject index entries, especially in the case of a classified catalogue. As the library grows, the need to prepare new class index entries for new documents decreases. If two or more books share the same class number (as usually happens), there is no need to prepare class index entries for the books other than the first.
10. Even a single class number, say, having four semantic digits, will require only four class index entries ab initio, while a permuted subject index would require $4 \times 3 \times 2 \times 1 = 24$ headings. Huge saving is obvious. The percentage of savings goes on increasing as the number of class numbers grows.
11. It works as a subject index to the main entries and retrieves the number of many books for a library user to make a choice.
12. If the classification schedule is available in an electronic format, then the chain indexing can be made a bit more automatic.
13. It is also used to prepare indexes for classification schedules. It is believed that Ranganathan got the idea of chain indexing from Dewey's Relative Index. Melvil Dewey used this method without giving it any proper name. He did not delve deep into it to make it a mature and objective science.

14. It can be used to derive feature headings for classified catalogues and bibliographies and shelf guides in stacks.

Limitations and Problems of Chain Indexing

1. It needs a logical and hierarchical scheme of classification. Chain indexing cannot be better than the scheme on which it is based.
2. It may not be easy to work with a classification system like the DDC, which only broadly groups documents on the shelves.
3. It works only well with rigorous systems, like the CC, which aspires to individualise every document on the shelves.
4. Any error in assigning a class number is more likely to be carried over into subject headings.
5. It is not mechanical, as assumed. Human intervention and experience are needed for (a) the selection of sought headings and (b) the editing of subject headings to remove unnecessary contexts.
6. It provides no guidance in discovering synonyms.
7. Ranganathan allows the replacement of derived headings by an axiomatic heading or a proper name if it exists (CCC fifth edition, KD3, p. 300). It requires knowledge of the subject and the language.
8. Dividing the line between sought and unsought headings is thin and hazy and requires a lot of discretion. Further, an unsought heading for one library may not be unsought for another. Moreover, today's unsought heading might become tomorrow's sought heading and vice versa.
9. As the headings broaden, the context goes on vanishing.
10. There is a problem of missing links to be provided by the indexer.

11. In the case of a classified catalogue, there is no sufficient guidance for 'see' and 'see also' cross-references.
12. It does not retrieve any specific document. The choice is a two-stage process, as stated earlier. Only the last link, if it is a sought one, refers to a specific subject of the document without naming it specifically by author and title.
13. It does not refer to collateral entries in the form of related subjects.
14. There are some unique problems to be sorted out while working with the DDC:

    (a) Problem of dual headings. Example:

597	Coldblooded Vertebrates	Pisces (Fishes)
954	South Asia	India

    Which of the two headings will be used for 597 or 954 for chain indexing? There are so many such cases in the DDC. In the DDC (twenty-third edition, 2010), these dual headings have been removed.

    (b) Problems of alternative headings:

    In many cases, there are alternative headings. Example:

    597 Pisces (Fish)

    381 Internal Commerce (Domestic trade)

    657.2 Recording (Book Keeping)

    A library will have to choose one of the two alternatives once and for all and make its subject authority record. And also, prepare 'see' references from the headings not used to the headings used. For example, if we prefer the term Domestic Trade then make the following 'see' reference: Internal Commerce *see* Domestic Trade.

    Cantered headings have their own problems.

    383–384 Specific kind of communications.

This is apart from the problem of the DDC being a broader grouping scheme, where the BNB had to use verbal extensions to make a number specific to or coextensive with the subject of the book.

For a dictionary catalogue, it provides only one specific heading derived from the full class number. A composite book dealing with a multiplicity of topics might not get adequately indexed.

(c) In a dictionary catalogue, lots of 'see also' references clutter the catalogue.

(d) Chain indexing rules for a dictionary catalogue, as given in the fifth edition (1964) of CCC, are tentative, if not rudimentary. Ranganathan urged for further research, but no further work has been done in this area for the last fifty years. Hence, chain indexing is old and dated to the era of OPACs.

EXERCISE UNIT 26 – UNIT 28

1. What is Sears List? Give an account of its historical developments.
2. What are the features of SLSH?
3. Write down the principles of vocabulary control.
4. What do you understand by SLSH? Discuss its principles and structure in detail.
5. What are the two types of headings in SLSH? Discuss in detail with examples.
6. Write a short note on the limitations of SLSH.
7. What do you mean by keyword indexing?
8. Write a note on the keyword indexing process.
9. What are the different variations in keyword indexing?
10. What do you mean by KWIC? Illustrate with the help of examples.
11. What do you mean by KWOC? Illustrate with the help of examples.

12. Write a note on the advantages and disadvantages of keyword indexing.
13. Define classified catalogue.
14. What is chain indexing? Discuss its mechanism.
15. Define unsought links in chain indexing. How are they different from sought links?
16. How would you prepare class index entries? Give an example.
17. Write a note on chain indexing for a dictionary catalogue.
18. Discuss the advantages of chain indexing.
19. What are the limitations of chain indexing?

Sample Question Paper

SAMPLE QUESTION PAPER 1

BLIS/MLIS **1st/2nd Semester**
PAPER: ORGANISING AND MANAGING INFORMATION **MAX: 80**
TIME ALLOWED: 02:30 HOURS **MIN: 32**

Attempt all the questions from sections A & B and only two questions from section C

SECTION A (**Short Answer Type Questions**) (**8×3=24 Marks**)

1. Define Genus-Species relationship.
2. What do you mean by ontology?
3. What do you understand by library catalogue?
4. What is the full form of MARC?
5. How is subject indexing different from cataloging?
6. What are the attributes of an indexing language?
7. What do you understand by semantic web activity?
8. What are the advantages of MARC?

SECTION B (**Medium Answer Type Questions**) (**4×8=32 Marks**)

1. Describe CC as a scheme of classification.
2. Highlight some of the problems while cataloging non-book material.
3. Discuss in detail the structure of an indexing language.
4. Define web indexing. Discuss its various types.

SECTION C (**Long Answer Type Questions**) (**2×12=24 Marks**)

1. Discuss in detail Ranganathan's five sets of canons for the work in the Idea Plane.
2. Discuss AACR-2R in detail. Highlight its genesis and structure in detail.
3. What do you understand by indexing principles? Discuss their need and purpose.
4. What is interoperability? Discuss its need and methods.

SAMPLE QUESTION PAPER 2

BLIS/MLIS **1st/2nd Semester**
PAPER: ORGANISING AND MANAGING INFORMATION **MAX: 80**
TIME ALLOWED: 02:30 HOURS **MIN: 32**

Attempt all the questions from sections A & B and only two questions from section C

SECTION A (Short Answer Type Questions) (8×3=24 Marks)

1. What are the uses of classification in a library?
2. Name some prominent classification schemes.
3. What is a microform catalogue?
4. What are the uses of CCF?
5. What are the types of headings in LCSH?
6. Define Thesaurofacet.
7. Write full form of ISBD and FRBR.
8. Define breadcrumbs.

SECTION B (Medium Answer Type Questions) (4×8=32 Marks)

1. Describe notational plane. Explain its need and purpose.
2. What is the purpose and scope of UNIMARC? Highlight its structure.
3. Discuss the criteria for the evaluation of an indexing system.
4. What do you understand by ontology? What are its types?

SECTION C (Long Answer Type Questions) (2×12=24 Marks)

1. Discuss DDC in detail. Throw some light on its three summaries.
2. Discuss International Standard Bibliographic Description (ISBD). Draw some light on its purpose and structure.
3. What do you understand by chain indexing? Discuss the steps involved in chain indexing.
4. What do you understand by term metadata? Discuss its types and cataloging tools.

SAMPLE QUESTION PAPER 3

BLIS/MLIS **1st/2nd Semester**
PAPER: DOCUMENT PROCESSING (PRACTICE) **MAX: 80**
TIME ALLOWED: 02:30 HOURS **MIN: 32**

Attempt all the questions from sections A & B and only two questions from section C

SECTION A (Short Answer Type Questions) (8×3=24 Marks)

1. How would you depict hierarchy in through DDC notation?
2. What do you mean by class in DDC?
3. Table 1 and Table 2 in DDC stand for.
4. What do you understand by order of precedence in DDC?
5. What do you mean by AACR-2R?
6. What do you mean by GMD in cataloguing?
7. Define classified catalogue.
8. Write a note on keyword indexing process.

SECTION B (Medium Answer Type Questions) (4×8=32 Marks)

1. How would you classify a title "central banks" using DDC? Mention the steps.
2. Illustrate simple synthesis in DDC using examples.
3. Discuss the need of a subject heading in a catalogue card.
4. What is chain indexing? Discuss its mechanism.

SECTION C (Long Answer Type Questions) (2×12=24 Marks)

1. Discuss step by step practical classification with DDC. Use suitable example.
2. What is the role, use and characteristics of "individual languages subdivision"? Give examples.
3. Discuss the AACR-2R cataloging of a document with shared responsibility with some suitable examples.
4. What do you understand by SLSH? Discuss its principles and structure in detail.

SAMPLE QUESTION PAPER 4

BLIS/MLIS **1st/2nd Semester**
PAPER: DOCUMENT PROCESSING (PRACTICE) **MAX: 80**
TIME ALLOWED: 02:30 HOURS **MIN: 32**

Attempt all the questions from sections A & B and only two questions from section C

SECTION A (Short Answer Type Questions) (8×3=24 Marks)

1. Name seven auxiliary tables in DDC.
2. Define subject analysis.
3. What do you mean by relative index?
4. What are different abbreviations used in the sub-entries of an index?
5. Define gross-reference in context of cataloguing.
6. What are the different types of entries in cataloguing?
7. What are the limitations associated with chain indexing?
8. Write down the principles of vocabulary control.

SECTION B (Medium Answer Type Questions) (4×8=32 Marks)

1. Classify "Drugs affecting nervous system" using DDC.
2. Illustrate multiple synthesis in DDC using examples.
3. Draw AACR-2R based catalogue for a document with multiple volumes.
4. Write a note on advantages and disadvantages of keyword indexing.

SECTION C (Long Answer Type Questions) (2×12=24 Marks)

1. Discuss different types of notes in DDC with examples.
2. What is the role, use and characteristics of "standard subdivision"? Give examples.
3. Discuss MARC-21 structure in detail.
4. How would you prepare Class Index Entries (CIEs)? Give examples.

Index